The Worst Of Broke-Ass Stuart

20 years of love, death, & dive bars

Stuart Schuffman

© Stuart Schuffman, 2025

This book, or parts thereof, may not be reproduced in any form, stored in any retrieval system, or transmitted in any form by any means— electronic, mechanical, photocopy, recording, or otherwise — without prior written permission of the publisher, except as provided by the United States Copyright Law. For permission requests, write to the publisher at the address given. Thank you for your support of the author's and publisher's rights.

ISBN 978-0-9990108-5-3

Cover by Jonah Price

Interior Art: Abby Wilcox, Richard Perez, Juan Leguizamon, Jon Sitch, Heather Tompkins, Robert Lui-Trujillo

Photo Credits: Nico Schwieterman, Victoria Smith, Tia, Griffin Wooldridge, Kevin Kelleher, Emily Trinh, Jennya Garibaldi, Kayla Brittingham, Peter Snarr, and Myleen Hollero

Campaign Poster by Lil' Tuffy; Photo by Chad Riley

Instagram: @BrokeAssStuart

Threads: @BrokeAssStuart

TikTok: @BrokeAss_Stuart

Facebook: Broke-Ass Stuart

Twitter: @BrokeAssStuart

Terran Empire Publishing

1761 Hillside Ct. Placerville, California 955667

www.terranempirepublishing.com

For anyone who has ever lived an unconventional life... or dreamed of doing so

Photo by Victoria Smith

The little bits of hand writing under the titles of pieces are where each was first published and when. Additionally, some pieces have hand written notes of explanation on how or why a piece was written and any important information regarding the article.

Contents

Introduction: Who the Fuck is Broke-Ass Stuart? Pg. 6

Slouching Towards Neverland (San Francisco) pg. 10

No One Ever Fell in Love At A Poetry Reading At A Startup Incubator (Bars) pg. 92

Let's Get Weird (Lifestyle) pg. 180

Jet Lagged, Hungover, and Homesick (Travel) pg. 215

Activism Is Not A Contest (Activism) pg. 259

Love Notes & Other Disasters (Love & Lust) pg. 293

All of This is the Natural Byproduct of Not Dying Young (Death) pg. 326

Acknowledgments pg. 348

Who The Fuck Is Broke-Ass Stuart?

Stuart Schuffman

Photo by Nico Schwieterman

Being a writer is a terrible way to make a living, but it's a beautiful way to make a life. And oh, what a strange and incredible life it's been. What started as a 33-page zine eventually led to me getting paid to travel the world and write about it, become one of the original social media influencers, create and host my own TV show, run for mayor of San Francisco, and found an award-winning website that's become embedded into the cultural fabric of the Bay Area.
And that entire journey is found in the pages of this book.

However, to understand how we arrived at this point, let's revisit the very beginning.

I was working in a candy store in San Francisco's North Beach when all this madness started. One day, a guy from the San Diego neighborhood where I grew up came into the store with his fiancée (they're now married). After we chatted for a bit, Melissa, the fiancée, handed me her card and told me to give them a shout next time I was in San Diego. After they left, I looked at her card, and it said she was a travel writer. I thought to myself, "Travel Writer? I wanna be a travel writer," and it was then that I decided to pursue this career path.

That was 2004, and I was living at 1907 Golden Gate, the sprawling 8-bedroom Victorian that served as the de facto clubhouse for the Cacophony Society and helped give birth to Burning Man. Many, many, many weird and important creative endeavors were hatched at 1907 over the 20 years that Miss P Segal and other misfits lived there. And Broke-Ass Stuart was the final one. Shortly after I started working on it, we were evicted, but I maintain that the spirit of creativity that was so infused in those walls helped inspire me to create Broke-Ass Stuart.

Broke-Ass Stuart's Guide to Living Cheaply in San Francisco was a 33-page zine that I physically cut, paste, and stapled together – and then made photocopies of – at a copy shop.

The first run of only 50 quickly sold, so I printed 100 in the next run. It was with these 100 copies that I began approaching bookstores around San Francisco and somehow convinced them to not only carry them, but also, in some cases, display them near the checkout counter. I sold around 1,000 copies of this first zine and won the "Best Local Zine" award in the SF Bay Guardian's Best of the Bay issue. Truthfully, my reaction to this minor success was, "Holy shit! I can't believe people really dig this stuff." So, I decided to create a second, larger BAS zine the following year.

Broke-Ass Stuart's Guide to Living Cheaply in San Francisco v.2 is everything really took off; I sold 300 copies of it in the first week (remember this is a zine with no PR and I was doing all the distribution by foot and mass transit). Lots of good things came about because of it; I was on TV a few times, on the radio, got "Best of the Bay" again, people recognized me at bars, I had some groupies, and ultimately, I got to write for Lonely Planet (I did the Ireland section for the *Western Europe* and *Europe on a Shoestring* books). I was finally, officially, a travel writer; I even had business cards that said so.

After Ireland, I decided that doing everything myself was too much work, and that if I was going to continue the Broke-Ass Stuart thing, I wanted to have a publisher so all I would have to do is write books and let them handle the rest. I blew every guy in Hollywood before I realized that the publishing industry was based in New York. Then (this part is actually real) I found Seven Footer Press on Craigslist and conned them into putting out my books...suckers.

Broke-Ass Stuart's Guide to Living Cheaply in San Francisco was published as a book in November 2007. Broke-Ass Stuart's Guide to Living Cheaply in New York City followed in November 2008. Shortly after, I launched BrokeAssStuart.com as an arts and culture website. In 2011, I achieved another dream: I created and hosted my own travel TV show, Young, Broke & Beautiful, and a book of the same name was also published. This time, it was a guide to living cheaply everywhere.

The show only lasted for one season, unfortunately, and so in 2012, I renewed my focus on BrokeAssStuart.com, paying more attention to writing about local things rather than traveling. It was during this time that I began freelancing for various local publications. I intermittently published things with *The Bold Italic* that always seemed to go viral. I also started a column at 7x7 called the Weeknighter, which was ostensibly a bar column, but more so a series of stories about myself and San Francisco, where the bar just happened to be the main character. After a couple of years, I moved the column to the *San Francisco Bay Guardian*, but when that shuttered a few months later, The Weeknighter was put to bed.

The San Francisco Examiner then approached me about doing a column, which allowed me to expand what I wrote about. Hell, I got to write about anything I wanted, so I took ample advantage of the opportunity. My Broke-Ass City column ran for over six years at the *Examiner*, and it was a fantastic opportunity to reach people who would never want to read something written by some loudmouth named Broke-Ass Stuart. Like so many things, though, that ended in the pandemic, which seemed like a fitting fate anyway. A little while later, SFGate asked me to be their Dive Bar Columnist, and I just couldn't say no.

During all of this, BrokeAssStuart.com continued to grow, allowing me to discover and amplify the voices of hundreds of writers who had important things to share with the world. And in a funny twist of fate, I got to publish work by Melissa Keith, the woman whose business card inspired the idea that I could be a travel writer back in the candy store in North Beach.

And so here we are, all those little lifetimes of words have finally caught up to me. The collected works that you hold right now span my entire career. There's a fine line between Broke-Ass Stuart and Stuart Schuffman, but I don't always know where that is. So, I guess, in a way, you're holding my whole life in your hands, hopefully though we're just at the halfway point.

I'm glad this book has found its way to you. I don't want to say that it's fate, because I don't believe in that shit, but you and I have both made the decisions that have landed this book in your hands, at this particular point in history.

And so, for that, I just want to say, I love you. I hope you enjoy reading this book as much as I enjoyed living it.

Slouching Towards Neverland

(San Francisco)

Stuart Schuffman

Through stories, articles, and poems, this chapter charts my journey from being an SF newbie to an ingrained part of the fabric of The City.

Twenty-three years and 30 pounds later, I'm still here. None of what I have would've been possible without San Francisco; my love, my muse, my favorite pickpocket. I've written more about this city than most people will ever read about it. Even before I started doing this whole Broke-Ass Stuart thing, I was cataloging my time here.

As you'll see, my first scribbles about this strange and staggering city begin right when I moved here for an internship in 2002. I hadn't even invented Broke-Ass Stuart yet. The name of the chapter comes from a zine of the same name that I put out in 2022. Some of the stuff here was in that zine, but there's a shit ton more that's been included since then.

Photo by Victoria Smith

I first moved to San Francisco in the summer of 2002 for an internship at Bill Graham Presents. At the time, it was the premier live music promoter in the Bay Area. This was before interns had to be paid legally, so instead, I received credit at UC Santa Cruz, where I attended school. Part of getting that credit was keeping a journal about my experiences, so technically, that was when I first started writing about San Francisco. If I recall, I tried to keep the journal for about two days and then bullshitted the entire thing after the summer was over. It's been 20 years, so I don't really remember, but that sounds like something I would have done. I mean, all the things I wrote probably happened, but who knows exactly in what order? What follows are a couple of funny excerpts from the journal. As far as I know, the only person to ever read this stuff before I put it in the *Slouching Towards Neverland* zine is Professor Eric Porter at UCSC.

BILL GRAHAM PRESENTS INTERNSHIP DIARY EXCERPTS

Slouching Towards Neverland Zine; 2022

Day 8

For its 1,000th episode, A&E Biography is doing a show on Bill Graham. In celebration of this, BGP is hosting a special, invite-only advance screening at the Fillmore. There is a minimum donation of $25, and all proceeds go to the Bill Graham Foundation. In honor of this gala, I spent all day stuffing invitations into envelopes and attaching address labels to them. The list of invitees was exciting, including James Hetfield, Ben Fong-Torres, and Chet Helms. It did not include me. That's quite alright, though; $25 is a little steep for the pockets of an intern, who, due to his inability to secure another job, has been living off two slices of pizza a day. I tried to get a job as a barback at the Fillmore, but from what I understand, by the time I get the job, my internship will be over. Maybe I'll try to conveniently "run into" Ben Fong-Torres and talk him into giving me a job writing for *Rolling Stone*.

Day 13

I am an intern, the lowest rung on the ladder, the smallest on the food chain, the plebe of the professional world. But as far as interns go, I'm a fucking god! I say this not out of conceit, for I imagine there are those who file and photocopy much more efficiently than I do. My god like status has nothing to do with my clerical abilities. It has to do with the fact that I get to see almost any show that comes to the Bay Area for free.

Stuart Schuffman

I've spent a considerable amount of time recounting my adventures at the BGP office; let me take some time to discuss the shows I've seen thus far.

The first show I saw was Keb Mo at the Fillmore. In all honesty, I went to see the show because I had heard of it before, and it was free. Dear reader, Keb Mo sucks. He's the Kenny G of blues. Fortunately, my friend and I were given free drink tickets, making the music tolerable. Unfortunately, we got the strongest drinks we could and became intolerable ourselves. I managed to get piss drunk at the first show I went to as an employee of BGP, and found myself saying shit like, "*In 1968 when Jimi Hendrix played here...*" to the president of the company as if I was teaching a history lesson. Luckily, he was unfazed. When Keb Mo began playing an appalling version of Bill Withers' "Grandma's Hands", we left with an overwhelming feeling of sickness. In retrospect, I'm not sure if it was the music or the Tokyo Ice Teas that made us sick, probably both.

My next adventure at the Fillmore was much better; I got to see virtuosity in action. Tabla Beat Science is like an all-star jam session featuring the world's best musicians. It's almost like live Bollywood music, and each player is *amazing*. The day after, I went to see New Orleans by the Bay, a concert that BGP performs at Shoreline Amphitheater. NOBB is two days of New Orleans music and commodified "culture" that happens every year.

They even have a wack-ass June Mardi-Gras parade halfway through the show each day. This year's headliner was Taj Mahal, and he was dope! For shows like this, BGP simply distributes a stack of tickets in the office and instructs all employees to take some for their friends and family. I did. And it was fun.

I'll share one more quick story about a show I saw. There was a beautiful girl who interviewed me for a job down the street from my apartment on Haight. Although I did not get the job, she did tell me to drop by sometime and say hello. Later in the week, I went by and invited her to go with me to see the Jim Rose Circus at the Fillmore. All I knew was that it was a sort of freak show, and after explaining this to her, she decided to accompany me out of pure intrigue.

Well, the show ended up being a mixture of a freak show and MTV's Jackass; she was appalled and decided to leave early. Needless to say, have not hung out since.

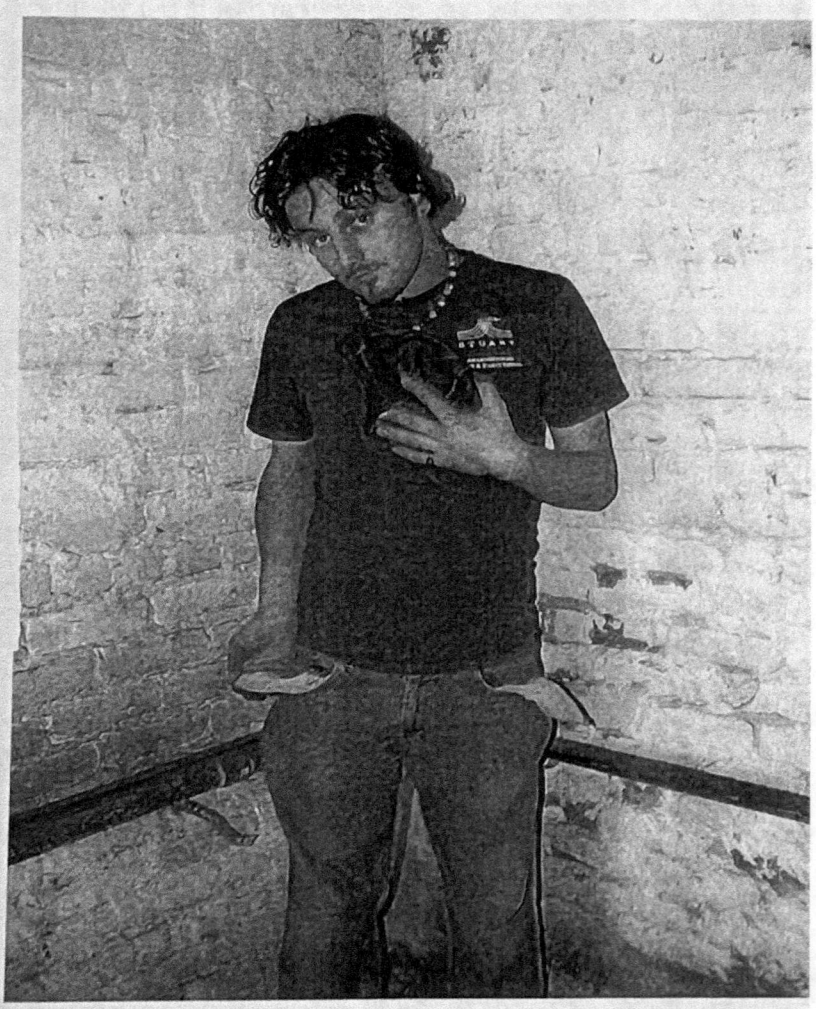

The first Broke-Ass Stuart zine. Cover photo by Tia

Stuart Schuffman

SAN FRANCISCO BOOK INTRODUCTION
Broke-Ass Stuart's Guide to Living Cheaply in San Francisco; 2007

I have absolutely the biggest crush on San Francisco. I mean seriously, have you ever met someone who's been to this city and said, "Nah man, fuck San Francisco. I can't stand that place."? Me neither. Sure, I've got friends who say they could never live here, but they still love it and can't wait to come back and sleep on my couch again. Why is that? I think in some part it's because, as far as cities go, this one is beautiful. It's got hills, lots of green parks, water on three sides, famous architecture, and of course, cute little cable cars. And, yes, we all know that San Francisco is an epicenter for all things related to good food and wine.

But really, all those things are peripheral in the grand scheme of things. What makes this city so fucking great is that everybody here has a little bit of freak and weirdo in them. Just look at Bay to Breakers, where tens of thousands of people either dress up in costumes or get naked, and push shopping carts full of beer for multiple miles across the City. Where else would something like Burning Man come from, but a city devoted to doing, whatever the fuck it is that you do? If US cities were people, San Francisco would be the weird art school kid who felt like nobody else understood him. Whether you live in the Mission or the Marina, there's a reason you chose San Francisco. You chose it because there was something about this city that spoke to you and made you feel like it was home. And you know what that means? You're just as loony as the rest of us, whether you like it or not.

Everybody knows somebody in San Francisco, which means that whether you're visiting from Australia or living in the Sunset, there's always a chance that you're gonna bump into someone you know. So just remember that San Francisco is a city where you can't escape your past. Not that that's a bad thing; I love it when I walk down Haight Street and bump into someone I met in Venice, Italy, when I was 20. One of the great things about this City is that everyone seems to know each other, or they are only separated by less than 3 degrees, making SF feel even more like a community.

Fuck, I guess what I'm trying to say through all this babbling is that there is so much to love about this City, and either you love it as much as I do, or you want to know more about it so that you can fall in love with it. I mean, why else would you have bought this book? Oh yeah, because you're just as broke as I am and you want to know how to live cheaply in San Francisco.

Well, pal, you've come to the right place.

China Fun Express: 211 Kearny St. @ Sutter St.

In general, I'm always a little bit skeptical of any restaurant with the word "fun" in its name. What's so fun about a Chinese food buffet that sells food for $4.98 a pound? Sure, it's inexpensive, but fun? Come on, Chuck E. Cheese's is fun. Chuck E. Cheese's has a 6-foot-tall rat walking around giving out balloons and hugs, and slides that drop you into a ball pit that smells like feet and is probably full of pink eye and lice. That shit is fun. I gotta tell you, China Fun Express, you should either change your name or put some god damn slides in your restaurant.

El Super Burrito: 1200 Polk St. @ Sutter St.

While some Mexican food restaurants have fancy and romantic names like El Farrolito or Taqueria Cancun, the people at El Super Burrito said, "Fuck that! Let's have our name tell people exactly what we do; we make big motherfucking burritos. That's what we do!" It'd be like a clothing store being named Very Comfortable Cotton T-shirts (believe it or not, one of the world's biggest telescopes is actually called the Very Large Telescope. These people can design a way to see light years away, yet can't think of anything better than the Very Large Telescope). Despite the uncreative name, though, the burritos here are good, and yes, they are very big. The jumbo burrito is easily big enough for two people to split, and it's only $5.50. They also offer all-you-can-eat chips and salsa. But the decoration here takes the cake; they have so many Corona streamers and *piñatas* hung up that you would think it was a five-year-old kid named Corona's birthday party.

The Magazine: 920 Larkin St. @ Cedar St.

Wow, I'm really amazed people don't talk about this one more. It's definitely one of those places that deserves mention in as many conversations as possible. It literally has one of the biggest archives of porno mags I've ever seen, and what's remarkable is the sheer variety. If you're into 18-year-old Inuit virgins in clown suits, being drenched in hot coffee, there's a 97% chance that The Magazine has what you're looking for. Sure, this store has old fishing and baking magazines and shit for like 35 cents, but who cares about that when there are back issues of Juggs? If you don't dig this place, you seriously have no soul (or a giant aversion to dirty old pervs).

The San Francisco Chocolate Factory: 286 12^(th) St. @ Folsom St.

Don't get your hopes up. There's no eccentric and snarky candy millionaire running around with a platoon of orange-faced musical little people, drowning fat kids in rivers of chocolate, and belittling elderly adults. No ma'am, not here, that's called heaven. Despite that one major shortcoming, though, the San Francisco Chocolate Factory is a great place because it does one thing really well: it makes delicious chocolate. Considering that these chocolates are a bit of a luxury item, they're fairly well-priced; yummy goodness starts at just $0.99. And they have a whole system where you can buy your goodies based on the percentage of cocoa in them. White chocolate is 31%, milk chocolate is 38% and the dark stuff ranges from 55% to 72%. Personally, I'm a 38%-er.

El Cachanilla: 2948 21^(st) St. @ Treat St.

If I were to guess what El Cachanilla translates to in English, it would be, "not fucking around". I know that's not the translation at all,but seriously, this place makes all the other taquerias in the Mission look like total pussies. Sure, I've seen other taquerias that sell tacos with *cabeza* (head fat), *tripas* (intestines), *lengua* (tongue), and even *sesos* (brains) before. Still, El Cachanilla one-ups them all and sells fucking *ojos* (bull eyes) too! If this were a prison movie, none of the other taquerias would mess with El Cachanilla because they'd be like, "See that guy over there? That dude is god damn crazy. I ain't messin' with him." On a slightly more serious note though, this place does have good, cheap food ($1.50 tacos), and a little walk up taco window for if you just wanna order to go. Yo, if you do end up eating the *ojos*, let me know.

Bow Bow Cocktail Lounge: 1155 Grant @ Broadway

I'm going to say this most plainly and honestly I can: I'm pretty sure Candy, the bartender here, is Dionysus disguised as a human being. It's the only logical way to explain the way she handles the position of bartender. It totally makes sense if you read any Greek mythology; gods used to come down to Earth in human form and just fuck around, all the time.

Look, if you go into the Bow Bow intending to have only one drink, just don't go, because I guarantee you'll have more than one. It's almost like she's using a Jedi Mind trick on you. And then once you've gotten nice and toasty and plan on leaving because you don't want to spend any more money, or you're too drunk, Candy starts *giving* you drinks! Sure, I can sit here and talk about how the place is kinda grungy and smoky and the karaoke sounds like a Siren PMSing, but the heart of the matter is this: Candy is the god of wine and debauchery incarnated into human form. If you don't believe me, go see for yourself.

TREADING THROUGH THE TREACHEROUS TENDERLOIN
Instant City; 2007

This was the first short story I ever wrote. It's about a night on the town researching for my SF book. It originally appeared in a shorter form in a literary mag called Instant City in 2007 and then as this full version in my SF book.

The night was winding down at the mediocre Italian restaurant in North Beach. My last table had just walked out the door, and Kenny was putting his final silverware roll-up in the appropriate basket.

"How much longer do you have?" he asked.

I took a look at the list of closing duties, "All I've got left is to take out the trash and do my roll-ups. Are you still down to come out and do research with me?"

Kenny got up from the counter and laughed, "I love how you call it research. I am absolutely down."

This was the night that I had planned on researching the Tenderloin for volume two of *Broke-Ass Stuart's Guide to Living Cheaply in San Francisco*, and in this case, "research" meant going to a bunch of different bars, taking notes, and drinking. It's really a tough manner of work, one that in fact required me to make use of a research assistant.

Luckily, Kenny had an extensive background in this field and volunteered for this particular assignment (that is to say, we drank together a lot, and I needed some company). This wasn't going to be a regular night at the Hemlock Tavern talking to average-looking hipster chicks about bands I couldn't give a fuck about, no, sir. This night we were hitting up some of the Loin's real dive bars, the types of places where the shit gets real thick on the first and fifteenth of every month.

We left the restaurant around 10:30 p.m., walked a couple of blocks down Columbus, turned right onto Stockton, and followed the street all the way until we were spit out on the other end of its filthy tunnel. We turned onto Geary, and it wasn't long before we were treading through the treacherous Tenderloin. It was at Geary and Jones that the neon lights of the Hightide drew me in like a goddamn mosquito to a bug zapper. Neon lights get me every time.

I was actually familiar with the Hightide; I'd hung out there a couple times about a year before when I'd been living with a girlfriend just up the street. I remembered it as a slightly dingy place with stiff drinks and a clientele mainly consisting of old man drunks and recently off-work cooks who spoke primarily Maya and hailed from the Yucatan Peninsula. From time to time, groups of nubile young travelers would wander in from a nearby hostel, but the overall feeling of the place would never have been described as sexy. Walking into the Hightide that night, a step or two before Kenny, I was shocked by a drastic change that had occurred sometime in the year of my absence. I acknowledged this mildly: "Holy shit, Kenny, there are girls in here and they're pretty!" Always an astute observer, Kenny had already picked up on this fact, replying, "From the looks of it, they have all of their teeth too. And I don't even see a single eye patch in the crowd."

"Aw, come on, dude, I didn't make it out to be that bad, did I?" In fact, knowing my tendency to exaggerate, I probably had, but at that moment, it was inconsequential. What mattered was that Kenny was correct; there wasn't a single eye patch or missing tooth in the whole place. I'd have to make a note of that. "Anyways, what are you drinking? I'll get first round," I changed the subject as we were now sitting at the bar and clearly within earshot of most of its patrons.

A pretty bartender approached us and asked what we'd like. "I'll take a Madras, please," I answered, pointing to Kenny, "and also, whatever the good doctor would like."

He ordered his drink, "I'll take a Pabst, please," and turned to me and asked, "What's a Madras?"

"It's vodka, cran, and orange juice," I answered, "I'm trying to be a little bit healthier."

"Wait, wait, wait... because orange juice and cranberry juice are both good for you, you're saying that the two combined must cancel out the awful things that the vodka does to your body?" he asked incredulously, and I nodded in agreement. "Wow! That has to be single-handedly the most ridiculous and," he paused dramatically, "brilliant thing you've ever said." The drinks arrived, and I paid the lady the measly price of six bucks, plus a tip.

"Denial is a beautiful thing, isn't it?" I took a sip and grimaced. The drinks were still stiff and cheap. I knew it was going to be a good night.

We left the Hightide and continued down Geary. I'd remembered that a new bar had opened up where Julep used to be, and I wanted to check it out. We found Whiskey Thieves almost completely empty; there were perhaps ten people inside, including the bartender. Kenny got us each a Madras, and we sat down at the back of the bar to soak up the atmosphere and take some notes. Enjoying my refreshing beverage, I concluded that in a neighborhood full of dive bars, Whiskey Thieves kinda seemed like the new kid who was desperately trying to fit in. It was the type of place you'd go if you knew that you weren't prepared for the caliber of shit that the Tenderloin had to offer. But us, we were prepared, and we knew it, so we finished our drinks and decided that the next bar would be the type of place where people go to drink their lives away. We like comedy.

It took about three seconds after walking in the door at Jonell's to realize that this was precisely the spot we were looking for. Named so because it sits on the corner of Jones and Ellis, Jonell's is the type of fine establishment where sitting with your back to the door might be the last bad decision you ever make. The patrons are generally drunk and leery old men who piss away all their money on booze and hookers, but the vibe is actually far from inhospitable. In fact, if you sit down at the bar, expect to get an earful of some of the most fucked up stories you've ever heard.

Settling down at the horseshoe-shaped bar, I saw a huge Samoan guy with a friendly but worn-looking face come out of the bathroom carrying a bunch of cleaning supplies. "Jesus Christ,"

I said to Kenny, under my breath, "Could you imagine having to clean that bathroom? It's gotta be worse than a dumpster behind a needle exchange."

Kenny was cringing, "I'm actually trying not to imagine the bathroom at all. Oh god, I'd hate to have to take a shit in there."

Another friendly but worn-looking Samoan face, this one female, approached us smiling and asked, "What'll it be, guys?"

"Hi," I smiled back, "can we get a couple of Madr ... ah fuck it, a couple of Budweisers please?"

"Sure, honey, I'll be right back." Just as she walked away, a man pushed through the door with the force of a house ripped from the ground and blown to Oz. The bar was pretty empty, but I knew he'd land right next to me. They always do.

Sitting down on one stool away, the man said a round of hellos. "Hey Suzy, hey Ricky," he greeted the couple who ran the bar. Then he greeted the only other people in the bar besides me and Kenny, a fat white guy who appeared to be completely catatonic, and an old black guy in a straw fedora, "Hey Fred, hey Willis." Finally, he turned to us: "Hey, new guys, I'm Mike." Before we got a chance to introduce ourselves, though, he began addressing the whole bar.

"Oh man, I just came from this huge fucking party where there was all this free food and free booze, and Jesus, shit man, you shoulda seen all the pussy in this place. Ya see, this guy I know, I gots all kinds of friends, this guy I know just opened this Cuban restaurant and tonight was the opening party. It was beautiful, my buddy really went all out, and the food, oh the food! Better than anything I've ever eaten, other than my mother's cooking, of course, God rest her sweet soul. This food was so good that I almost went to the store to buy some sandwich bags so I could sneak some out, but I figured I didn't want to look sleazy in front of all those rich people. But fuck 'em anyways. Ya guys ever had Cuban food? Them fucking Cubans really know how to shake some pots and pans, ya know what I mean? Look, I even brought a menu so you could see what I'm talkin' bout. Here, pass it around." At this point, Mike pulled out a folded-up paper menu and handed it to Suzy, the bartender who had just dropped off two Buds for Kenny and me, and a glass of whiskey for Mike. "Thanks, Suzy, how'd ya know what I wanted?"

"Cuz you get the same damn drink every night," Suzy answered sweetly while taking the menu that Mike had handed her. Suzy read over the menu and then passed it around while Mike proudly looked on as if he were letting his friends touch a piece of the true cross he'd found in Jerusalem. The menu got around to me, and I'll have to admit, the food did sound pretty good.

"Looks good, man," I answered his awaiting eyes. Mike looked like his 50 or 60 years on this Earth had been rough; you could tell he'd definitely been around the block a few times. But he was jolly in his roughness, and he was energetic and also pretty tubby. He kinda reminded me of an all-grown-up, alcoholic, bearded version of "Chunk" from *The Goonies*. I got the feeling that Mike was a good guy, just a little overzealous.

"You're fuckin-A right, it looks good. And it tasted even better," he answered. "Ha! And shit man, the women in there were so hot they wouldn't even fucked me when I was you're age. How old are ya, 21, 22? What are young bloods like you doing in here anyways? If you're looking for pussy, this ain't the place, but you can buy some pussy on Polk Street if you want. Be careful though; check for an Adam's apple, cuz some of them women ain't exactly women. Know what I mean?"

He followed this with a wink.

"But then again, maybe you're into that fag shit anyways. If you are, it don't bother me none, but from the looks of it," he gestured around the room, "you ain't gonna get any dick in here either. Except for maybe Fred, I don't know cuz that son-of-a-bitch don't talk. Now what'd ya say you guys are doing here?"

I took the last sip of my beer and made the international sign for "two more" to Suzy. Then I turned to Mike, "Well, we're here doing some research. I do this book/zine/guide thingy called 'Broke-Ass Stuart's Guide to Living Cheaply in San Francisco', and we're out here doing research for volume two. Jonell's seemed like a perfect place for my book." At this point, I pulled out a copy and showed it to him.

"So, by research, you mean you're going around to a bunch of different bars, drinking, and taking notes," Mike asked. He was flipping through the book, looking amused.

"Exactly," I answered.

"You making any money doing this?"

"Nah, not really. And anything I do make just goes right back into the book."

"How much for a book?" Mike asked as he reached into his back pocket for his wallet.

"Five bucks," I said. I couldn't believe I was making a sale in Jonell's, of all places.

"Well, I've got your Fin right here, and I'll do you one even better." He put the five-dollar note on the table in front of me and proceeded: "The best bar in the world is just a few blocks from here. You ever heard of the Brown Jug over on Eddy and Hyde? Best bar in the world. My old lady's been working there for 22 years—beautiful American-Indian broad. We been married 30 years; can you believe that? Man, they got some nice atmosphere in there and a great jukebox, and boy, my old lady can really pour a drink. Take my advice," he looked down at the book, "Broke-Ass Stuart, that's a good name. Take my advice, Stuart—go in there and ask for Shelly. Tell her I sent you and tell her that I send my love."

How could I say no to that? I knew that if this guy Mike said the Brown Jug was the best bar in the world, it had to be a pretty fucking strange place. I almost felt like it was my civic duty to go check it out. Kenny and I settled our tab, said goodbye and thanked our new friends, and set out for Shelly and the Brown Jug.

My first impression of the Brown Jug was that it looked the way that redneck biker bars always look in movies. There were framed posters of motorcycles on the wall, and a neon Budweiser light that kept trying to end its miserable life, finally flickering out for good. But here's how we knew we were getting into some weird shit; instead of playing the expected music, like Lynyrd Skynyrd or David Allen Coe, the jukebox was blaring mid-80s adult contemporary light rock, like Level 42 or Hiroshima. A bit confused and caught off guard, we sat down at the bar and prepared to order some drinks.

I addressed the bartender who was drying some glasses behind the bar.

"Hi, are you Shelly?"

She eyed me suspiciously and said hesitantly, "Yeah."

"Cool," I said, "We just came from Jonell's, where we met Mike. He's a really nice guy. He told me to tell you 'Hi' and that he sends his love."

At this, she shook her head, chortled a bit, and walked away to grab some more glasses. Now I was really confused and felt a little uneasy. She came back and I tried once more, "Mike's your husband, right? He's the one who told us about this place. He said it was the best bar in the world."

Shelly put down the glass she was working on and spit out her reply, "I don't talk to that motherfucker when he's been drinking. Shit, I don't even talk to that motherfucker when he's been thinking about drinking, that rotten piece of shit." Um ... *awkward!* Shelly then picked up the glass again, took a breath, and said, "Now what the fuck can I get you?"

"Two Budweisers," Kenny answered.

I was really glad not to be talking to Shelly anymore. She brought over the beers, and Kenny paid her while I did my best not to look him in the eye for fear that I would lose my shit and burst into hysterical laughter. I turned to my right and saw at the end of the bar a lady looking like a washed-up, drunk as hell, Diana Ross making weird scrunched up faces at her drink. She and I made eye contact, so I waved to her and said, "Hello." She replied by giving me the finger. She continued to do so every time I looked over there for the rest of the night.

I turned to Kenny, holding back a giggle, and said, "You can't win 'em all," and then pulled out my notebook and began writing a few notes.

Meanwhile, Kenny somehow befriended the lost Supreme. I overheard him ask her, "So why don't you like my friend?"

"Cuz he's white! That's why! You're alright cuz ... what are you Chinese or something?" she asked.

"Uh, Taiwanese," he said.

She cut him off and mumbled, "Yeah, cuz you're Chinese or something. But he's white! Waving at me and smiling and shit." At this point, I looked over at them from my notebook and was once again met by her middle finger.

"Fuck it," I thought, and turned to my left, where I saw a crumpled-up old man who looked like he'd been sitting on the same bar stool every night since 1948. I smiled at him and nodded, but got no response. Just as I was about to return to my notebook, some cheesy song that only gets airplay on your mom's love song stations, like "I Go Crazy (Each Time that I Look in Your Eyes)" came on (okay, so I secretly love that song, but don't tell anyone). The old guy next to me suddenly got all animated and started silently waving his cigarette around in the air and grinning like someone who just had their first taste of baby flesh and realized that they loved it. This was the point when I realized that the Brown Jug probably *was* the best bar in the world, but that it was far too much for my fragile soul to handle. It was like having your mind opened up to all the secrets of the universe and realizing that maybe you didn't want to know those secrets after all. I gathered Kenny, and we walked out the door.

* * * *

"That was *amazing*," Kenny said as we were walking down Hyde towards Market Street.

"Dude, I know. I seriously can't wait to write about that shit. Like, I really gotta hand it to Mike; I think that old blowhard was right about the Brown Jug," I answered.

"Yeah, but I've got the feeling that the reason he thinks it's the 'Best Bar in the World' and the reason we do might be at odds with each other."

"You're probably right, but goddamn, I'm still really blown away." By this point, we'd had a good five or six drinks, and my stomach was telling me it was time to put some food in it. Call it the drunk munchies if you want. We were approaching Market. "Hey man, you hungry?" I asked Kenny.

"Yeah, I could eat. What's open?"

"Lemme think ... oh! *Yes! Yes!* Carl's Jr. at like 7th is open! Dude, have you ever had a Western Bacon Cheeseburger?"

"Nah man, I don't really eat fast food," Kenny said as we turned onto Market and I started leading us to the Promised Land of curly fries and milkshakes.

"It's not fast food! It's the fucking Western Bacon Cheeseburger! It's like in the upper echelon of man's achievements, with like, fire and space flight!" Kenny laughed, but I continued.
"I'm not fucking joking. This is serious; we're going. You don't have to have one, but I sure as hell am."

We went to Carl's Jr., where we both sat and ate our delicious Western Bacon Cheeseburgers amidst the homeless, the fluorescent lights, the rancor, and the stench that is Market Street at 2 a.m. I was satiated, and it had been a good night. I was ready to go home. Kenny and I walked out of Carl's Jr. and grabbed the first cab we saw.

The cabbie looked to be about our age, and he had a thick accent that sounded like he had grown up in a former Soviet republic, such as Russia or possibly Ukraine. Since he was driving one of those nice new cabs that Desoto always has, the car had a CD player. He was playing some Tupac. Just after I told him where to go, Kenny asked him, "Hey man, do you think you can turn that up?"

At this, the driver got all excited and, through his thick accent, said, "Oh, so you like Tupac? I love *him*! Tupac is my n**ga!" He then bumped the music and, as if to prove how big of a fan he was, rapped/screamed along with the lyrics— "How do you *vant* it? How do you *feel*? *Comen* up as a n**ga in *dat* cash game, *Liven* in *dat* fast lane, I'm for *real*!" The rest of the short ride consisted of the cab driver playing his favorite Tupac songs for us while he and Kenny discussed their theories about why Pac really wasn't actually dead. I was fucked up enough that I couldn't even tell if Kenny seriously thought Tupac was alive or if he was just egging this guy on.

We finally got dropped off in the Mission. Kenny lit his last cigarette contemplatively and said, "So, what a boring night, huh?"

I went along with it, "Yeah, nothing interesting ever happens to us."

"Did you at least get some good stuff for the book?"

"Nah, I think under the Tenderloin section I'll just put 'BORING' in big letters and leave the rest blank." We laughed at ourselves. "Thanks for coming out tonight, man, it was a lot of fun."

"Yes, it was. I'm glad we did it. You'll have to let me know when the next research trip is. I'm totally down to go." "Cool. I'm doing the Marina sometime this week."

"The Marina? Um...," Kenny blew out a puff of smoke, "scratch what I just said. You're on your own for the Marina."

"Fair enough," I said, and then we did the whole handshake/ man-hug thing and I went home and passed the fuck out.

WHEN SAN FRANCISCO FAILS THOSE WHO LOVE IT
San Francisco Examiner; 2018

"This really is an amazing city," Quincy said as we drove past the Panhandle on our way to dinner in the Sunset. She had just returned from traveling extensively through Germany, France, and England and was tying up loose ends before returning to London to continue graduate school.

"Sure, most of the soul has been sucked out," she continued, "but the city itself...there's no place quite like it." Quincy and I had been roommates for over 3 ½ years. Outside of just a handful of people, Quincy is the person I've lived with the longest since leaving my parents' place when I was 18. And now her time as a San Franciscan was officially ending.

San Francisco has long been a transient city – people would move to town because they'd always wanted to live here, stay for a few years, experiment with various lifestyle choices, get at least one questionable piercing or tattoo, and then move someplace else. The ones who stayed longer realized that they hadn't chosen San Francisco; it was San Francisco that had chosen them.

All that started changing around 2011 when the second tech boom kicked off. The siren call that had attracted so many to San Francisco wasn't crashing them into the rocks; it was now banishing them from the kingdom. Evictions skyrocketed, rental prices soared, and communities were wrenched apart, all so that people could be imported from around the world to fill the jobs being created in San Francisco, which weren't going to San Franciscans. And while the city itself remained a picturesque, fogged-in mini-city on the edge of the continent, the humans who made it truly special were rapidly being expelled.

No matter where you live, getting older is a series of life changes you'll need to get used to. The people I frolicked with in my mid-20s are different from the ones I hung out with in my early 30s, and those folks are different from the ones I spend my time with now. Sure, certain individuals remained constant during these times, and there, too, are others who pop in and out of the timeline like a recurring cameo in a Netflix series. There are also the ones who are now just people whose lives I see on Facebook. All of this is the natural byproduct of not dying young. If you live long enough, your life goes through changes; that's just how it works.

The difference with growing older in San Francisco is all the vitriol that has gone along with it over the last few years. I saw too many friends, lovers, and acquaintances leave, not because they wanted to, but because they no longer had a choice. Some were just too tired of fighting so hard for something that no longer loved them back.

It was heartbreaking for those of us who stayed to watch, but for those who left, it was devastating. So many of those who moved away felt a true love had betrayed them, and as they crossed a bridge in a moving truck or boarded a plane for their next chapter, they said, "To hell with San Francisco! I can't stand this place anyway."

Driving out towards dinner the other night — the car filled with Quincy, her sister Sasha, and our other roommate Nancy — I thought about how burnt out on San Francisco Quincy had been before her travels. She had finally hit that wall, and like everyone else, she did what came naturally: she left.

So, it was good to hear her speaking so lovingly about our city. "I missed this place so much," she told us as we turned onto Lincoln Way. "Despite everything, it really is a special place."

After dinner, as she dropped Nancy and me back off at the apartment, Quincy said, "It's weird to think that I don't know if I'll ever come back. Sure, I'll be back to visit, but I don't think I'll ever be able to live here again." I knew she meant that she wasn't sure if she could afford to live in San Francisco again. But she also meant something else: Once you give up on San Francisco as an idea, can you ever fully embrace it as just a place?

I guess those of us still living here are trying to answer that question every day.

Stuart Schuffman

SAN FRANCISCO'S INDEPENDENT HEART AND SOUL
Indie Mart Zine; 2009 or 2010

BACK in the LAte 2000's and EARly 2010's there WAS Indie MARt, A DAY Long PARtY where All Kinds oF LocAL ARtists, MAKeRS, WRiteRS, and CRAFteRS would Set up Booths and Sell their WAReS. It WAS A PReCuRSoR to Shit Like RenegAde CRAFt FAiR. This Piece is FRom A ZiNe that WAS GiveN out there. You cAN tell BY ReAding it. that SF WAS Still AN EpiCenteR FoR ARtists + WeiRdos.

From a city built on gold dust and denim to one tenaciously rebuilt after an earthquake and fire, San Francisco has a history of saying, "Fuck it, dude, I'll just do this shit myself." DIY culture runs deep here. Whether talking about longshoremen striking to create their own labor laws in the 30s, or hippies liberating their minds with rock and LSD in the 60s, or the nerds inventing Web 2.0 in the 90s, this city's pride has always been in looking at the surrounding culture and deciding to do something different. And that spirit is as alive today as it ever was.

Take the Indie Mart, for example. It started off in Kelly's backyard because she wanted to sell the shit that she and her friends made. And now look where it is, it's a god damn block party with over 100 vendors and thousands of attendees. Or look at what's happening in the Mission right now with all the food carts. A handful of people, fairly independent of one another, looked around and realized one day that San Francisco was severely lacking in street eats. Suddenly, carts are popping up all over the place, selling everything from muffins to curry and from *crème brûlée* to cookies. And maybe none of those people would have thought of doing such a thing if the Tamale Lady hadn't started her own DIY food trend nearly 15 years ago.

Yes, San Francisco is proud of her independent movers and thinkers, those who build, create, and tinker. And I'm proud of them too. I got my start making itty-bitty zines, like the one you're holding. I didn't do it to make money, I just did it to make *something*. And in a way, what makes this city so special is not just that people set out to create things simply for the sake of creation. What makes it special is that the rest of the community sets out to support these creations. Without that, we wouldn't have Burning Man or the Indie Mart or Power to the Peaceful or even Pride, for that matter.

So, consider this a toast to San Francisco, to the independent spirit, to DIY ethics, and to all you freaks and weirdos who consider this your home and make it so by both being creators and by supporting one another. Now let's have a drink.

AS THE MUNI BUS GROANS HYDRAULICALLY WHEN IT KNEELS TO LET SOMEONE ON
Previously Unpublished

As the sun rises over the building cranes outside my window
As the exhaust fans hum and whir from the Thai restaurant next door
As the fog sits wondering if it will stay or go
As the madman in the street bellows at monsters only he can see
As the bears walk hand-in-hand down the sidewalk in leather gear
As the paleta guy jingles his bells before taking a break in the shade
As the Muni bus groans hydraulically when it kneels to let someone on
As the girls in yoga pants promenade with rolled up mats
As the all-day drunks lean against each other while bumping music outside of 16th St. BART
As the gaggles of guys in Patagonia fleeces gabble about money
As the little Chinese grandmas carrying pink plastic bags elbow me to get on the bus
As the muralist adorns an empty building on Market St.
As the flocks of wild parrots squawk merrily from the trees above your head
As the Tenderloin simmers with sinners and saints, heartbreak and hope
As the independent bookstore sets up the sidewalk dollar bin
As the person ensnared by fentanyl nods off while standing up
As the brunchers cackle while day drunk on bellinis
As the perfect 65-degree weather keep us cool while the rest of the world bakes
I'm so glad to be home.

LIVING IN SAN FRANCISCO MEANS...
The Bold Italic; 2011

This was the first piece I did for the Bold Italic. It was their first thing to go crazy viral, helping put them on the map. It's also the first time I went viral. If you've never had something go viral before, let me just tell you, it is surreal.

Living in San Francisco means hearing your neighbors fuck. The noise comes through the walls, through the ceiling, through the floor. The sound of muffled moans and love murmurs in Spanish, in Cantonese, in Tagalog, in English, in Arabic, in French, in...

Living in San Francisco means having worked at a start-up, made lattes, mixed Bloody Marys, sold shitty clothing, waited on morons, and invested your heart, your soul, and all your energy into a nonprofit. It means still walking dogs, still trimming weed, still babysitting, still doing random gigs from Craigslist, still participating in clinical test studies at UCSF, still doing whatever the fuck it takes to pay rent in this city. It means thinking that half a million dollars for a one-bedroom condo is totally normal.

It means having fucked your ex-roommate, which is exactly why they're an "ex" roommate. It means walking into a party and encountering at least three people who've seen you naked. It means falling in love with someone you met at a free concert in Golden Gate Park.

Living in San Francisco means moving to the Mission and complaining that it's getting gentrified. It means knowing that the Marina isn't actually that bad after all, and recognizing that Nopa is a restaurant, and that the neighborhood is called the Western Addition. Knowing that Upper Haight is always about five degrees colder than Lower Haight. That 6th and Mission is both sad and shady. That the Outer Sunset and Outer Richmond are more than just fog-engulfed neighborhoods with fine ethnic food. That there's a certain magic in North Beach, as long as you don't go there on the weekends. That the Financial District is full of suits, Noe Valley is full of babies, SOMA is full of condos, and the Castro is full of gays. Actually, every neighborhood is full of gays.

Slouching Towards Neverland

Living in San Francisco means continually dealing with impermanence. It means having places you love close up forever. It means having friends get married and move to Oakland. Friends who leave to join the Peace Corps. Friends who go to rehab. Friends who lose their minds. Friends who move back to wherever the fuck they're from. Friends who OD and never move again. It means dreading the inevitable earthquake that will ultimately wash this city into the sea.

Living in San Francisco means never leaving the house without wearing layers, having just one wardrobe, and owning lots of hoodies. Owning lots of scarves. Owning lots of hoodies and scarves for your dog. It means having pale legs that get sunburned every time it's warm out. Calling in sick to work because, for once, it's 80 degrees and you want to drink a 40 in the park. Enduring the cold summer months and savoring the warmth and festivities of Indian Summer. It means being worried that the term "Indian Summer" may not be politically correct.

Living in San Francisco means embracing any cause for celebration. It means having a costume box for events like Bay to Breakers, the Love Parade, Burning Man, Halloween, Decompression, the How Weird Street Faire, or whatever new dress-up holiday gets added to the calendar this year. It means accidentally buying blow in the Beauty Bar and having a medical marijuana card. Getting 86'd from Zeitgeist for doing something stupid. Getting 86'd from Zeitgeist for no good reason at all. Drinking with 75-year-old Beat poets at Specs. Dancing in the streets when Obama won. Dancing in the streets when the Giants won. Dancing till 4 a.m. at The Endup, at Club Six, at 1015 Folsom, at some underground warehouse in the Bayview where the directions weren't even sent to you until 10 that night.

Living in San Francisco means having friends who are sex workers. Friends who have PhDs. Friends who have PhDs who are studying sex workers. It means having gay friends, straight friends, and friends who are somewhere in between. It means being open-minded about people—unless, of course, they're Republicans.

Living in San Francisco means waiting an hour for a cab if there's the slightest bit of rain. It means riding the Night Owl and thinking you're gonna get mugged by the teenagers in the back. Taking the 22 from the Marina to the Dogpatch and observing the city's vast spectrum of existence. Sitting on BART and trying not to think about what lives inside those cushions. Riding Muni and seeing feats both beautiful and wretched within seconds of each other.

It means walking these streets and witnessing broken beings weeping, sleeping, peeing, drinking, shitting, fighting, smoking crack, shooting up, screaming, bellowing, raging against some hellish torment that only they are privy to. It means having a local bum you kinda look out for, slipping her a buck or two, even though it's been her "40th birthday" every day for the past five years.

Living in San Francisco means coming over the Bay Bridge and having your heart race a little when you see the city's skyline. Crossing the Golden Gate and smiling at the way the fog sits right on top of it. Snaking up the 101 and Candlestick Park being the greeting that tells you you're almost home. It means visiting Middle America and being thought of as some kind of socialist gay hippie. It means traveling Europe and being considered one of the enlightened Americans. It means missing burritos, missing pho, missing Tapatio. It means missing Dolores Park, missing farmers' markets, missing the ability to walk wherever you need to go. It means flying back from two and a half months in South America and getting a little teary-eyed watching *Doctor Doolittle*, just because it's set in San Francisco.

Living in San Francisco means the midday smell of pot. Cold winter winds that cut right through you. Sweet summer strawberries are grown not too far away. Crisp salty air by the ocean. The occasional sound of gunshots. Being able actually to count the number of stars visible in the sky. Warm whiskey and late-night chatter on a new friend's rooftop. It means walking by bodily waste and unfortunately being able to tell that it's from a human, just by the way it smells. It means feeling the hum of the city as it gets revved up for another Saturday night.

Living in San Francisco means loving this city for all its fantasies, its freedoms, its fuckery, and its follies, and being excited to read something that begins: Living in San Francisco means...

SAN FRANCISCO SUNDAY MORNING
Instagram; 2016

In 2016 there was a ballot measure in SF called "PROP Q" that aimed to take tents away from homeless people. Despite its cruelty (why would you take shelter from them without offering some in return) PROP Q actually passed... Not that it's been enforced.

Walking home from your place
at 8 in the morning
on Sunday
still early enough that
people haven't come out to find
their car windows smashed yet

I play "Ivy" by Frank Ocean
And then I play it again

The City is still wet and sleeping
from last night's parties and rain
The homeless are soggy
and defeated and yet people who live in homes
want to take their tents away

SAN FRANCISCO IS MORE THAN A MUSE, IT'S A LIFE PARTNER, A LOVER, AND A BEST FRIEND
A zine put out by the bar Monarch. 2013

In one of our drunk, late-night bouts of revelry, my friend Kelly said something every single person who loves San Francisco feels, "I don't want a relationship that gets in the way of my relationship with San Francisco." I understood exactly what she meant. I write about San Francisco all the time, but to say that she's my muse would be incorrect. This is partially because it's cheesy, but even more so because it's not entirely true. San Francisco is more than just a muse; she's one of the most important things in my life.

Stuart Schuffman

We don't choose San Francisco, San Francisco chooses us. We arrive by train or plane or car and she emits a whisper that hits a frequency not everyone can here. Like an ancient mermaid saying, "We are for each other" and when you know it's true, you do everything you can to be with her. You pay stupid fucking rents and you work stupid fucking jobs. You live with too many roommates and you simplify your life, becoming ok with not having things like a car, a dishwasher, laundry machines or pretty much all the little comforts that come with living in the 21st Century. In a way, you're sacrificing modernity to be living in a city that, ironically, is working so desperately hard to redefine what the word means.

I believe in San Francisco; I believe in its whys and its hows. I believe in the way that even the slightest amount of fog can effect how the light looks. I believe in the magic of dancing in the streets in costumes just for the fuck of it. I believe in being able to smoke pot and drink outside without being hassled. And I believe in a city that is full of people with open minds and open hearts who really, at their core, want to see the world become a better place.

But sometimes San Francisco scares me. It's not the shards of thuggery that occasionally explode into your world, physically taking your wallet or bag by force. And it's not the itty-bitty pieces of car windows that litter the concrete like street diamonds. It's far bigger than that. It's the systematic dismantling of all that we find holy in this city. What is San Francisco when we start telling people they can't be naked in the Castro, or that the Tamale Lady can't sell her wares, or when we start kicking out old pensioners who just want to hang out and play chess all day on Market Street?

What is San Francisco when we start bowing to big tech companies and giving them everything they want? How can we be the same city that disallows a chain to have more than 11 locations, but then give tax breaks to other huge businesses?

The San Francisco that we love, the one who we don't want any relationship to get in the way of our relationship with, seems to be getting chased away in front of our eyes. Places that would've been underground warehouse spaces 10 years ago are now offices full of people who view The City, not as a place to build community, but simply a place to make money. As the people who've made this city such a strong and vibrant place, full of weirdos and underdogs, get pushed out, it just reinforces the fact that those of us that stay here have a responsibility. We have a responsibility to keep San Francisco strange, to keep it funky, to serve as ambassadors for *the other*, and most importantly, to stick-up for and fight for the people and the places that are still here.

San Francisco is more than a muse, it's life partner, a lover, and a best friend. As long as there are still strong beats, and heavy base, and circus freaks doing circus freak things, this will always be our city. Let's just make sure that, as a community, that we do everything we can to keep it that way.

FOGUST IN SAN FRANCISCO
San Francisco Examiner. August 2016

The Fog is one of the things I adore most about SF, so I wrote a beautiful little love letter to it. The "Burnt Buildings" comment is a reference to fires that some folks saw as caused by greedy landlords.

It's Fogust here in San Francisco. Our Great Grey Dame can even be seen sashaying through the Mission District, leaning gently into the husks of burnt buildings as if she's peering in with sadness. The downtown skyscrapers, those monuments to industry and wealth, look as if the sky got tired of being scraped and decided to throw a blanket on them. The Sunset and the Richmond have been lost altogether, and the search party says they won't be found again until September.

Yes, Fogust ... it must have been Fogust when the person who is not Mark Twain made that famous Twainian remark about the coldest winter being a summer in San Francisco. That person must've been relatively new to San Francisco because there's a hint of incredulousness in there. Newbies view our foggy summers as something they have to endure, unfortunately. Those of us who've given ourselves completely to The City view this as the time we feel most at home.

I was up in Lake Tahoe last weekend, doing things you can't do in San Francisco, like breathe in fresh pine air, swim in temperate water, and wear shorts. It was in the 80s each day, and people basked in the sun while lying on the beach. It was nice to see what summer felt like to the rest of the world.

Driving back through the Central Valley, the temperature reached as high as 110 degrees — an ugly number that would make the entirety of San Francisco melt like wax. Then, crossing over the Emperor Norton Bridge, as the fog draped across The City like someone passed out peacefully on a couch. I sighed with love as the temperature tumbled down to Fogust numbers. It's always wonderful to come home, and I look silly in shorts anyway.

It was the fog that shrouded the Golden Gate from Sir Francis Drake when he sailed up the coast. He had no idea what kind of magnificence he passed by on his way north. The fog hid the entire Bay from him. And in a way, that's what Fogust does to those who can't wait around for September.

As far as I know, the jury is still out as to whether or not the term "Indian Summer" is racist, but they have brought back a verdict saying that September and October are the best months to be in San Francisco.

Nobody appreciates nice weather like San Franciscans. We may feel most at home during our cold and foggy summers, but come September, The City springs to life all twitterpated and ready to mingle. By that time, the tourists have mostly gone home, and every weekend has some sort of decadent splendor — Folsom Street Fair, Hardly Strictly Bluegrass, Fleet Week — all of it hitting a crescendo with Halloween before it peters out into our (hopefully) rainy months.

But right now, it's Fogust, and the best way to honor that is to do what San Franciscans have been doing for a century and a half: Walk through the evening, arm in arm with someone you might be in love with, and use their scarf to pull them closer while you lean in for a kiss. Or sit in a dark bar, occasionally looking out the window, while you scribble poetry about the one that got away. Or stay up late on a rooftop with new friends, drinking whiskey and telling stories. Or stay

Photo by Griffin Wooldridge

in early, reading a book about all the places you've yet to see.

Fogust is romance thrown into the atmosphere. Just when you feel like you're too busy or too old or too jaded to feel romantic about anything ever again, step outside and realize that at least you'll always have Fogust.

RENT CONTROL IN SAN FRANCISCO IS A GOLDEN HANDCUFF

BrokeAssStuart.com; 2014

I wrote most of this drunk one night after being at the bars. I got up the next day and was surprised by how good it was, so I cleaned it up, finished it, and put it on my site. It resonated with Alot of people. At dinner that night someone leaned over and thanked me for writing it.

Stuart Schuffman

It's a hell of a thing to know
that once you have to move,
you can never come back again.
That this is the last place you will ever live,
in San Francisco,
The City
that you love and that you've given so much to.

Having already chosen a life of semi-austerity
where you skip many modern comforts
like washing machines,
and dishwashers, in exchange for the low rumble of Mission Street mornings.

To live like you're in a perpetual state of being a college student,
in the sense that,
you reside amongst mini generations of other people's stuff.
Mixed matched spoons and cutlery;
a revolving door of roommates and their things.

Often times no one knows or remembers
where these droplets of ephemera even came from,
but now they are part of the house
and essentially part of your life,
because you can never leave.

Living in San Francisco,
and having rent control,
has become a sort of golden handcuff.
If you ever need to move,
or get evicted,
you have to essentially trade in your San Francisco citizenship.

The Visigoths are at the gates
and will gladly take your place,
thinking that they've moved into something special,
without realizing,
they are pushing out the specialness like spin art.

You are the drops of paint that make the color,
but the faster things spin,
all that's left,
are the streaks showing where you used to be.

Slouching Towards Neverland

Artwork by Abby Wilcox; courtesy of The Bold Italic by GrowSF

I wrote this in October 2011 for the Bold Italic. I'd been a San Franciscan for almost a decade and felt like I knew almost everything there was to know about this place. So, I was excited to explore a legendary underground SF tradition. I was also excited to get paid decently for it. This was from the first iteration of the Bold Italic. I think we're on the fifth now. There are some minor edits in this piece because, as it was initially intended for the web, I had to remove links and instead add words to ensure the sentence makes sense.

Stuart Schuffman

DO YOU KNOW ABOUT THE CUTTY BANG, SF'S HOMEGROWN LIQUOR STORE COCKTAIL?
The Bold Italic; 2011

I was sitting across from a guy who was dating, or fucking, or somewhere in between, a friend of mine. "Have you heard about Cutty Bang?" he asked. "My friend Serg, out in San Francisco, who runs this blog called Beer And Rap, told me about it. There are a bunch of bodegas in SF that take airplane bottles of booze, mixers, and a cup with ice, wrap them together with a rubber band, and sell them. Cutty Bang is the most famous, but there are all different kinds."

What the fuck? I hadn't been that interested in our conversation, but at this point I perked up. How could I not know about this? How could there be something so elusive and underground in San Francisco that I, someone who almost fetishizes such things, hadn't heard about it? The second I got home, I'd have to look into this. It would be my great white whale. My mythical beast. I would hunt down this so-called Cutty Bang, and I would drink it. Then I'd write about it.

Unfortunately, the day I got home, Serg had published an article about Cutty Bangs on the Uptown Almanac blog. So, I decided to let the story go and tried to put it out of my mind. It just didn't work. Every once in a while, I'd think about the drink and its brilliant possibilities, and then the TayDaTay song "Cutty Bang" would play in my head. Goddamn you, TayDaTay, you twisted genius! Finally, I reached out to Serg both for his blessing and his guidance. At the current moment, I have a fridge full of airplane bottles and mixers rubber-banded together in little baggies. This is how it all went down.

Sorry Charlie.

I started at Charlie's Pharmacy in the Fillmore, apparently one of the main players in the Cutty Bang game. Rumor was these guys sold so many Cutty Bangs and its variations that they even had a menu with pictures. I approached the counter and the dude rocking a Giants shirt standing behind it. "Hey man, you guys sell Cutty Bangs?"

"Nope," he answered.

"What're all those little bottles and mixers grouped together over there?" I pointed to a few shelves behind him that were filled with exactly what I had asked for. Well, almost... I didn't see the combo of Seagram's, Tanqueray, Bacardi Limon, and pineapple juice, the sum of which equals a Cutty Bang.

"Well, we used to sell Cutty Bangs, but we don't anymore. Too many people started copying us, so we stopped naming them and instead just assigned them numbers. To stop the copycats, we switch up which number is which every once in a while. In a few months, I may put the Cutty Bang back in rotation."

The man behind the counter is Nick Shoman, one of the store's owners. He went on to tell me that copycats aren't even the whole problem; the real issue is Johnny Law. Apparently, a city ordinance was passed that made it challenging to sell these hallowed drinks. While liquor stores could still package and sell the ingredients together, they were banned from vending them alongside the cups and ice.

This, of course, irked Shoman. His take was this: The cops got on his case for selling the drinks because people were drinking them outside his store, but why didn't the cops do anything about the people who were actually drinking them? Good question, Nick.

Name of the Game.

Before leaving, I had to find out where the hell these names came from (back when names were used) and what kind of magnificent bastard created these elixirs. The answers were simple. The names came from popular songs, whatever was in the news, or off the top of Nick and his brother's heads.

And the drinks? Nick and his brother put together whatever they think sounds good. They must have a knack for this, considering they've been doing it for 10 years. Nick was cagey about revealing the names of the drinks because he was worried about the competition stealing his shit. He allowed that the #7 was the Obama and was made from pineapple juice, Don Julio, Bacardi Limón, Sour Apple Pucker, and Bacardi Big Apple. I bought an Obama just in case the president wants to throw one back with me next time he's in town.

I walked out of Charlie's Pharmacy feeling dejected by the fact that, technically, I hadn't found what I was looking for. Satisfaction wouldn't be had until I walked out of a place with a Styrofoam cup and ice, as well as the potent baggie of booze. The Cutty Bang was turning out to be my mythical beast after all.

Legendary Status.

I headed down to Bayview Liquors on Third Street and Newcomb. According to legend, this is where the Cutty Bang and all her siblings originated. I walked into the liquor store and asked if they sold Cutty Bangs. At first, I thought I'd scored; they had them! But then the other shoe dropped. I'd have to get the cup and ice somewhere else. Sammy B, the young cat behind the counter, said the cops cracked down on Cutty Bangs and their ilk because of the litter they created. Apparently, before the heat, Bayview Liquors sold nearly 20 drinks a day.

I looked into the deli fridge and saw a handful of drinks packaged together in sandwich baggies.

"Which is the most popular?"

"The High Speed," he replied.

"Which is what?"

"Two Bacardi Limóns, Seagram's, and a Red Bull."

"Which is the best tasting?"

He thought about it, reached down, and put a filled baggie on the counter: "The Freaky. It's got Skyy vodka, Cîroc vodka, Bacardi, and cranberry-grape juice."

"And what's this?" I pointed to an extra-colorful one, and Sammy placed it on the counter next to the Freaky.

"This is the Freak Me."

"It's different than the Freaky?"

"Yeah, it's fruity. It's got cranberry juice, Bacardi Melon, Watermelon Pucker, Cîroc vodka, and Tanqueray."

"Is it good?"

"Yeah."

Speed Freak.

Just as Sammy finished, a chick in her mid-twenties came in the door, saw the bundle, and said, "Oh shit! Who's buying the Freak Me?"

"I am," I said, and then asked, "Is that your favorite?"

"Fuck yeah," she said. "It's the best!" I liked her enthusiasm. I bought it.

Just then, a flamboyant dude looking like Sisqo, minus the millions he made off the "Thong Song," walked in. He followed me outside and told me that next time I got a High Speed, I should get it with an energy drink called "Hunid Racks." He informed me that his name is Anthony, and that not only is he a singer, but he's also somehow involved in the "Hunid Racks" business. How wasn't precisely clear.

After hitting a couple more stores, only to be met with the same answer, my bag was overflowing with airplane bottles and mixers. I stopped at a Subway to get a cup with some ice and treated myself to the Hunid Racks version of the High Speed in honor of my new friend Anthony. It was a light turquoise color, but not very appealing.

Crazy Town.

Finally, I set my sights on the Tenderloin. Where else in San Francisco (or the developed world, for that matter) are laws so flagrantly disregarded? I mean, crack heads are buzzing through the streets like goddamn velociraptors at any hour. I doubted the cops could give two shits about whether or not a bodega was selling Cutty Bangs.

I started on a random stretch in the heart of the madness. The first-place yielded questioning looks and indifference. In the second place, the dude knew of the High Speed and could put one together for me, but again, no cups and ice. As I walked out, I got stopped by an old timer who looked like the absolute worst of what the Tenderloin could do to a person. The world had kicked this guy's ass. He said, "Thanks for being here. The neighborhood is changing and coming up. Thanks for being part of it." And then walked away. I'm like catnip for crazy.

As I walked into my third liquor store in the TL, I was resigned to the fact that the glory days of the Cutty Bang were over. The sun had set on this elusive beast, and I'd missed my chance to do what any free human deserves: to make a ghetto-ass cocktail and drink it on the street in front of the store he bought the fixins in. If the Cutty Bang was dead, then a tiny part of America was also dead. And a little part of me, too. My great white whale had gotten away.

Ice Cold.

I walked up to the counter to give it one last try. "Hey man," I said, "do you sell Cutty Bangs?" The old guy behind the counter looked at me like I was a fool. "Of course, my friend. And the High Speed, too. Which is it you want?"

"Yeah, but do you have cups with ice?"

The same look of exasperation came over his face. "Of course! Did you not look in the freezer?" He pointed behind me. I went over and opened the door. Sure enough, there was a plethora of cups and ice waiting to be plucked from the bowels of the freezer and filled with the cocktail of my choosing.

I walked out of there with a smile on my face and a Cutty Bang in my hand. The good guys had won for once. And if I ignored the human feces on the sidewalk and the crack head zombies fluttering around me, all was right with the world. Plus, I had a messenger bag filled with airplane bottles and mixers. At least my fridge would be full of something for once.

Do it Yourself.

Wanna get your own Cutty Bang or some variation of it? Stop in to Charlie's Pharmacy at 1101 Fillmore. The #7 may still be the Obama. Check out Bayview Liquors, the original home of the Cutty Bang, at 4700 3rd St. to get tons of different kinds of these little liquor-store libations. As for the spot in the Tenderloin, I'm not trying to get anyone busted, so you'll have to find that one yourself.

SEE YOU IN THE PARK, SAN FRANCISCO
7x7; 2013

It's already 70 degrees outside and the day's not even half over. The weather thingy on my computer says the high is gonna be 78 today, but what the fuck does it know? In my experience here, anytime it's predicted to be above 73, it invariably ends up being in the 80s. And there's nothing worse than a gorgeous day in the Bay Area in the middle of the work week.

It's demoralizing. Really nice days in San Francisco are our snow days. Granted, schools and businesses don't close, but they might as well. Workers who are otherwise excellent and punctual suddenly come down with the kind of food poisoning that can only be cured by drinking beers in the park, going for a hike, driving to Bodega Bay, or, actually, like for realisies, going to lie out on one of San Francisco's beaches. I want to do all of the above right now. I just texted a friend who works in the Presidio that we should both play hooky and frolic out there in search of its famed pet cemetery. She has a better work ethic than I do, apparently, as evidenced by her response with multiple sad emoji faces.

But that's just it: There just isn't a sufficient combination of emoticons to adequately express how we as San Franciscans absolutely lose our fucking minds when the weather turns this warm. When a city renowned for its open-mindedness and disregard for rules receives what amounts to a moral get-out-of-jail-free card, it truly turns hedonistic. People stay out late drinking, smoking, and screwing even more than they usually do with an air of abandon that says, "This literally may not ever happen again." And that's how it really feels. We're so used to layers of clothes and layers of fog that collectively, as community, as a city, as a county, we take up a single voice and say, "Fuck this. I'm going to the park."

Yes, San Francisco, you are going to the park today, and guess what? Everybody is gonna be really good-looking. While we gush about the millions of reasons why San Francisco is the best city in America, we often follow the sentence by muttering something to the extent of, "But people here just aren't as good-looking as they are in New York or L.A. or San Diego." While that may or may not be the case, a large part of it is the fact that it's perpetually autumn in San Francisco. You don't even know what the person you're dating knees look like until the first time you get them naked. It's like Karl the Fog has somehow managed to make us adhere to Victorian standards of decency just because he fancies himself a history buff. But all that changes on days like today. Suddenly, the hipster girls who dress like flirty grandmas show some skin, and you realize they have nice figures under all that ill-fitting frumpery. The nerdy tech guys wear tank tops, and you notice that all that time they spend in the gym after work is shamefully being obscured by the fact that they wear hoodies all year long.

And here I am, sitting in my sweltering room in my underwear, typing away on my computer, just trying to figure out a way to end this piece so I can, in fact, play hooky. Fuck emails, fuck writing, fuck worrying about paying my bills. Fuck scarfs, fuck sweaters, fuck having the chills. It's beautiful outside and I need to take part in it. I just hope a cold front comes in soon so I can get back to work.

I'll see all you beautiful people in the park, San Francisco.

Artwork by Richard Perez/Skinny Ships; courtesy of The Bold Italic by GrowSF

WHY ARE ALL MY FRIENDS MOVING TO OAKLAND?
The Bold Italic; 2013

My friends say they are moving to Oakland because San Francisco has let them down. The douchebags are winning. Divis is clogged with Google buses. Valencia is drowning in shmancy new restaurants. North Beach is full of knuckleheads. Mark Zuckerberg bought a house in the Mission. The artists are leaving. The city is gentrifying.

My friends say they're moving to Oakland because the rent is cheaper. The landlords aren't looking for ways to kick you out. You won't have to share a room with six roommates. You won't get outbid for a room by some dot-com fuckface. You won't have to be a mildly well-known writer just to get invited to interview for an affordable room. When you break up with your girlfriend, you won't have to keep living with her for two months since neither of you can afford to move out. They say they're moving to Oakland because it's the town that could, not the city that already did.

Slouching Towards Neverland

My friends say they're moving to Oakland because it has heart. Because it's less cynical and less self-conscious. Because it's more diverse and more friendly. Because you actually get to know your neighbors instead of just nodding to them in passing on the stairs. Because there's no one from the Marina. They say they're moving to Oakland because it has a thriving art scene. The kind that murmurs as a monthly street fair. The kind that shapes late at night in underground warehouses, in community workspaces, as wheat paste in the streets, as protest in Oscar Grant Park.

My friends say they're moving to Oakland because there's more space. They extol the many merits of Lake Merritt. They're moving because there's room to park your car. There are parks in the hills from which you can see stars. They'd rather see the view of San Francisco from afar. My friends say they're moving because they can have a backyard. You can have a vegetable garden, chickens, dogs, and potbellied pigs. Actually, one of my friends doesn't know if she can have a potbellied pig. But she really wants one.

My friends say they're moving to Oakland because it's far less disgusting. They say Oakland doesn't smell like piss and shit. That they don't have to step over syringes and crack pipes each time they leave their homes. No 6th Street zombies and no Tenderloin. No 16th Street BART crackheads and no 24th Street BART drunks. They say they're moving to Oakland because there's no human feces sprayed against the wall like some utterly demented Jackson Pollock painting.

My friends say they're moving to Oakland because the weather is better. Because Oakland is always 10 degrees warmer. They get an actual summer, one where you don't need a space heater and you might even be able to get a tan. Because fuck Indian Summer. And fuck always wearing layers and fuck having hoodies for your dog. They say they're moving because on New Year's Eve and the Fourth of July, you can see fireworks light up the whole goddamn Bay Area and not just pop in muted colors through the cover of fog.

My friends say they're moving to Oakland because they can. They say they're moving because it feels like something special is happening there. They compare it to Brooklyn because of the bridge and the tunnel, as well as the exodus of artists and working-class people. They say it's like Portland but with way more black people. Some of them say they are moving to Oakland like they think they're some kind of pioneer settlers. Just like some kind of pioneer settlers, they'll realize there were people there before them.

They're moving to Oakland so they can rep it, wearing shirts that say, "I Hella ♥ Oakland."

My friends say they are moving to Oakland for the restaurants and bars. Because they love Bakesale Betty, Zachary's, Miss Ollie's, and Dogwood, they love Flora, Heart & Dagger Saloon, Cafe Van Kleef, and Beer Revolution. They Love Linden Street Brewery, Eritrean food, taco trucks, and the Tamale Guy. They say one of these days they'll finally try Giant Burger.

My friends say they're moving to Oakland because it's edgier and imperfect. The robberies, the gunshots, the Oakland PD. The rioting, the protests, the Oakland PD. They say they are moving because they see the writing on the wall, the beginning of a gold rush. They want to establish roots and grow with Oakland as it grows, creating a community and actively participating in it, while raising their kids within it and owning property. Helping shape what might be the next great American city.

My friends say they're moving to Oakland because all their friends seem to be moving there. They say San Francisco is done. That Oakland is now like the San Francisco they remember, or the one they wished they lived in, or the one they imagined when they moved here from wherever it was they came from.

My friends say they're moving to Oakland because it's just across The Bay, and they say, "You'll come visit, right?" and you say you will. And this time you might be actually telling the truth.

But I'm not moving, I'm staying in San Francisco. I'm staying because I can walk everywhere I need to go. Because no matter how much they raise the rent, this is still a city of freaks and misfits. Because no one gushes in adoration for their city the way San Franciscans do. I'm staying because my city loves me. And fuck, do I love her back.

Also, I've got pretty damn good rent control.

OUTSIDE THE GOLD RUSH
Slouching Towards Neverland Zine; 2022

I wrote this in 2013 for the Bold Italic but it never got published for some reason. You can tell that things were really starting to go off the rails in SF at this point. In this case "Tech Boom" refers to what happened to SF in the 2010's while "Dot Com" is what happened in the 90's.

Ca-CLANK, Ca-CLANK, Ca-CLANK, go the shopping carts outside my window, shuttling between anywhere and nowhere, filled with cans and glass and bits of lifetimes lived within bottles and bindles and needles and numbness. Passersby play urban hopscotch, skipping and jumping over smeared and chunky plops of human shit that pepper the sidewalks. One of those luxury liners of the street lumbers by, whisking away tech workers to parts not unknown, just uninteresting. I feel I'm caught in between, that pretty soon, I won't be rich enough or poor enough to live in San Francisco, the city that is my home.

    I moved to San Francisco in 2002, a time I like to call "between gold rushes." The fervor and swagger of the first dot-com boom had not so much burst as it had flown around the city like a balloon with the air let out, taking down everything it crashed into. San Francisco had ridden the dot-com monster into the 21st century on a wave of optimism and massive change, and not unlike the original gold rush that created this place, more than just a handful of people ended up with obscene wealth. And then, like anything too good to be true, it ended with a whimper, causing those who hadn't managed to strike a vein of digital ore to leave and pick up the pieces and create something of their own.

    This is the San Francisco I moved into. That stretch of the Western Addition, centered around Divisadero, was still, for the most part, a Black neighborhood, and the real estate people hadn't yet figured out how to make it sound less like one by renaming it NoPa. The Tenderloin was as heartbreaking as it is now, but its residual influence stretched a bit further beyond its borders. The Mission was recovering from the initial influx of yuppies that had occurred during the dot-com gold rush, and then from the purge that followed its end.

It was quickly filling up with young people like myself who fancied themselves painters, writers, musicians, or anything else that falls under the category of artist. At the time, we wouldn't have said we were gentrifying these neighborhoods because we didn't really realize it. We mainly were just young, broke, and idealistic, looking for a place to call home where the rent wasn't too steep and the hills weren't either.

Since that time, I've gone on to write three books, founded a fairly popular arts and culture website, and created and hosted my own travel show. But despite all that artistic success, I'm still as broke and struggling as ever. I've loudly added my voice to the cultural patchwork of San Francisco, and I've put in my goddamn time here, 11 years of it. And despite all of this, I'm getting more and more worried that there may not be a future for people like me in San Francisco. This has long been a city full of creators, doers, and participants. People who make things in the long hours of the night just to share them with others who might similarly revel in the uniqueness of the moment. People who create things like Burning Man, Bay to Breakers, or the Internet. Yes, I see the irony there.

The internet probably wouldn't have become the thing it is today without the "Hey, let's try this!" culture that permeates the Bay Area. So, it's ironic that the internet is the very thing that seems to be choking that culture out so desperately. And here's the thing, I don't feel like it's on purpose. People aren't being like "Oh fuck all these weirdos, I want to institute some homogeneity here." In fact, it's the opposite; many of the people who are attracted to the spirit of this place are the ones who are killing it. Like a non-native plant being introduced to a new environment, these people are looking around and saying, "Hey, I think I like it here. I can really spread out." And that's exactly what they end up doing. Take Jason Evanish, for example. He seems to really dig San Francisco, but in his viral article "25 Things I wish I knew before moving to San Francisco," he has no fucking clue that there's anything here that is not related to technology.

Where does that leave the people who make the city run? People who work at city hall, people who drive Muni buses, people who put out fires, people who show up when you call 911? What does it mean for a city when those people can't afford to live there? And where does that leave people like me, people in the arts who just wanna make cool shit; things that make people laugh, things that make people appreciate the world around them and see that it's full of wonder? These sidewalks scream poetry, literally. Elvis Christ puts them there. And this city is beautiful. It makes you want to fall in love and be happy to be alive. There are literally hundreds of songs written about San Francisco. Who's gonna write those if the artists are gone? And how many of those songs do you think were written about your fucking app?

What I'm trying to get at is that not all worth can be measured in dollars. Jack Hirschman is worth more than your startup. Vicki Marlane was worth more than your startup. Harvey Milk was worth more than your startup. We're in the midst of yet another gold rush. In contrast, the original one led to an explosion of population, culture, and ideas, ultimately resulting in the creation of one of the most cosmopolitan cities on earth.

This one might leave us with something that San Francisco has never been called in its 150+ year run: Fucking Boring.

NO ONE IS REALLY EVER ANONYMOUS IN SAN FRANCISCO
The Bold Italic; 2013

I used the terms "Junky" and "Crackhead" in this piece. If I were writing it now, I definitely wouldn't have used those words since they are kinda fucked up things to call people who are already getting the shit kicked out of them by life. Hopefully they've gotten the help they needed and gotten back on their feet.

Reno calls itself the "Biggest Little City in the World." That's bullshit. Anyone who's lived in San Francisco knows that's a title that should be wedged between "Baghdad by the Bay" and "The City That Knows How" in our pantheon of monikers. If you've been here long

Stuart Schuffman

Artwork by Juan Leguizamon, courtesy of The Bold Italic by GrowSF

enough, it's impossible not to run into someone you know; it's one of San Francisco's many charms. We encounter pieces of our past in the random people we run into daily. This can occasionally be awkward, depending on which chapter of your biography opens itself in your path, but mostly it feels like being part of a wonderful community.

There are people within this community, though, who float around the peripheries of our existences whom we notice, but who don't always notice us. Some are people we've had brief encounters with, but who don't remember us. Others are folks we've seen around for years, silently witnessing the way they wear the triumphs and failures that life indiscriminately hands out. We see them on the bus, on the street, in the park. We see them at the café, at the bar, on BART. They are tiny question marks or ellipses in the stories of our lives, and they don't even realize they're part of it.

Think for a second about the "anonymous" San Franciscans in your life. Got them? Now read about some of mine.

The Junky Homeless Lady Who Has Gotten Her Shit Together

I've seen her around 16th and Valencia for as long as I can remember. Looking sallow and scabby, she always asked me for change, each time having a different story as to why she needed it. Just the other week, I saw her walking down Folsom Street looking amazing. She had on new shoes and clothes, and possibly had a new set of teeth. There was a healthy color and fullness to her face. Dangling from her neck was an enormous crucifix. It seems like finding God helped her find herself.

The Guy Whose Name Might Be Frank

He worked with me for a couple of weeks at a mediocre Italian restaurant in North Beach. Our boss had seen him help an old lady across the street and hired him on the spot, although the Guy Whose Name Might Be Frank had never waited tables before. He was terrible at being a waiter and ended up quitting a few weeks later. He has the look of someone who enjoys camping/hiking/rock climbing and was probably an Eagle Scout/Marine. I saw him sitting in the window at Four Barrel recently and wondered if he still helps old ladies cross the street.

The 16-Year-Old with Blue Hair

I see her more often than the others here because she works at a popular breakfast place. I met her when I was 21 and smoking a joint on Hippie Hill. She ambled up to us, plopped down, and then told us she was 16 and on mushrooms. She had blue hair, and we gave her some of our joint. A few years back, I ran into her at a bar and mentioned this, but she was drunk, so I don't know if she recalled either of our meetings, or maybe she pretended not to.

The Eritrean Guy Whom I Spent Christmas Eve With

I see this guy in bars or walking down the street, but he never notices me. I met him nearly 20 years ago on Christmas Eve at a bar called the Red Room, which no longer exists. The place was filled with a dozen or so people who had nowhere else to go, so we found each other on barstools and shared stories and loneliness. I'd never heard of Eritreans or Eritrea before that night, and he explained the history of the Ethiopia/Eritrea conflict to me. There were a few other people who hung with us that night whom I doubt I'd ever remember. Sometimes I wonder if they've seen me around and recognize me, but I don't recognize them.

The Crackhead Homeless Lady Who Has Definitely Not Gotten Her Shit Together

In fact, she's gotten worse. I met her many years ago at 3:30 a.m. in Orphan Andy's. It was one of those late-night discussions, the ones that feel important, though you can't recall what they were about — the kind in which all eight people in the late-night diner get involved.

Many of them were pretty bad off, but she was the worst, tweaking and twitching throughout the conversation, contributing when she could. With her high cheekbones and big eyes, she might have been beautiful at one point, but years of drug use had ravaged her. These days, I see her on corners like 16th and Mission and 11th and Howard, among piles of possessions. She's often wearing some strange wig and a few dresses that, just like her, might have once been magnificent.

The Older Mexican Man Who Used to Live Next Door to Me

In my early and mid-20s, I lived near 23rd and Guerrero. Next door to us was a duplex in which three generations of a family lived. At least once a month, they would host an awesome party attended by their larger extended family. *Mariachi* and *Ranchera* music would play loudly from the garage, and a feast of food and beer would continue all day long. I'd always walk by on my way home and say hello, secretly wishing to be invited in for a beer and a taco, but it never happened. I still occasionally see the patriarch on Mission Street wearing his cowboy hat and boots. The one time I smiled and nodded at him, he responded, but he seemed to have no idea who I was. I still wanna go over for a beer and tacos.

SAN FRANCISCO IS SLOWLY SHIFTING AWAY FROM BEING OUR NEVERLAND

The Bold Italic; 2015

Hooo boy did this thing light up the internet when it came out! Everyone had an opinion about it and some douche nozzle at SF Magazine even wrote a hit piece in about me and the article in response. The internet giveth and the internet taketh.

My mom always asks me when she's going to be a grandmother. Most of the time, it's in jest, but sometimes, when it's just she and I in the car running errands, she gets more serious about it. "You're not so young anymore," she tells me, not in a mean way, but in a mom way — meaning that it comes from a place of love, but also that she won't be dancing around some shit.

And she's right that I'm not so young anymore. I'm 34 years old and living like I'm 24. I have three roommates whom I met on Craigslist. I'm in an often-unsteady relationship (due in part to my Peter Pan Syndrome), and I want nothing to do with anything that requires me to be responsible for anything or anyone other than myself. And the thing is, I can't imagine having any other kind of life... and I'm not sure I want to.

We always refer to San Francisco as Neverland. But as more and more Peters and Wendys and Lost Boys and Tinker Bells are pushed out of the city, I wonder if we can continue with this fantasy. Can a Peter Pan like myself survive in a Neverland diaspora?

It's easy to be forever young when the landscape that you live in doesn't support adulthood. Shirking grown-up responsibilities like car payments is simple when you can ride a purple fuzzy bike everywhere. When the concept of owning a home is unfathomable, you just continue living with a bunch of roommates like a college student. But if I were suddenly evicted and forced out of this bubble of Victorians, fog, and hills, would I find that maybe my development had been arrested after all?

Before the current housing crisis, most of the people I knew who left San Francisco did so because, for them, it was time to escape the fantasy. They wanted normal grown-up shit like dishwashers and laundry machines and a multiple-bedroom house with a yard where their Tenderloin-studio-conceived kid could play. A cultural rift developed between those who decided they wanted out and those who wanted to continue playing make-believe. Many of us who stayed continued to do things like go out drinking on weeknights, have casual sex, and fuck around with mind-altering substances. A savings account was just the place where your money hung out until you transferred it to your checking account, and the concept of a retirement fund was ludicrous, because who the fuck has any money for that anyways? If you're never gonna grow up, who needs a 401 (k)? Lately, though, for those of us who continue to play along, it's felt like there's a crack in the snow globe, and the vagaries of time are slipping in.

These days, it seems possible to play at Peter Pan only if you've got VC funding. Silicon Valley bankrolls buy the trappings of eternal youth, like Foosball tables and PlayStations at open offices. But it all seems contrived: going to an office in the first place and working for someone else sounds a lot like growing up.

I may not have realized it at the time, but I made a choice a long time ago to live a life devoted to creating things—stories, poetry, spectacles, moon dances; the wild stuff that makes being alive worth it. I've always been content being monetarily broke but creatively and experientially rich. The things I create (books, TV shows, articles, poetry, web content) are highly consumed, and as a result, my lifestyle far exceeds my bank account. From free meals to free booze to free tickets to shows, I get taken care of very well everywhere I go in SF, and that, combined with rent control, has always made being a broke artist viable. But here's the thing: I am terrified of being evicted. I've managed to cobble together a life where bartending a few times a week supplements the little bit of money I make through my endeavors. But if I lose my rent control, I pretty much have to move out of the city, and I worry that I'm too old to start all over again and build this someplace else.

I have always been a motherfucking hustler, but right now I'm hustling harder than I've ever had to in my life. The fear of losing my apartment and the torment of having been so successful artistically yet so broke, is pushing me to work 12-hour days most weeks. I've always worked under the assumption that if I just keep making dope shit, I will finally pass over the tipping point that my career has been on for so long. But faced with the reality that San Francisco now only seems to support your dreams if you dream in code, I'm grinding doubly hard, trying to make my projects profitable instead of just cool, because I'm not ready to leave.

The strange thing about worrying when I'll get pushed out of Neverland is that I'm just as nervous about what happens if I don't. I've seen a lot of people who, like me, never fancied the idea of growing up, and they are still living in the same broke-as-fuck situation as I am. I look at some of my heroes and I see my future in them and it terrifies me, because if it's this hard now, I don't see how it can get any easier as I get older.

These are the people who, given the choice between chutes and ladders, chose the chutes every time because it was always a hell of a lot more fun than climbing up somebody else's fucking rungs. Idealism can be a dangerous thing when you live in a place that so thoroughly encourages it, but it's even more treacherous when it feels like that place is crumbling away. When you've built your whole life around living in San Francisco and not ever really growing up, what do you do when San Francisco grows up without you?

No matter how much I want to stay young and play make-believe forever, the forces of time and economics are conspiring against me. And as the city that so supports our fantasies also succumbs under the weight of gold, it makes me wonder what to do next. Do I leave Neverland and finally grow up? Or do I stay here with what's left of the pirates and the fairies pretending to be young forever, until one day when I just can't pretend anymore?

Riding in the car with my mom, we head off to the next errand, continuing to talk about her nonexistent grandchildren. "I look at Harriet, and she's my current hero," she smiles at me. "She didn't become a grandmother until she was 70. To be honest, honey, I just want you to be happy," she says. For the moment, living this weird life of uncertainty, where I hustle hard every day to both pay rent and create meaningful art, I think that might be precisely what I am. Happy. Let's just hope I can figure out how to make this shit last.

AS SAN FRANCISCO GOES, SO GOES OAKLAND
San Francisco Examiner; 2015

The last time San Franciscans talked this much about Oakland was in 1906. The City was ablaze, and 100,000 residents fled across San Francisco Bay, many never to move back to San Francisco. They say the population of Oakland doubled in roughly 72 hours.

There's a funny analogy here. San Francisco is currently ablaze again, and amid changes that, while not on the scale of a three-day fire, will forever change the physical, cultural, and demographical landscape, just like in 1906. New buildings and cranes scrape The City's skyline while people who call themselves San Franciscans are being pushed from their homes by forces out of their control. Cataclysms are not always caused by nature.

And once again, Oakland is there to take the brunt of it, pick up San Francisco's pieces, and be forever changed by thousands of refugees just looking for a place to call home. Too bad no one asked Oakland how it felt about it.

I was out in Oakland this week with my good friend Sayre, who's been living in The Town for seven or eight years and is one of its biggest cheerleaders.

At one point, we ran into Boots Riley, front man of the legendary hip-hop group The Coup and writer/director of the hottest movie in America right now, Sorry to Bother You. Boots, an Oakland native involved in radical politics, cares deeply about his city's plight and the role of capitalism in it.

Boots and I became friendly when he was on my talk show, *The Kinda Late Show with Broke-Ass Stuart*, and we have been in touch ever since. We were at Legionnaire, one of the many new bars that have exploded into downtown Oakland in the past couple of years, jamming out to the music of Motown on Monday, a party that originated in San Francisco. Marvin Gaye was bumping through the speakers, and Soul Train was being projected on the screen. The crowd was far more diverse than any I've seen in San Francisco recently.

"So, how do we stop Oakland from becoming the Mission?" I yell-talked at Boots over the blaring Motown. It was something that Sayre and I discussed often, but this was the kind of thing Boots focuses on in both his music and his activism.

"We need to begin with functional rent-control laws," Boots yell-talked back to me, "and focus on bringing in jobs that pay real living wages for the people who are already here. Neither of which are things that City Hall has any intention of doing."

Later on, Sayre pointed out other things Oakland could do, such as implementing occupancy requirements for new residential construction and penalizing property owners in places like West Oakland who just sit on fallow land until the price rises high enough for them to sell. But we all know City Hall won't do that.

I've spent so much time over the last few years lamenting the things that Mayor Ed Lee's administration has allowed to happen in San Francisco, yet I never even thought about what his counterparts were doing just across the Bay. I didn't realize that Oakland's City Hall was as deeply entrenched in the same "capitalism at any cost" ideology as our own.

And maybe that's at the heart of what's happening in Oakland.

When you live in San Francisco, it's the center of the world. We like to think the things created here reverberate around the globe, but we fail to notice how the serious issues we view as just our own are actually affecting the communities around us.

There's an old saying (that I'm completely making up right now) that goes "As San Francisco goes, so goes Oakland." And for Oakland's sake, I hope it doesn't.

SHOWING THE TECHIES SOME LOVE
San Francisco Examiner; 2015

I feel bad for the "techies." I'm not talking about the ones like Jack Halprin, the Google lawyer who tried to evict seven units, mainly comprised of teachers, so that he could have his own mansion. And I'm not talking about the venture capitalists using their money and influence to try to create a San Francisco in their own image. Those people are wankers.

I feel bad for the thousands of people who have been lucky enough to get a job that pays them to move to one of the most wonderful cities in the world. These are not the millionaire CEOs of tech giants; these are the people who work for them. And most of them have gotten in far too late to be part of that big "getting acquired/going public" pay day. Or they've come to San Francisco with an idea they really think might change the world. Who says no to an opportunity like that?

So, why do I feel bad for them? Because they've never been given the chance to be San Franciscans ... and most of them don't even know it.

It must be a hell of a thing to move somewhere for a job and be told that you are the cause of most of that city's problems. What somehow gets lost in all the finger-pointing and hand-wringing is that the bad guys in this housing crisis aren't the people looking for a place to live. The real villains are the rapacious real estate developers, landlords, brokers, and speculators making monumental fortunes, and the politicians who are in their pockets. The smartest thing these devils ever did was allow the general public to blame The City's newest transplants for the mess their greed fed upon. It's easy to blame your new neighbor for moving in when you can't see the landlord who evicted your previous one.

But that's not the only reason the "techies" haven't been given the chance to be San Franciscans. The entire startup culture has knowingly or unknowingly created an insular society apart. We live on the streets in San Francisco. We don't sit in our cars all day commuting to work; instead, we bike, walk, or take mass transit. We explore local restaurants and get to know neighborhood shop owners.

We become part of this city by drowning ourselves in it. That all changes when you take private transportation to work, where they feed you so you don't have to leave, and they clothe you so you can be their billboards. After working ridiculous hours, the culture justifies it pithily as #StartUpLife. It's easy to opt out of San Francisco by simply using an app to order anything else not provided.

So, I want to get this message out there to all the "techies:" It's time to become San Franciscans. If you're gonna be here, BE here. I'm tired of all this you/we bullshit that I just did in the previous two paragraphs. What I'm inviting "you" to do is to become part of the "we."

San Francisco is on the precipice of losing its soul, and if you're tired of being blamed as the problem, be part of the solution. There's a movement fulminating right now that's centered around issues like ending evictions, building affordable housing, tackling homelessness, and keeping the arts in The City. And I'm asking you to be part of it.

Register to vote, get involved in progressive politics, and start caring about San Francisco, not just its tech scene. If you genuinely want to be here, then we want you here too.

SAN FRANCISCO ISN'T NEVERLAND, IT'S LATERLAND
San Francisco Examiner; 2016

I'm currently sitting in my parents' kitchen. It's hot in San Diego. Hell, it's been hot all over the state this past week, and I'm so glad that places in SoCal have air conditioning.

Visiting San Diego is always different from what I imagine it's like for most other people. Most people see San Diego as a beautiful city to visit: hit the beach, cruise the Gaslamp Quarter, gawk at the zoo, and admire the fancy people's stuff in La Jolla. For me, it's where I come home to have a smaller, quieter life. In fact, I don't really have much of a life here. I have a huge one in the Bay Area, but in San Diego it's relatively tame.

A large part of that is because I left San Diego for UC Santa Cruz when I was 18, and I haven't really lived here since. The other part is that all my friends who are still here, or those who've left and come back, live very different lives from the ones I do. Most are married and/or have kids. They've got mortgages and early morning schedules and can barely fathom the idea of being out past 10 p.m. other than for special occasions.

As for me, at 36, I'm not quite old, but I'm certainly not that young. Living in The City, though, creates an entirely different relationship with time. San Francisco isn't exactly the Fountain of Youth, but it might be the recyclable water bottle of it that we've all made sacrifices to drink from ...

San Francisco allows us — or maybe forces us, depending on how you look at it — to be young longer, at least in terms of lifestyle. We rent and live with roommates and don't own cars, because our lives both facilitate and require it. We postpone things like marriage and children because we're busy with our careers, or cuz we really enjoy being single, or we still need to get some shit out of our systems.

There always seems to be more time down the way. I'd use the Neverland analogy, but it's gotten tired. Let's just call San Francisco "Laterland" instead. In Laterland, time moves slowly, and space is something we all lack.

The funny thing about Laterland is that, when you exit, even just for a few days, you understand how insulated it actually is. It's like refrigeration. You leave, and suddenly the aging process speeds up. Visiting your hometown and seeing your parents grow older makes you realize that you are, too.

Experiencing the lifestyles of your peers, with their planning and play-dates and procreating, makes you think about what you're not doing with your life and where you want to be. And then you start wondering if you want what they have ... until you head back to Laterland, and that dream fades the more you try and grasp it.

Life in Laterland is superb. I don't make much money, but I also don't have many responsibilities: no wife, no kids, no mortgage, no car payments, no pets. I can pretty much do what I want, when I want.

And for now, living in Laterland sounds just about perfect. I love my life. It's magnificent not just because of the lack of responsibility, but because of the vast and wonderful experiences that lack of responsibility allows me to have. But every time I return to Laterland, I come back with the question: "What happens when that changes?"

Laterland doesn't stop time, it just slows it. And the answer is something we all have to figure out for ourselves. I just hope that my answer comes with air conditioning, because it's way too hot right now.

DAMN IT FEELS GOOD TO BE A SAN FRANCISCAN
San Francisco Examiner; 2015

The West Coast woke up to something monumental on Friday. The Supreme Court voted to allow LGBT citizens the right to marry anywhere from sea to shining sea. It was like Manifest Destiny for San Francisco values. Suddenly, our queer siblings and parents and friends and hairdressers and selves could marry the people they loved in every state in the Union. Yes, even those states.

And it felt good. Like really good. Because, whether or not any of us had consciously realized it, we really needed a win. Too many mornings lately, we've woken up to bad news. From racially based police brutality and murder, to terrorist mass killings, to the evictions of our friends and loved ones...every time we watched or read the news (or turned on Facebook), the world seemed to be going to hell.

And then Friday happened, and it felt damn good.

I got the news in a hotel room in Seattle that I was sharing with my gay brother Ross. He burst in the door, waking me up, and said, "Oh my god! The Supreme Court just made gay marriage legal! You gotta get up and watch the news!" So I did, and sat there crying tears of joy and relief, while the past couple of years of national hatred and heartbreak washed out of me...for at least a little while.

Once the initial jubilation wore off, the first thing I thought was, "I can't believe I'm not in San Francisco." My city, who gave lives for this very day, and which rioted in the streets for it. My city, who legalized love in 2004 and took Pride, one of the most powerful words in the English language, and emboldened it to mean something more. My city, who had been fighting for this day for decades, and who at this very moment got it, exactly when we needed good news the most. Damn, it felt good to be a San Franciscan, which is a feeling many of us hadn't had in a long time.

Now, don't get me wrong, I'm not dogging Seattle by any means. It's an incredibly progressive city with a vibrant LGBT community and a badass gay/hipster/hipster-gay neighborhood called Capitol Hill. Plus, they even have an openly gay mayor, Ed Murray. I was thrilled to be on a trip with my family and spend Pride weekend with them, celebrating this momentous occasion. But as the photos kept rolling in on social media, I couldn't help but get little twinges of "I wish I were there" because I knew that in my heart, I was there.

By the time you read this article, the news cycle will be on to the next thing. Your Facebook feed will be clogged up with some terrible news about an atrocity in the Middle East or a police murder in New Jersey or the shameful eviction of somebody's grandmother in San Francisco. But when that happens, remember last Friday and let it give you hope. Let it remind you that we can change things and we can make the world a better place. It may take years, and it may take struggle and setbacks, but last Friday was proof that, with enough love, hard work, and organization, the tide of history can be pushed forward.

Last Friday was a good day to be an American. I'm really looking forward to saying that again soon.

HAVING ROOMMATES IS INTEGRAL TO LIVING IN THE CITY
San Francisco Examiner; 2016

I first moved to San Francisco when I was 21 for an internship in the booking department at Bill Graham Presents. It was the summer of 2002, a simply magical time in my life, and the genesis of the nearly 15-year love affair I've had with The City.

At some point during the internship, I learned that one of the talent bookers lived with a roommate. This blew my mind. Given that he was much older than I, maybe 40, the fact that he lived with a roommate fascinated me. At the time, I was sharing a converted living room in the Upper Haight with a friend, and both of us slept on air mattresses. There were two other roommates in the tiny apartment as well. Considering that I was still in college, living with a bunch of people seemed normal, but the idea of a grown-ass man having roommates seemed... well, odd.

Today I'm 35 years old and once again sleep in a converted living room. This time around, I have a real bed and don't share the room with anyone, but I still have three roommates. When I moved here in 2002, I had no idea how integral roommates were to the San Francisco experience. In fact, they are often the only thing that allows us to afford this city.

Take a second and think back to all the different roommates you've had over the years. For those unfamiliar with the urban experiment that is city life, the idea of living with strangers can be strange. The funny part is that they don't even know how strange those random people can be.

Over the years, I've lived with an amazing cast of characters. There was the roommate who, after passing out drunk in the living room, would somnambulate back to his room in the middle of the night. When his bare feet hit the linoleum of the kitchen, his brain would think it was the bathroom. It took us a long time to figure out why there would be puddles of piss in the kitchen.

There was the motley crew of artists and freaks I lived with at 1907 Golden Gate. The ages ranged from 23 to 50 and included a lawyer, a personal valet, and a social worker. The illustrious Miss P Segal held court late night around the kitchen table, smoking cigarettes and regaling me with stories of the early years of Burning Man and the

Cacophony Society.

There was the girlfriend I lived with in the Mission for three and a half years. We had an epic Cold War about the importance of form vs. function with regards to the throw pillows on the couch. When we broke up (don't worry, it had nothing to do with throw pillows), I couldn't move out for another two months because, unfortunately, that also seems to be an integral part of the San Francisco experience as well.

There have been so many other roommates in my time in S.F. Luckily, I love my current ones. We all have our own things going on, but sometimes those things coincide, and we hang out. Nobody is too clean, nobody is too messy, and nobody pees on the kitchen floor. I don't know if I'll still be living with other people when I'm 40, but if so, it really won't be that odd. I'll just be glad that I can still be in this city, where having roommates makes you far less strange than living alone.

MAGIC LIVES IN NORTH BEACH
San Francisco Examiner; 2016

North Beach is where magic lives. Neon strip club signs throw color at the pavement below while Coit Tower sits illuminated on Telegraph Hill, like God's own fire hose nozzle. Smells of garlic and sauce drift from restaurants whose large windows teem with people from around the world. Street barkers do their best to pull you in, and whether they're peddling pasta or tits and ass, their coo is the same: "What you've got going on out there will never compare with what we have in here." And sometimes they're right.

This is the San Francisco that still feels like San Francisco. Part sideshow for the tourists, part midnight movie for the locals, North Beach can be anything to anybody as long as they are willing to say "yes."

Unfortunately, I've got the shakes this morning from too much yes-saying last night. I was at Spec's, where you can flirt with pretty girls and hear stories from weird old men. I did both. But I could've been at Vesuvio, or Gino and Carlo, or Tony Nik's, or, or, or ...

It doesn't really matter where I was, as long as it was in North Beach.

The written word is still a sacred thing in North Beach, as is art. Hovering over a corner at the intersection of Broadway and Columbus, large illuminated books seem to be flapping their wings to fly. The art piece by Brian Goggin and Dorka Keehn, titled "Language of the Birds," is an homage to the literary brilliance that has emerged from San Francisco, particularly North Beach. Across the street is San Francisco's literary anchor, City Lights Books, and kitty corner to that is the Beat Museum. One of the finest things you can do in this neighborhood is sit in a bar and read a book.

The other is to drink like a madman. This is usually the path I take.

Though I don't live in the area, I'm there frequently. I can show up alone and know that I'll run into friends somewhere, because North Beach is still an actual neighborhood, where people act like neighbors.

Stuart Schuffman

I know Mikey might be smoking outside Grant & Green, and Matt might be making pizza at Capo's, and Laura might be pouring stiff ones at Columbus Cafe. And even if I don't run into friends, I know that I'll make new ones on a barstool at some point in the night, because this is North Beach, and that's just what you do.

It's a weird thing to be in love with a neighborhood in which you've never lived. It's strange to know all its alleys and street names and colorful characters. But who am I to fight against magic? How can I resist the ghosts of the Barbary Coast? How can I say no to the staccato echoes that still reverberate with Allen Ginsburg's "Howl" or combat the lure of Jeremy Fish's artwork on the side of buildings?

For me, the answer is simple: I don't.

Yes, magic lives in North Beach. Hopefully, I'll run into you on a barstool there soon.

A TALE OF THREE CITIES
San Francisco Examiner; 2016

"After the past few nights, I've realized San Francisco is a tale of three cities," I say to the little group of people I'm smoking and drinking with.

We're sitting on cushions in somebody's "Zen room" at least a dozen floors above Market Street in the Nema Building, a brand-new high-rise apartment complex in the heart of The City. Given its proximity to so many tech companies, it more or less functions as a very high-end dormitory for tech workers.

"You see, the three cities are high-rise, low-rise, and no-rise," I said to them. "High-rise is obviously where we are now. It's the folks whose entire relationship to San Francisco is seen through the lens of making money from the tech boom. Those who live in the 'low-rise' city are the people who were already here and are fighting to keep San Francisco a place for everyone. They generally don't live in high-rise buildings. And those who live in the 'no-rise' city sleep in tents at the foot of the high-rises."

"It was the best of times, it was the worst of times, and it was the far, far worse of times."

I was a little stoned and a little drunk, but as far as semi-poetic generalizations go, it was pretty good, especially considering the previous few nights I'd had.

A couple of nights before, I'd joined with thousands of other activists in shutting down Interstate 880. We were protesting the recent police killings of Alton Sterling and Philando Castile and the hundreds of years of systematic violence that police have inflicted on communities of color. It was powerful and peaceful, with mostly low-rise residents, despite the presence of some high-rise people.

The night at the Nema building was completely different, though. It had started at the Modernist, a brand-new private club where an annual membership costs $3,000 and all you get from it is access to a bar and restaurant, where a vodka soda is $16. Nick and I were allowed in because we were there for somebody's birthday. The bar was full of tech-industry millionaires, for whom San Francisco was a gold mine. We left shortly afterward, chased out by incredibly expensive booze prices and offensive techno music, and headed to an apartment party at Nema.

It was then that I realized we were living in three separate cities. The party was full of young, well-paid tech workers who were most likely employed by the people who belonged to the Modernist movement. The only books on the shelves were about coding, and the biggest framed thing on the wall was a collection of stock certificates from some technology company.

"Where the fuck am I?" I asked Nick. He works at a well-known tech company but has been in San Francisco long enough to be part of the struggle to keep San Francisco, well, San Francisco. He's like a bridge between low-risers and high-risers.

"Yeah, man, it's like I told you," Nick said, "a lot of these people may live and work in San Francisco, but they aren't actually in our San Francisco. They go to work, then go to restaurants and bars that primarily cater to tech money, then live in a building that only houses tech workers. It's like a parallel universe."

"Or a completely different city," I replied.

Worse yet, they were out of booze. So, we went to his friend's place to get some and ended up in the "Zen room," where I made up my unified theory on our tale of three cities.

Stuart Schuffman

SAN FRANCISCO IS JUST NOT THAT INTO YOU
San Francisco Examiner; 2016

Is it enough to love the way the fog tiptoes through the trees in the Presidio? Can the 47 hills that undulate across The City keep you satiated? Will the skyline that nearly scratches heaven be able to stop you from wandering away? Is the staggering beauty of San Francisco enough to keep you here?

The low huff and fizz of cars passing by trickles in through my window as I sit at my desk. This room is my office, my living room, and my bedroom. The other night, I put out a funny little thing on Facebook that said, "'I really want to have a living room one day' is the most San Francisco thought I've ever had."

It was one of those jokes that managed to cut right to the bone.

The amount of reaction it got was incredible; people shared all the different things they've given up just to live in San Francisco. It was the kind of laughing you do to keep from crying. It was one of those stark moments when you remember the place you've given your heart to might not love you back. Maybe San Francisco is just not that into you.

It's not like all of us haven't been sacrificing things in exchange for living in San Francisco for a long time. But lately, more and more people have been concluding that it might not be worth it after all. First, it was the evictions that pushed our friends and loved ones out of The City, but now so many of them seem to be wandering off on their own.

"That's why I left," said one commenter. "That's why I'm leaving," said another. For some, it's easy to cut the cord and go; for others, it's like Fleetwood Mac's song "Landslide": "Well, I've been afraid of changing 'cause I built my life around you."

They've left for Oakland, Portland, New York, and L.A. They've scattered to New Orleans, Chicago, Toledo, and abroad. It's like a great San Francisco diaspora, spreading the seeds of tolerance and weirdness across the world. But with all these people taking their love someplace else, how much of what makes San Francisco special leaves with them?

What keeps you here? What's stopped you from looking at the corruption, greed, selfishness, and sadness that's come to define San

Francisco, and kept you from packing your bags and splitting town?

For me, it's partially the beauty. I am literally awestruck every time I cross the Bay Bridge and see my city shining back at me. Another part of what keeps me here is the community. Sure, most of my really close friends have left, but that's also pushed me toward finding new communities that care about San Francisco and are willing to fight tooth and nail for her.

Another thing is that I've built a really wonderful life here. I've been able to cobble together this weird existence, in which I manage to make a living by creating cool things. And the people here support me and cheer me on ... except for a handful of assholes.

Yet, what might be the biggest thing that keeps me in San Francisco is that I'm almost scared to leave. How do you leave the greatest love of your life? It's like losing your religion or devoting your life to studying alchemy and finding out it's all a lie.

Instead, I try to focus on what I love about this city and fight to keep it the magnificent place I've always known it to be: a city for everyone. Because without people like you and me, this would just be a collection of hills, big buildings, and trees.

SAN FRANCISCO VALUES IN LOCKSTEP WITH HALLOWEEN

San Francisco Examiner; 2017

Even though Halloween isn't until Tuesday, the festivities have already begun. Every city in America does Halloween, but nobody does it quite like San Francisco. Not only is Halloween a *bacchanal* of beautiful vices barely masked by costumes and frivolity, but it also marks the end of our festival season. Starting in May with the How Weird Street Fair, San Franciscans have endless ways to celebrate the wildness that still runs through The City, even if it's become more subdued in recent years. Then, after all the street fairs, park concerts, block parties, and decompression events, the season comes to a close with ecstatic fervor.

Depending on which day of the week Halloween lands on, this erupting insanity can last for nearly a week.

Yes, this is a Halloween town. We use any excuse throughout the year to put on a weird costume and party in the streets, but

Stuart Schuffman

Halloween is the main event. People spend more time and money on Halloween than on New Year's Eve. If there are five evenings of shenanigans, there's just cause to have five different costumes — and sometimes an extenuating circumstance can cause you to change costumes midway through the madness.

Last year, I dressed as Disco Stu from "The Simpsons." At a late-night party, a guy asked to try on my wig and then disappeared with it. I spent the rest of the Halloween week dressed as a robber baron.

Christians co-opted the pagan festival Samhain and turned it into All Hallows' Eve to help convert the Celts to their god. And All Hallows' Eve eventually became Halloween. Back when mystics and druids roamed the earth, Oct. 31 was when the veil between the spirit world and our world was the thinnest, and people could commune with the dead.

In a way, Halloween is still a time when the veil is thinnest in The City. I don't necessarily mean people can talk to spirits on Halloween, but it lets us channel the freakiness that this city used to represent. It's a nearly week-long celebration where you can quite literally be whoever or whatever you want. Isn't that at the core of what San Francisco stands for?

Halloween marks the transition from our warm months to our rainy ones. It's like the gods of San Francisco hold back on the waterworks just because they like to see us at our best. Shortly after, we put away our costume boxes, the skies cloud up, and the rain pushes us inside for a few months.

At least, that's the way it was for many years. After a nearly five-year drought, we were fortunate to have all the rain we did last year. But, as we've seen in the news lately, climate change is impacting places all over the world. San Francisco most likely won't be any different. So, if there is no rainy season to offset the festive one, what does that mean for us?

Even utter hedonists, like me, need some sort of balance in our lives. We can't just party forever. Thankfully, *Día de Los Muertos* comes right after Halloween. Even if the weather doesn't change, *Día de Los Muertos* grounds us. These days, it's the real veil between us and the spirit world. The procession through the Mission and the altars at Garfield Park remind us that our time here is short, but that our ancestors are with us wherever we go.

What's always made this city special is that it's been a place where cultures are less likely to collide than they are to dance with one another. For many of us, the tandem of Halloween and *Día de Los Muertos* is the ideal representation of that — they're the perfect dance partners. One night you're chasing the spirits, and the next you let them chase you.

Happy Halloween week, my lovely witches and warlocks. Be safe out there and get the last bit of madness out of your system because if we're lucky, we'll soon have lots of rain.

NOTHING IN SAN FRANCISCO IS SHOCKING ANYMORE
San Francisco Examiner; 2018

Many of the things we shrug off as normal in San Francisco don't happen in other places. Like when I heard someone outside my window yelling, "Honor your father and mother!"

Without looking, I knew it was the old Filipino guy who is always shouting through a bullhorn at Market and Powell. Or how you're more likely to hear someone say, "My boyfriend's wife has a girlfriend," than, "I'm a Republican." Or how running into someone you know in a fast food joint is more embarrassing than seeing them in the waiting room of an STD clinic ...

A while back, my cousin's wife was visiting from Phoenix for a work thing. She hit me up and said she wanted to have a wild and crazy night. So, I took her and another suburban soccer mom out to Industrial Goth Night at The Stud, followed by a Hubba Hubba Revue burlesque show where the theme somehow fused the Easter Bunny and weightlifting bros. A wild night for them is usually having the babysitter stay late so they can have an extra margarita at Applebee's, so our night in San Francisco blew their freaking minds.

For those of us who've lived in The City for a while, it takes a lot to get us to raise an eyebrow: A dude walking down the street wearing nothing but a Giants cap and a cock sock? We call that Tuesday. A lady who's dyed her dog's fur pink to match her own? That's just Lisa. Paying $900 a month at age 37 to have three roommates and no living room? That's called adulthood.

There are oodles of quirky things we take for granted here. Still, there are also sad ones to which we've become all too accustomed: Expecting your car to get broken into if you leave so much as a few visible pennies—being able to walk by poop and know if it's human or animal just by the wafting smell—seeing the sidewalk littered with needles and having neighbors who sleep in tents each night. Having friends and loved ones evicted and pushed out of The City due to rampant greed. Watching someone rant, scream, and thrash at some invisible foe—all of these daily occurrences.

School board president Matt Haney, who's also running for District 6 supervisor, recently wrote on Facebook about showing members of New Zealand's parliament around San Francisco and how shocked they were at our city's "brutal inequality."

"It crowded out everything else, unavoidable, relentless, omnipresent, but normalized," Haney wrote.

"Normalized" is the key word; for those of us who live here, none of it is shocking. It's just our everyday lives.

Think about the last time you were truly stunned by something you saw in San Francisco —something that made you stop what you were doing and say, "Wow..."

Mine was a couple of years ago. I saw a homeless man coming up Market Street wearing little more than filthy rags with newspapers stuffed into his clothes. As he walked, huge clumps of human feces, the size of a small fist, skittered out of the holes in his clothing. Seeing this poor man, reduced to such wretchedness, was so shocking that I stopped in my tracks and said to myself, "Oh my fucking god." Then, I looked up and saw all the cranes building skyscrapers for billionaires and thought, "How can these two things be happening on the same block?"

Maybe that's what really defines this place, what truly makes San Francisco special. A handful of people are becoming unfathomably wealthy while a larger group of people are so unconscionably poor that they have no choice but to defecate in the street. And the rest of us... well, we're just doing our best to survive while trying not to step in shit.

WHEN THE CITY YOU LOVE DOES NOT LOVE YOU BACK
San Francisco Examiner; 2018

Back in 2011, I had a travel TV show on IFC that I created and hosted called *Young, Broke, and Beautiful*. It was an incredible experience. I got to gallivant around the US exploring the weird and wonderful in different cities. We visited New Orleans, San Diego, Memphis, Boston, Baltimore, and Detroit. Unfortunately, it didn't get picked up for a second season, and that was that.

Before we got the green light to make the show, we shot a couple of sizzle reels — mini 10-minute pilot episodes — to show proof of concept. One was for New York and the other was for San Francisco. Just the other day, I rewatched the San Francisco episode, and damn if it didn't get me right in the gut. Seeing that episode we shot in 2010 brought me back to how enamored I was with San Francisco at the time. It was a love letter to a city I was deeply enthralled with, a city I described in the introduction as "full of dreamers and believers, seekers and preachers, people who don't fit in anywhere else, and never wanted to anyways."

Watching it made me miss San Francisco even though I still live here, and it reminded me of how much we'd lost. Over the weekend, I also re-stumbled upon an old quote from the late journalist Herb Caen that nailed how so many of us feel these days: "The city is cruel to the weak, deaf to those who love it, and subservient only to those who are wrecking it. Like all neurotics, the city hates its friends, and loves its enemies."

Old Herb wrote that in 1972 about the people he saw while strolling through down-and-out 6th Street (at least some things never change), but now it makes Caen seem like a prophet. I can't think of a better way to describe where San Francisco is in 2019.

Back in the 2000s, most of the people I knew gushed about San Francisco. They loved this place and wanted people to know it. Sure,

The City had problems, and there were plenty of folks who came here, tried it, decided it wasn't for them, and left. But many of the people who had chosen to be here felt they had found home.

That was the underlying theme of the episode we shot. There was Poet Laureate Jack Hirschman talking about how he'd left a professorship to become a North Beach street poet, and trans-activist and entertainer Vicki Marlane telling stories about how SF had opened its arms to her, and the circus performers in the Bohemian Carnival who thrived here because of how the community supported them. San Francisco had saved everyone we talked to in some way or another.

I don't know anyone who talks about San Francisco in that way anymore. I imagine the handful of people at the top making vast fortunes probably glow when they discuss this city. But even well-paid people who work for them, those making six figures and still struggling, complain about the burden of living in San Francisco.

And those who are far less fortunate than they are doing everything they can just to avoid ending up on the street. Herb Caen was so right. It's scary. This city is cruel to the weak. It is deaf to those who love it. And it is subservient to those who are wrecking it...just look how the late Ed Lee handed developers and tech giants the keys to the city while he was Mayor.

San Francisco hates its friends and loves its enemies, and damn, this place breaks my heart. Nine years ago, SF was quite possibly the greatest love of my life. I know many of you are going to comment along the lines of "Well, why don't you leave then?"

Where can I go when my entire income is based on thinking, writing, and talking about San Francisco?

Plus, maybe deep down inside, I still do love this place, even if it doesn't always love me back.

SALESFORCE TOWER LOOKS LIKE A GIANT BUTT PLUG
San Francisco Examiner; 2017

For most of my time at the SF Examiner they pretty much let me do whatever I wanted. So I wrote this gem. It got so much traffic that the Examiner put a poll on their site asking "Do you think the Salesforce Tower looks like a giant butt plug?"

To be fair, it looks more like a dildo than a butt plug, but that was too on the nose. So I took some creative license.

As I look out my window, I see it stretching toward the heavens. The large glass windows are filling in, reflecting the fog and the Bay. At night, it's illuminated like a beacon, screaming, "I am the symbol of a company so powerful that, if they want to, they can completely alter The City's skyline. And by God, they want to." Similarly, at night, the little cranes at the top make it look like the building is throwing its arms in the air in victory.

The Salesforce Tower has been climbing skyward for months, but we're finally at the point where you can see it from almost anywhere in the Bay Area. It is huge. It is imposing. It is the ultimate symbol of the role tech has played in the transformation of San Francisco.

And to be honest, it kind of looks like a butt plug.

Yes, dear reader, the soon-to-be tallest building this side of the Mississippi looks like a sex toy designed to be inserted into the rectum for sexual pleasure ... only, you know, bigger. And so, because of this, I am hereby giving the Salesforce Tower its new nickname: The Butt Plug. Salesforce can call it anything it wants, but we, the citizenry of the San Francisco Bay Area, will call it what we damn well please. And that's The Butt Plug.

There are plenty of famous buildings around the world that have legendary nicknames. A big building in London that resembles an egg is called "The Gherkin," because it also somewhat resembles a cucumber. The new addition to the Stedelijk Museum in Amsterdam is called "The Bathtub" because people saw it and said, "Huh, that sure looks like a bathtub." And the Centre Pompidou-Metz in Metz, France, is affectionately called "The Chinese Hat," because the architects were said to be inspired by the wonders of the Chinese hats.

Now, I'm not saying the wonders of butt plugs inspired the architects of The Butt Plug, but I'm also not saying they weren't ...

This is San Francisco, after all. We've been on the forefront of every sexual revolution, so it's only fair that we become the first city in the world to have a building named after something you or your partner puts in your butt. This is our legacy. This is who we are as a community. We deserve this. Plus, it's pretty fitting considering how many things we've had rammed up our asses these past few years.

The City of San Francisco should get behind this, too. Think about the revenue it could make by selling butt plugs that looked like The Butt Plug! They could raise millions of dollars to help fund essential projects locally or donate the money to colon cancer research. Can you imagine how many butt plugs could be sold at Folsom Street Fair? Wouldn't you be so proud of our city if they were the reason colon cancer was wiped off the face of the earth?

I can see it now: Butt plugs celebrating The Butt Plug for sale right next to the San Francisco fleece jackets in the tchotchke shops on Powell Street. Plus, it's not like this is the first sexually suggestive building in San Francisco. I mean, come on, Coit Tower is about as beautiful of a phallus as you can find in the world of architecture.

So please join me in the christening of this new building. From now on and in perpetuity, we shall call the large skyscraper at 415 Mission St. The Butt Plug. Say it with me now: "The Butt Plug!" Feels good, doesn't it?

Thank you, Marc Benioff, for once again giving so much to the people of San Francisco.

Slouching Towards Neverland

Artwork by Jon Sitch, courtesy of The Bold Italic by GrowSF

LIVING IN SAN FRANCISCO MEANS... (REDUX)
The Bold Italic; 2015

This is the sequel to the 2011 piece. In the first one you can tell how in love with SF I was. In the Redux you can tell that I've been disenchanted by all the fuckery brought on by the Tech Boom.

Living in San Francisco means being torn apart. It means watching people you love get evicted and seeing cultural institutions replaced by trendy cocktail bars. Moving to this city for a job in technology and getting vilified for being the reason for higher rents, even though you can barely afford your own. Reading the news and getting sick to your stomach because the elderly, the mentally disabled, the working class, and the creative class keep getting "displaced," which is a euphemism for "thrown out of their homes in the name of greed." It means reading the news and being enraged that a 98-year-old lady is getting evicted. It means reading the news and worrying about when you're going to get evicted yourself.

 Living in San Francisco means seeing someone you know in the Planned Parenthood waiting room. Seeing someone you know at the DMV. Seeing someone you know at the grocery, the gym, a sex party, the airport, Vesuvio, Ike's Place, the Warfield, in Oakland (where you find out they've been living for the past two years). It means meeting someone for the first time and being weirded out because you have 77 Facebook friends in common. It means meeting someone for the first time and being even more weirded out because you have zero Facebook friends in common. It means living in the biggest little village in the world.

Living in San Francisco means being matched with a hilarious amount of your friends on Tinder. It means making plans to go on a date with someone you met on OkCupid for Sunday, but running into them in a bar on Friday, realizing how bad the dating scene has gotten for women here. I was chatting with someone on multiple dating sites eight months ago, but we never met up. Then, I saw them at the Independent, and I have friends who are just friends but used to be friends with benefits. Having social circles in which, at some point or another, most people have slept with each other. Knowing it's impossible to date someone who hasn't fucked someone you know.

Living in San Francisco means hearing people say that art is dead in the city. It means hearing people say that music is dead in the city. Hearing these things and saying "fuck that" by going out to spray-paint and wheat-paste, hanging weird mobiles from the telephone wires, having shows in your living room, joining flash mobs, organizing new local festivals, and dressing as bananas and handing out PB&J sandwiches to homeless people. It means wandering past the open-mic poetry night at 16th and Mission and smiling because art will never die in San Francisco. It means feistly starting your own business doing the thing you love.

Living in San Francisco means being enamored by the legend of Emperor Norton. It means seeing Frank Chu and telling him, "Give 'em hell, Frank!" Wondering when Omer, a.k.a. "Bum Jovi," stopped playing horrible guitar on Valencia. Being terrified of the Filipino guy with the megaphone screaming about "honoring your mother and father!" at the cable-car turnaround. Mourning the death of the Bushman but not being sure which one died. Realizing that the death of the Brown Twins is really the end of an era. It means being absolutely gutted when you heard about Robin Williams, because he represented San Francisco at its very best.

Living in San Francisco means knowing that local politics are completely crooked. It means knowing that Willie Brown still runs this town, even though he hasn't been mayor since 2004. Well, he and Rose Pak, anyway. It means knowing Ron Conway and Reid Hoffman are trying to buy this town, and that Ed Lee is giving it to them.

Knowing that David Chiu's backroom deals with Airbnb were shady. Worrying that SF isn't as progressive as it used to be. Worrying that all the new people who moved here won't vote or care about local issues. Worrying that "San Francisco" will no longer represent an ideal, but will now just be a place. It means crying into your keyboard when you heard the *San Francisco Bay Guardian* has shut down.

Living in San Francisco means thinking that jaywalking while smoking a joint and drinking a beer in front of a cop is totally normal. It means seeing a men's knitting circle in a café in the Castro and thinking it is totally normal. Seeing Deep ride by on his trike, blaring Prince, and thinking it's totally normal. Seeing people walking around dressed in bondage gear and thinking it's totally normal. Seeing people wearing strange costumes at any hour of the day on any day of the year, and thinking it's totally normal. It means seeing 13 people sleeping on the sidewalk during your walk to work and, unfortunately, thinking that's totally normal too.

Living in San Francisco means knowing someone who worked somewhere that got acquired or went public or some other shit and became rich. It means always wondering just how rich they really are, having friends at some of the most powerful tech companies in the world who can actually help you when their technologies don't work as intended. Being a guinea pig for every imaginable app that launches. Having six different ways to call cars to get home and being able to order Thai food, a plumber, toothpaste, booze, smoothies, and never even having to pick up the phone, wondering if you're losing the ability to actually talk to people in person. It means co-working, ride-sharing, renting your car out by the hour, renting your extra room out by the night, and renting your couch out by the week. It means knowing that the "sharing economy" isn't a movement; it's a business plan for companies who don't want to pay their taxes ... but fuck, it makes life easier.

Living in San Francisco means having a tattoo of the Golden Gate Bridge, Sutro Tower, or a California bear, a California poppy, or the city's skyline, but definitely not one of Coit Tower. That would look too much like a dildo. It means hearing "Nobody's got it better than us" and really believing it. It means cringing when people say "San Fran," and actually, kinda, maybe warming up to the name "Frisco."

Stuart Schuffman

Living in San Francisco means knowing your neighbor's schedule, even though you've never met them, using the word "hella" as often as you breathe air. Being excited for pumpkin and strawberry It's-Its. Having long-standing arguments about which is the best taqueria. Having conversations, wondering when this bubble is gonna burst. Having conversations about weird guys in the park who make giant bubbles. Having a bike you love stolen. Having a bike you don't even like that much stolen is frustrating. Knowing at least seven people who've been hit by cars while riding a bike. It means words like "scaling," "pivoting," and "disrupt" are part of your vocabulary, even though you work in a restaurant. It means knowing a remarkable amount about wine varietals and cooking techniques, even though you work in tech.

Living in San Francisco means acting like you never have to get old but worrying that you really are. It means being in your thirties, with all your friends now married and having kids, while you're still living with three roommates you found on Craigslist. It means being in your twenties and hopping from job to job, trying to find something you actually believe in. It means being in your forties and doing work that you believe in, but still worrying about paying your bills. It means starting to consider what it would be like actually to move out of San Francisco. Considering Portland or Oakland or even LA – yes, really, LA – but knowing how much it would break your heart to leave the city you've given so much of yourself to.

Sunset on the Golden Gate

THERE IS NO SAN FRANCISCO WITHOUT SAN FRANCISCO
The End of the Golden Gate: Writers on Loving and (Sometimes) Leaving San Francisco; 2021

I wrote this essay during one of the deepest parts of the pandemic, July 2020. It's from the collection: The End of the Golden Gate.

It felt like moving trucks were parked on every block in town. There was a low hum of activity as friends, frenemies, lovers, ex-lovers, sometimes lovers, parents, stepparents, drag parents, and day laborers hired from in front of the U-Haul place on Bryant Street, all carried furniture out of buildings throughout the city. It was July 1, 2020, five months into the COVID crisis, and San Francisco was hemorrhaging residents. Apparently, all it took was a literal fucking pandemic for thousands to realize they'd finally had enough of this place.

All this time we'd been saying, "Just wait till there's a big earthquake and watch all these people scurry back to Ohio or Wisconsin or wherever the hell they came from." Little did we know that something far more microscopic would actually be the thing that sent them running.

The surprising thing was that it wasn't just tech bros and social media managers fleeing. People who had been here for ten, fifteen, twenty years—who had come not for the tech industry, but because they were in love with San Francisco, or at least the idea of it—were now leaving, too. It wasn't just programmers and marketers who were looking for exit signs but poster artists and poets, servers and writers, and bartenders and blues musicians. The people we had hoped a catastrophe would make more room for were also being swept out.

Obviously, all the death and economic fallout is the last thing anyone wanted, but was this emptying of San Francisco the thing we'd been hoping for for the past decade? Were we finally getting our city back, or would San Francisco just be a taller, emptier version of a place that was getting harder to remember?

I've spent nearly twenty years in San Francisco, and for the first half of them, this city was the true love of my life. Some friends and I had a saying that went, "I don't want any relationship that gets in the way of my relationship with San Francisco." But over the past decade, that relationship has become more of an abusive one.

I love San Francisco. And I fucking hate San Francisco. This place gives so much while simultaneously taking so much away. I'm constantly inspired by the activism and the community building I see here. And I'm repeatedly gutted by the greed and selfishness that have come to define this place, making it a cautionary tale of what happens when a handful of very wealthy people actually get almost everything they want.

There was a time when I thought San Francisco was the future of America, even if I didn't know which future it would be. Would it be a Dickensian dystopia where the ultra-wealthy frolic while the rest of the population is either homeless or a couple of bad breaks from being so? Or would it be one where progressive ideals pave the way for a more equitable country where everyone has healthcare, housing, and education? With just a little more political will, San Francisco could be the city where such unfathomable wealth could be used to actually make sure everyone had a place to live, a decent education, and food to eat. We could be the shining example the rest of the country needs to see to make this a nation that is truly for everyone.

When I moved to San Francisco in 2002, I fell deeply and utterly in love with it. The city was full of misfits, dreamers, artists, and weirdos. It had spent the past half century as the place where you went if you didn't belong anywhere else. Whether you were a refugee from Latin America or Middle America, this city opened its golden gates and said, "Welcome home." Being a San Franciscan was something to be proud of because it meant you lived in one of the most special places in the world.

A decade later, Mayor Ed Lee gave substantial tax breaks to several big tech companies to keep them in the city, and this set off an avalanche of fuckery. Rents and property values reached unfathomable levels, record numbers of evictions happened as rapacious landlords tried to cash in, and newly evicted people with nowhere else to go often ended up on the street, causing our homeless population to become ever-growing.

On top of that, the newcomers to San Francisco didn't love the city like we did. They arrived from around the world to work for companies that only seemed to be creating apps to do the tasks your mom wouldn't do for you anymore. They worked too many hours, getting fed and boozed at work, which meant they didn't spend nearly enough money at the local businesses that made SF unique. Not that they had much money left over, considering they were paying $3,000 a month to live in our loved ones' former apartments. For many people who moved here, San Francisco was merely a temporary destination to work and earn a living before returning to their original home. They often didn't know, or didn't care, about the cultural carnage they were unintentionally part of as they created massive wealth for a handful of people and their investors.

Those of us who, through a combination of rent control and dumb luck, were able to survive this maelstrom watched as the city that was such a part of the way we defined ourselves as people became nearly unrecognizable. The betrayal was gut-wrenching; it was like going to high school and your best friend from middle school became the bully who picked on you.

So, what's kept me here? Part of it is that I have nowhere else to go. I make my entire living by thinking, writing, and talking about San Francisco. My work is synonymous with what's going on culturally and politically in San Francisco, and a massive part of that is distilled through my two decades of personal connections and insights into this place. Considering the Venn diagram of my life, where media, activism, and the service industry intersect, it would be impossible to build that anywhere else. For me to leave the Bay Area, I'd have to pick a new profession, and really, a new life altogether.

But what's also kept me here is still catching glimmers and glimpses of the place I fell in love with. Whether it's a guy walking through the Castro wearing only a sun hat and a cock-sock, or the fact that city hall lights up pink, blue, and white for Transgender Awareness Week, or that Democratic Socialists get elected to public office, or that you can't walk down the street without running into someone you know ... there is still some real magic and it out- weighs most of the bullshit most of the time.

Stuart Schuffman

* * * *

My fiancée, Kayla, is sitting on our couch, morosely wondering out loud, "Do I have any friends left here?" Lately, we've gone to several going-away parties in various parks, and the exodus is getting to her.

The history of San Francisco is a series of booms and busts, but this one feels different. As home and rental prices plummet, I find myself wondering if anyone will be around to capitalize on the drop. Suddenly, thousands of people have realized that there is no San Francisco without San Francisco.

By which I mean: They've begun questioning the point of living someplace that's dirty, expensive, and full of heartbreaking homelessness when they're stuck inside their apartment. If none of the things that make this place special are available, why even be here?

For all the people who've left, that question was already answered. Over the past decade, we've seen our favorite places close down and get replaced by yoga studios and high-end cocktail bars. Just take the corner of Sixteenth Street and Valencia in the Mission District as an example. What used to be a Latino *tiendita* was replaced by an upscale version of a corner store, where instead of buying *panaderia* pastries for a dollar, you can buy high-end versions for five dollars. I don't think you can get a more literal example of gentrification. Or when the Lusty Lady—a peep show and the only worker-owned strip club in the nation—closed down, there was talk of turning the space into a peep show–themed cocktail bar. Thankfully, that atrocity didn't come to fruition.

Slouching Towards Neverland

San Francisco is a city that's been thoroughly plagued by wealth, greed, and gentrification. Yet, when it finally looks like much of what caused this is fleeing like locusts after a feeding frenzy, what's left behind is far less than what was here before.

The people we love have moved or are moving. The places that make this city wonderful are closed or are closing. And what's left over is a beautiful city full of empty buildings and far too many people sleeping in the streets instead of inside those buildings.

* * * *

Recently, I was walking around the Mission, seeing haunting fliers for shows that never happened and murals painted on plywood that covered the windows and doors of places that I love. And it hurt my heart. But I also realized that the murals weren't just beautifully crafted Closed for Business signs, they were actually shouts of hope from a city that always rises back up. The fact that when the world went to shit, a group of people figured out how to pay artists to take that shit and make it pretty... well, that just felt like the San Francisco I fell in love with.

And that got me thinking: Maybe this is San Francisco's chance to get it right. We've stood at the crossroads and seen two possible paths—hell, we even ventured a little too far down the dystopian one. Perhaps this culling of people and companies, this exodus of exes and friends, can act as a reset button. Perhaps this is our opportunity for San Francisco to embody the ideals it preaches truly.

After a decade of fighting greedy landlords, destructive venture capitalists, rapacious housing developers, and nearly omnipotent tech giants, it feels like we can finally catch a breather. As these forces of displacement choose to displace themselves, those of us who somehow withstood the onslaught can fill those spaces with art, community, and people we love. And I mean spaces quite literally. Just imagine what kind of cool and creative places can open up when they don't have to worry about a landlord raising rent by $30,000 a month.

That's not to say we don't have a lot of work ahead of us, but maybe once again, San Francisco values might mean something more than just the value you can generate in San Francisco.

Stuart Schuffman

HOW SAN FRANCISCO CHANGED MY LIFE
San Francisco Examiner; 2020

I first moved to San Francisco during the period between the gold rushes. It was 2002; the dot-com bubble was a laughable memory to most of the people I knew, and the City was full of people who, given the choice between sinking and swimming, decided to float.

It was the summer between my junior and senior year at UC Santa Cruz, and I was in town for an internship at Bill Graham Presents. I was 21 years old and slept on an air mattress in a door-less room at Haight and Central that I shared with my friend Mani and his air mattress. I had barely enough money for food, rent, and a couple of $2 beers at Murio's Trophy Room. It was absolutely glorious.

Nearly 20 years later, as I'm about to pass a significant milestone and turn 40, I'm thinking about how that summer changed my life and pushed me towards where I am now. That was the summer I first fell in love with a woman, but more importantly, it was when I first fell in love with San Francisco.

After the internship was over, I went back to Santa Cruz to finish my final year of school. The girlfriend I'd met that summer was still in San Francisco, so every other weekend I'd take a bus over Highway 17 to the San Jose Caltrain station and then grab the rail up to Fourth and King. No matter how many times I took that ride, I'd get butterflies in my stomach and my heart would race a little bit as we passed the 22nd Street Caltrain station, heading into downtown.

Sure, part of it was because I was going to be seeing my lady, but mostly I was twitterpated at the thought of being back in San Francisco. The City had gotten under my skin in a way no other place ever had before, and each day I was here felt imbued with the potential to meet someone fascinating and discover things not just about the world, but about myself.

San Francisco felt both cosmopolitan and quaint. Expansive yet accessible. Each time I approached by night, I sensed it vibrating, like the whole city was roiling with underground magic, reverberating like the world's biggest bass drum. And those whose ears could pick up the frequency knew it was for us, and we did everything we could to be there and drink in the things that young people thirst for.

As soon as I graduated, I moved right back to San Francisco. I bounced around apartments (Russian Hill, Tenderloin, Western

Addition) and jobs (gay bar, hat shop, candy store), doing anything I could to stay in this luminous city of "yes." Because that's what San Francisco seemed to say with conviction, Do you want to be surrounded by people who accept you no matter your gender or ethnicity or class? Yes! Do you want to move into a warehouse with eight other people and work a job in a café so that you can spend the rest of your time making art? Yes! Do you want to make a zine, sell it from your backpack, and somehow turn that into a writing career that's now lasted nearly 20 years? Hell yes!

That last one was obviously me. I'm sitting here thinking about how I've given nearly half my life to this city and how it has paid me back in spades. The fact that San Franciscans saw a scrappy kid who made a zine about cheap things to do and not only supported him, but cheered him on, well, that spirit is what made me truly fall in love with this place.

So much of what I do now, so much of my devotion to this problematic, maddening, beautiful, brilliant, heartbreaking, mystifying city is tied to the way San Francisco made me feel when I was in my early 20s. It was a city of dreamers and believers, seekers and preachers, people who didn't belong anywhere else, and never wanted to anyways. It was a city of "hell yes!" in a world of too much "no."

I used to have a saying that went "Some people run away to join the circus. Others run away to San Francisco. Those of us who live here know it's the same thing." And for those who read my writing and scratch their head about why I lament S.F.'s changes, that's the reason why.

I'm embarking on a new decade at a time when San Francisco is experiencing yet another massive shift. About 10% of The City's residents have left since the pandemic began, and tech companies continue to flee. I'm excited to see where this takes us and maybe, if we're lucky, some of the magic that made this place so special will seep back in and fill up all the space left empty.

Stuart Schuffman

I'M FINALLY HOPEFUL ABOUT THE FUTURE OF SAN FRANCISCO

San Francisco Examiner; 2021

When I wrote this for the Examiner in Feb 2021, the vaccines were set to start rolling out and everyone who was still in SF really wanted to be here. For the first time in a long time, I was optimistic about what the future of SF could be. And all it took was a fucking pandemic.

For the first time in a long time, I'm optimistic about the future of San Francisco. I know that's a weird thing to say, considering most of us barely leave the house, tons of people don't have jobs, and many of our favorite institutions keep closing down. But honestly, I can't remember the last time I felt SF was so full of hope.

The reason for this is that almost every person in San Francisco is here because they want to be here. Whether they're transplant or native, rich or scraping by, tech worker or artist, nearly everyone here looked the pandemic in the face and said, "Not even you can make me leave San Francisco."

Of course, some folks wanted to leave but couldn't afford to, and there are plenty of people who wish they could be here but aren't, but everyone I talk to in this city is excited to be part of building the San Francisco that comes next. It's actually exhilarating.

And it makes sense. We spent the last decade in a culture war where one side didn't care enough about this place to even participate in the culture war. We saw our loved ones evicted, our rents skyrocket, and our favorite places shut down (well, I guess some things don't change). And all this was to accommodate tens of thousands of people who only planned on being here for a short time anyway.

And now they're gone. One hundred thousand of them. Yes, some of the people who left actually did love SF, but the pandemic's toll was the final thing that made them buckle. You know who you are, and we miss you. For most people who left, being able to work from home meant they no longer had to live in San Francisco, as it wasn't their home. And that's fine — farewell, good luck, and please try not to ruin things wherever you end up.

For those of us still here, it's a brand-new day. Suddenly, for the first time in a decade, people can afford to move from the golden handcuff of a rent-controlled apartment to a better one. They can finally leave dilapidated buildings or unhealthy living situations without their rent being tripled. They can make decisions that benefit them more holistically, rather than sacrificing safety and sanity just to pay rent because that's what so many of us have done just to live here. That's how much we love this city.

And the best part is, the strife we endured over the past decade has led to many more renter protections and discouraged some of the most egregious speculation. If these laws had been here 10 years ago, many of our loved ones would still be in The City. But maybe now some of them can come home.

So, hell yes, people are optimistic.

Even the blight is filled with possibility. While the empty commercial spaces we see around places like Union Square are unsettling, people are already scheming to see what kind of beauty they can create once things open back up. Commercial landlords will have to lower rents to meet the diminished demand, and quirky shops owned by local people may take over where corporate flagships once existed. The Westfield Mall downtown is already paying attention. They plan to open up space previously occupied by large brands, allowing local artists, designers, and craft makers to sell their wares instead.

The performing arts are starting to adapt to the new normal as well. The Midway in the Dogpatch is beginning to book seated, outdoor dining experiences with fantastic live performances. And last weekend, Red Light Lit, the sexy literary series, had a live reading at Chambers in the Phoenix Hotel. While most venues don't have the outdoor space and capacity that these places have, it shows the creativity folks are using to move forward, taking the performing arts off of Zoom and back into real life.

The most important part of my current optimism is the fact that vaccinations are real and they are happening. (My parents just got their second shots last week, YES!) There is light at the end of the tunnel. The vaccinations obviously aren't just a San Francisco thing, but that combined with everything above fills me with hope.

We are just beginning to emerge from one of the most trying and traumatic periods any of us will likely live through, and what we might find on the other side is exciting. San Francisco has a bright future ahead of it because the people who live here believe in this place. I'm looking forward to whatever comes next, and I'm glad we will be experiencing it together.

No One Ever Fell In Love At A Poetry Reading At A Startup Incubator

(Bars)

Stuart Schuffman

In 2012, I started a column at 7x7 called The Weeknighter. While it was initially supposed to be about the best deals and things happening in nightlife in SF, that would've bored me. So, I created a series of stories about my life and history in San Francisco, where each featured bar became the main character. After a couple of years, I moved the column over to the *San Francisco Bay Guardian*, but it closed down about six months later. So, I didn't write much about bars for a while until *SFGate* approached me in 2022 about being their Dive Bar Columnist, an offer I could not refuse.

I like to write about bars because, for many people, especially folks in their 20s and 30s, that's where life happens. You go to them to celebrate, you go to them to mourn, and you go to them just to make things happen. Even if you don't drink, you'll love the stories in this chapter because, if nothing else, they are all about what it's like to be beautifully flawed humans.

Photo by Kevin Kelleher & Emily Trinh

NO BAR IN SAN FRANCISCO HAS A MARK ZUCKERBERG ANECDOTE AS GOOD AS PHONE BOOTH'S
SFGate; 2022

"That bandanna makes you look like such a hipster," Mike Heartless said, busting my balls as he leaned against the bar, drinking a Tecate.

I had just gotten back from my first and only Burning Man, so it must've been September 2004. After wearing a bandanna around my neck for a week in case I needed to breathe in a sandstorm, I thought I might work the accessory into my regular style. But apparently my friend Mike, in the skin-tight black jeans, black leather jacket, black

No One Ever Fell In Love At A Poetry Reading At A Startup

Buddy Holly glasses, and perfectly trimmed stubble, thought it was too hipster. Back when people cared about such things, hipsters reminded me of junkies, in the sense that they thought everyone else was one but themselves. Guess I was a hipster, too.

It's funny that all these years later, no one really talks about who's a hipster anymore. Still, bandannas are a popular accessory, not for surviving sandstorms but as a makeshift (and unfortunately ineffective) means of stopping the spread of a deadly disease. But I digress ...

While I'm not sure if it was the first time I ever went to the Phone Booth, that bandanna story is my earliest distinct memory of that wonderfully quirky dive bar at the corner of 25th Street and South Van Ness. I spent a lot of time at the Phone Booth in that first decade of this extraordinary century. It was during that short but monumental period when Myspace was all the rage. Suddenly, this thing called social media made it so that we could amplify and project any version of ourselves we identified with at that very moment, so people I hung out with had names like Mike Heartless and Lisa Poisongirl. I think they still have these names in my phone, even though they're now in their 40s with kids.

The Phone Booth was smoky back then; it was one of the last bars in SF that allowed lighting up. But the impressively cheap drinks, exquisitely curated jukebox, delightfully campy decor, and weirdo clientele made smelling like an ashtray the next day almost worth it.

What's remarkable is that, in a city that's seen so much change over the past 20 years, not much feels different since I started drinking there ... other than the smoking, thankfully. Then again, to a bar like the Phone Booth, 20 years is nothing.

Sitting down at the end of the bar next to the aforementioned legendary jukebox, husbands and co-owners Steven Spingola and Jared Wendt explain that they believe their bar is at least 80 years old. While there aren't any records earlier than the '60s or so, a friend gave them a matchbook from what appears to be the 1940s when it was called the Phone Booth Cocktail Lounge and the owners were "Marge and Jim."

As for where the bar got its name, there's a huge old Pac Bell building a block away called the 25th Street Telco Building, which was built in 1949 and full of telephone operators and other phone company employees. But considering there was a previous phone company building next door to the Telco building as early as 1909, the Phone Booth could potentially have had this name for even longer than Steve and Jared suspect.

What is known for sure is that Jared started working at the Phone Booth around 1996. Then on April 1, 1999, Jared and Steve (a third-generation San Franciscan) bought the joint from Linda Pancost, who Steve described with a loving smirk as "a notorious owner of this bar and a notorious woman in her own right in San Francisco."

At the time, it was an off-the-beaten-path old man gay bar that was "beige inside with lots of mirrors and no beer on tap." A man named Eddie played piano on the weekends. The neighborhood was quite different, too. It was before the Mission really gentrified, so most residents were Latino, including a lot of immigrant families.

The Phone Booth that we know and love today, with the famous Barbie doll chandelier and signed photos of Tom Selleck and Barry Manilow, came into existence when Jared and Steve took over.

"When we bought it in 1999 ... we put in all the tap beers and built all of this stuff and put in real liquor, and we got a jukebox that I take care of," Steve told me over our second drink. He was in a band called Outer Circle, which was signed to Enigma Records in the '80s, and he's still a musician and a songwriter today. Jared is the creative force behind the decor — he built the chandelier himself.

Neither Selleck nor Manilow have ever stopped in for a drink, but the list of famous people who have is long and eclectic. I mean, sure, we all expect John Waters to have drunk at the Phone Booth (he's done so twice), but so have Chloe Sevigny, Michael Fassbender, Spike Jonze, Michael Stipe, Andy Samberg, Hope Sandoval, and many more.

"So, Mark Zuckerberg has been here," Steve tells me during my third drink, "which was a fiasco. Because he walked up to the door with his entourage, and the doorman, Andy, who is a bartender here, too, said, 'I need to see your ID.' And his friends are going, 'Don't you know who he is?' And [Andy] goes, 'I don't care who he is. I need to see your ID.'"

To Jared, that exemplifies the kind of bar the Phone Booth is. "There's not one person working here who would make a big deal

No One Ever Fell In Love At A Poetry Reading At A Startup

about anyone [famous] walking through the door. Drew Barrymore can walk in here and play pool and sit here punching holes in warm cans of beer, and no one says anything or makes a deal or even wants a photo."

This, of course, makes me wonder why Drew Barrymore was punching holes in warm cans of beer (maybe she was shotgunning them?), but, to stay well within the vibe of the bar, I don't ask.

When I began hanging out at the Phone Booth nearly two decades ago, the clientele was a mix of local drunks, queers, hipsters, queer hipsters, and local drunk queer hipsters. It was probably 70/30 gay/straight, and there was always a tangle of old-timers and younger folks. And they got along marvelously. Liz, the bartender that evening, has worked at the Phone Booth for 16 years, and at the mention of the older crowd, she pipes in, "They make friends with everyone."

Times change, though, and there's only about five or six old-timer regulars left. But that's not all that changes. The fellas explain that, unlike back in the day, the clientele doesn't really see themselves as gay or straight. "There's more fluidity," Jared tells me.

Regardless, the crowd is still mostly musicians, artists, and service industry people.

As I finish my fourth and final drink, I ask the most important question of all: how they've survived through the pandemic. Jared and Steve both admit it's been incredibly rough. Up until the pandemic, they had always been profitable, but the past two years have put them into debt for the first time. Steve and Jared are optimistic, though, things are picking up, and they're starting to crawl out of it.

"We've gone through, over the years, just so many of those ups and downs and been able to maintain it through all of them," Jared tells me. "I never thought I'd be a bar owner ... and I also never thought that we would own the bar for as long as we have. I always thought we might have it for five, 10 years, but time flies."

As I say goodbye, the bar starts to fill up with that wonderful assortment of interesting humans that's always seemed to populate the place. Walking out the door, I think about how lucky we are to have the Phone Booth still alive and kicking in San Francisco. I think the next time I pop in, I'll wear a bandanna for old times' sake.

Stuart Schuffman

SAN FRANCISCO DIVE BAR KILOWATT OPERATED UNDER A 'BDSM TOWER'
SFGate; 2023

Most of the people I used to hang out with at Kilowatt have left San Francisco. Anthony is down in Aptos, just south of Santa Cruz. Jeremy is in San Diego. Marina has moved to Los Angeles. Angie has gone to wherever loud, brassy cartographers with lots of tattoos and crazy hair go when they pass away. But Kilowatt is still here. Hell yes, Kilowatt is still here.

Anthony used to call Kilowatt "Kil-a-game" because we never met any girls there. Then again, we didn't really meet girls at very many bars to begin with. We were single and in our mid-20s, and since this was nearly a decade before Tinder, bars were where you were supposed to meet people, but we mostly just spent our bar hours hanging with friends. And many of those hours were spent at Kilowatt.

The bar was always full of dogs, pool players, and Detroit Red Wings fans. Loud punk and metal thrashed through the speakers, and if it was your birthday, you were given a very cheap bottle of champagne and a Polaroid camera to use for the night. Phones didn't have cameras on them back then.

Those days are gone, but after all these years, Kilowatt is not only still here, it's gotten a brand new shot in the arm. At the end of 2022, it was announced that Kilowatt had been sold. Normally, when a well-loved mainstay changes hands, it causes trepidation. But this time it was exciting news. After 28 years, owner Peter Athanas was retiring, and he was selling it to three folks who'd been bartenders at Bottom of the Hill and Thee Parkside for years.

"Peter wasn't going to sell to just anybody," Katie Rose McCarthy tells me as we sit at one of Kilowatt's booths alongside her co-owners, Peter Niven and Rick Eusey. "In fact, when we asked if it was for sale, he said, 'Who's asking?'"

According to the new owners, it was their relationship with the bar's previous proprietor that was critical to making sure the bar was passed into their stewardship.

"He saw that we liked what he had done, what he built for the last 30 years," McCarthy explains. "We wanted to keep the name, we wanted to keep that energy, just breathe fresh life into it."

And they were undoubtedly going to need his help to get through the process of buying the bar. Athanas sat down in the office with them nearly every day as they transferred everything over.

How the hell do you open a bar in San Francisco?

San Francisco is a harrowing place to open a business. Beyond the absurd cost of ... well, everything, projects get held up for years by mountains of red tape, bureaucracy, and prolifically greedy landlords.

"It was nearly impossible," Eusey answers when I ask about the difficulty of opening the place. Niven expands on this, saying that despite working in bars for years, the process is still an administrative nightmare: "Everything is like — 'Do you know about this permit? Do you know about that one? Do you know how to get the permit for your permit for your permit?'"

McCarthy, Niven, and Eusey might not have even gotten the bar if it weren't for the pandemic. Seeing all the sadly shuttered businesses and learning that Athanas was on the verge of retiring created the perfect push to take late-night, post-shift "We should open a bar, man!" riffing to dive bar reality. Well, that, and a little helping of San Francisco magic.

"It was like a chain reaction," McCarthy ruminates. "One person we'd meet would help us and then give a leg up that led to another person, and this whole thing became relationship after relationship after relationship. It feels like this was built on a mountain of good people and community."

During the time they shut the bar down for renovations and upgrades, it seemed that nearly every day someone would randomly pop by with a pizza and a paintbrush, asking what they could do to help. "This experience fundamentally changed the way I look at people," McCarthy discloses. "It makes me think people are good. You know?"

The wildest example of this was when there was a knock at the door, and Adam Pfahler, the drummer from legendary SF band Jawbreaker, was there with tacos. He said he'd been watching the Kilowatt crew's Instagram stories and figured they needed some lunch since they didn't seem to have time to eat or sleep.

If that's not a wee bit of the old San Francisco magic, I don't know what is.

Kilowatt's musical legacy.

Beyond being an active member of the San Francisco community (Pfahler founded Lost Weekend Video), there's probably another reason someone from Jawbreaker showered Kilowatt with extra love and attention. The bar had been a popular venue in the 1990s where the band played numerous times.

In fact, lots of '90s bands treaded the boards of the tiny Kilowatt stage when they were up and coming, including Pavement, Murder City Devils, and Neutral Milk Hotel, whom one of Niven's friends saw in 1996 (and booed the notoriously dissonant songwriter).

There's also a very unsubstantiated rumor that Nirvana played at Kilowatt, with Eusey recounting a woman at the bar recently who claimed to have heard the band play "Smells Like Teen Spirit" there.

While there's no verification of her story at the moment, the Kilowatt Three found lots of very real musical artifacts in the basement during renovation, including old concert posters and photos by SF music photographer hero Peter Ellenby. But possibly the best thing they found was a logbook of show notes from the Kilowatt's stage manager in the '90s with details like how the band sounded and how big the crowd was.

And apparently, he was uh... kind of a dick. One description from 1996 of a well-known band (the Kilowatt folks wouldn't tell me who) read, "Nobody drinks. Losers." Another one read something like, "Norwegian rock band. Very loud. Shirtless," and yet another one was something to the tune of, "Rude. Played a 20-minute set. Terrible."

In the logbook, you can also see how much each band made, and apparently, the Murder City Devils — one of McCarthy, Niven, and Eusey's favorite bands — only got paid $100 to play.

By the time I started going to Kilowatt in the early 2000s, the only thing left of the bar's legacy as a venue was old show posters, including the one for the final concert in 1997, headlined by The Oblivions. It's still on the wall and says, "The Kilowatt is dead! Final f—king show!"

The musical legacy was significantly influenced by the original booker, David Kaplan, who was also managing several bands at the time. There are conflicting accounts about whether Kaplan's departure resulted in the end of live concerts or owner Peter Athanas pulled the plug himself, but Kaplan's career continued without Kilowatt. Soon after his tenure at Kilowatt, Kaplan moved to New York to manage a little rock 'n' roll duo named the White Stripes.

Crucially, though, Athanas had continued to keep the live music permit up to date, which made it infinitely easier for the Kilowatt Three to get the city's blessing for shows when they took over.

Kilowatt's fiery past.

If you're looking at Kilowatt from across the street, and you're familiar enough with San Francisco architecture, you'll notice that the building was once a firehouse.

According to the history shared with me by Eusey and by GuardiansOfTheCity.org — a fascinating website about the history of the San Francisco Fire Department — the current building is the third firehouse built on the site. The first was built in 1854. The second one was constructed in 1868 for the newly organized Engine Company No. 7 and their horse-drawn steam engine. This one was destroyed as a result of the Great Conflagration of 1906. When it was rebuilt in 1908, it was still set up for the horsey fire brigade. It wasn't until 1918 that this fire company got a motorized engine. The structure remained a firehouse until 1968, when Engine Company No.7 was moved to 80 Digby St. in Diamond Heights, and the family who currently owns the building bought it.

"I know for a fact that it was a bakery at one point, probably the '60s," Eusey tells me. "There's an older gentleman that keeps coming in, shooting pool, and taking photos and stuff. And he's like, 'I remember, the oven was right here...'"

One of Eusey's friends said it was also once a restaurant owned by some family friends called Firehouse BBQ. It wasn't until the late '70s or early '80s that it first became a venue called Firehouse Seven. In the late '80s and early '90s, it was called Paula's Clubhouse, of which author Michelle Tea fondly remembers, "The first place I kissed a female in San Francisco is now the Kilowatt, but back then it was a queer punk dance club called Paula's Clubhouse."

And then in 1993, Peter Athanas bought the joint and named it Kilowatt because he was an electrician by trade.

Stuart Schuffman

Photo by Kevin Kelleher & Emily Trinh

But possibly my favorite story from the long history of the Kilowatt building is the guy who had the "BDSM tower." Apparently, at some point in the past 30 years, a guy upstairs had wild BDSM sex orgies. This building was meant for it. Not only does the top floor have group showers left over from when the firefighters used to live there, but the tower that sits above it also has a bunch of hooks that are remnants from when it was a working firehouse.

"Anytime you go to a fire, when you come back in, the hoses are all wet, so you have to hang them up," Eusey, who was a firefighter for Cal Fire, explained. Because of this, there are a bunch of hooks in the tower that were used for hanging hoses (pun unintended but completely unavoidable), and the guy who lived there would use them in his kinky play.

"Wait," Niven cuts in during Eusey's explanation. "Those hooks were for hanging hoses? I thought that old horny guy just hung them up there for BDSM."

Kilowatt's bright future.

While discussing what it's like being the next chapter in Kilowatt's history, McCarthy told me, "It's such an honor and privilege to be a part of keeping that going for people. I was blown away by seeing what this space means to people. I never get tired of when somebody comes in and you can just see all these memories flashing through their eyes."

And I, too, am one of those people. Every time I walk through those doors, I can't help but think about my wild nights running around the Mission in my 20s. And I'm so glad that Kilowatt will be around for future generations as a place to get drunk and make friends, lovers, and poor decisions.

THE HEMLOCK TAVERN IS TRYING TO KILL YOU
7x7; 2013

I really just LOVE this piece. Unfortunately the Hemlock is closed now. The building that replaced it has a space where the bar used to be and it's for corporate events or some shit.

Socrates died from drinking hemlock. He was too smart for his own fucking good, and they killed him for it. Those in power tried him and sentenced him to death by drinking a beverage laced with that poisonous plant. He was apparently a real asshole, though, the kind of guy who couldn't take the hint that you just want to sit at the bar, have a drink, and not be asked hundreds of questions like, "But who are you really?" and "Do you wanna hear about my app?" He was that kind of asshole.

It kinda fits that Socrates was killed by hemlock, though, because the Hemlock Tavern is also trying to kill you. And I mean that in the best way possible. It appeals to all your vices: The drinks are cheap, there's a heated smoking patio, loud rock n' roll bands play in the back room, the jukebox is free, and it's a good place to get laid. Plus, it's in the Tenderloin, so if the bar doesn't have what you're looking for, you can pretty much walk out the door and find anything else you might want.

The Hemlock Tavern is part of the San Francisco I moved to 11 years ago. It was a period I now refer to as "between gold rushes," when things on Polk Street were grittier, gayer, and stranger, and the people who now yell stupid shit like "YOLO" from the windows of May's and McTeague's were too scared to cross Broadway, let alone California. These days, the douchery of the Marina is creeping down Polk Street like hemlock (does hemlock actually creep? Regardless, it just works so well here), but the Hemlock Tavern has managed to stay the same.

The bartenders are still sweet and sour, the bags of peanuts are still hot, and you're still guaranteed to run into your ex's roommate, or an old co-worker, or one of the thousands of people that drift in and out of your life, only to show up again years later at a dive bar in the Tenderloin. There's an old Oscar Wilde quote that goes, "It's an odd thing, but anyone who disappears is said to be seen in San Francisco." If he'd lived here, he would've known that you just have to go to the Hemlock to find them.

If you've been reading The Weeknighter all this time, you know that I often end up waxing nostalgic. It's hard not to when the places you go and the people you love are so intertwined, and when the city that you've given your heart to is changing so rapidly before your eyes. If you haven't figured it out by now, these are not fucking bar reviews; these are reveries. These are meditations, and these are love poems.

These are for the people who need San Francisco almost as much as San Francisco needs them. For the drunks and the dancers, the protesters and the pot heads, the fighters and the fuck-ups. These are for people who want to spend their lives in San Francisco but have landlords who feel otherwise. It's my way of pinning down San Francisco to what it is now, like a time capsule, so hopefully future people can look back at it with wonder.

The Hemlock Tavern is just a bar—a really great bar, but just a bar. I'm using it as a vehicle through which to tell you a story about how much I love San Francisco and how much it breaks my heart sometimes. They killed Socrates with hemlock.

I hope the Hemlock Tavern keeps killing it.

TITTIES AND FRIED CHICKEN AT THE GOLD CLUB
San Francisco Bay Guardian; 2014

"Come on, Stuart. Titties and fried chicken. How can you, of all people, say no?"

They were cajoling me via Twitter. There's probably some hip slang for that, twijoling maybe, but I don't know what it is. Regardless, Mik, Ed, Dottie, and Cait were really giving it to me. And of course I caved. Willpower isn't one of my powers. Plus, Mik was visiting from New York, and I'd been meaning to go for so long anyway.

I said to myself, as I was putting on some clothes, "I don't wanna live a life where I can't drop everything and go to a strip club in the middle of the day for a free buffet." I slipped on my shoes and responded to their latest tweet with, "Fine. On my way. I'm gonna make it rain chicken wings."

I first heard about the Gold Club's legendary Free Lunch Buffet at the Gold Club when I was compiling info for *Broke-Ass Stuart's Guide to Living Cheaply in San Francisco*. An ex-girlfriend from college stripped at the Hustler Club, and she'd heard about it from one of the girls she danced with. As I neared the Gold Club that day, I thought about how this was one of those SF things I'd always wanted to do, and I was excited to be crossing it off my list finally. Walking in the front door, a girl behind a counter told me that there was a $5 cover charge. I gladly paid it and went to find my friends.

"I fucking love this place!" Dottie yelled at me over the pulsing Top 40 music, "I come here every year for my birthday!" She'd just pulled her face out from between a stripper's boobs and slipped a couple singles into the elastic of the girl's thong.

"So, wait, today's your birthday?" I asked.

"No, but it sure feels like it," she said with a big shit-eating grin. Just then, Mik, Ed, and Cait sat down with plates heaped with food. There was chicken wings, slaw, biscuits, corn, mac and cheese, and so much more. I was about to tell them how amazing it looked when the strip club DJ boomed in his strip club DJ voice, *"Let's give it up for the lovely Jasmine! Jasmine everybody! Now, coming to the stage is the sensuous Cinnamon! Let's hear it for Cinnamon!"* Cinnamon began working the pole to a Lil John song.

"So is the food actually good?" I bellowed over the music.

"Hell yeah, it is!" Mik yelled back.

"I'm on my second plate!" Ed said.

So, I got up to find out for myself. I don't go to many strip clubs, but the Gold Club was the nicest one I'd ever been to. Someone had spent a lot of money making it the most attractive place to get publicly undressed in SF. Considering the club's location, and that it was just after noon on a Friday, the place was full of men and women in business suits, tech guys in tech guy clothes, and Financial District workers wearing North Face fleeces.

Surprisingly, there were only one or two guys in sweatpants. I sat back down with my plate of food. "Goddamn, this is good!" I screamed over a Van Halen song. The crew just nodded in agreement. I got a second plate full and wolfed that down too. After a succession of girls with fragrant-sounding names took off their clothes to mediocre music, it was eventually time for each of us to get back to our respective works.

As we parted, we agreed it was the best lunch break in the history of people having lunch. "We'll have to do this again next time Mik is in town," I said, and we all went our separate ways.

I never did get to make it rain chicken wings.

'OPEN A BAR IN THIS NEIGHBORHOOD?' THE SAN FRANCISCO DIVE THAT TOOK A BIG GAMBLE

SFGate; 2024

If you look just to the right of Club Waziema's front door, you'll see a photo of a man who is clearly in the midst of cleaning up an unholy mess. Linger on the photo a second longer, and you'll realize that the hoarder's dream in the picture is actually the interior of Club Waziema.

"That was after we worked on it for maybe two months," Nebiat Tesfazgi tells me as we sit in what is now a very uncluttered Club Waziema. "It took us eight months to clear."

Today, as you hang out under the dark, moody lighting amid the posters of Ethiopia and the beautiful velvet wallpaper, it's hard to imagine Waziema ever being an indoor junkyard. In fact, for anyone who moved to San Francisco this century, it's hard to think of the spot at 543 Divisadero as not always being San Francisco's best and only Ethiopian restaurant/neighborhood dive bar.

"It took us eight months to clear." A vintage shot of the effort to launch Club Waziema.

But 543 Divisadero has a long history that stretches back to when the neighborhood was called the "Harlem of the West," and even beyond that, and includes cameos by some of the world's most well-known musicians.

The birth of Waziema.

I don't recall when I first learned about Waziema. It was probably around the time I moved into the infamous Burning Man/Cacophony Society house at 1907 Golden Gate, just a few blocks away. This was in 2004 when the neighborhood was still called the Western Addition and real estate agents were just beginning to experiment with naming it NoPa. The area was at the tail end of its long and mighty run as a historically Black neighborhood, and the storefronts along Divisadero were far more likely to be selling essential oils or braiding hair than they were to be serving $25 hamburgers or topiary in bespoke earthenware.

Although I don't recall when Waziema entered my life, it's been one of my favorite spots on Divisadero ever since. I've been there for birthday parties, first dates, and fundraisers. I've sat at tables having earnest catch-ups with friends, attended raucous gatherings of dozens where we took over the back room, and had quiet, contemplative drinks alone at the bar before heading to a nearby show. And no matter why I was at Waziema, the vibe was always warm and welcoming, the kind of place that would be my local bar if I still lived down the street.

But it took a million hurdles for Nebiat and her husband, Giday Beshue, to make Waziema what it is, the first of which was coming to the United States. They grew up together in Adwa, Ethiopia, where Giday was the best friend of Nebiat's older brother. Nebiat came to the U.S. in 1982 as a refugee, while Giday got a scholarship to study in Canada. He joined Nebiat six years later in San Francisco. You'd think that if they could navigate making it here from Ethiopia, opening a bar would be a breeze. Then again, this is San Francisco ...

"People laughed at us and thought we were crazy," Nebiat tells me as she explains what it was like when she first opened Club Waziema. "Police officers walked in and said, 'Are you crazy? You want to open a bar in this neighborhood?'"

When Nebiat and Giday began the project of getting Waziema off the ground in the mid-'90s, the Western Addition was a neglected neighborhood, and Divisadero had relatively few businesses. Because of this, the California Department of Alcoholic Beverage Control claimed it was a "high-risk" area and didn't want Nebiat and Giday to open the bar. This led to four hearings with the Board of Supervisors, who also denied them. So, they got 700 or 800 signatures on a petition and hired themselves a lawyer. Finally, after about four years of pushing, they officially opened in 1999. But they were only granted a license for beer and wine and had to close at midnight. It wasn't until 2007, after 11 years of fighting against the ABC, that they were allowed to serve liquor and stay open until 2 a.m. every night of the week.

The jockeying to open Waziema ultimately led to them serving food. Since there was a dearth of dining options in the area, the neighborhood wouldn't let them open if they weren't also a restaurant. Nebiat explains, "We said, 'Well, in that case, we have to do Ethiopian food since that's we know.'"

And then there was the junk.

The building's landlords, Mr. and Mrs. Robinson, also owned several buildings and businesses around town. When one would close, they'd use the space at 543 Divisadero to store all the junk that came out of it. Which is how it came to be that Nebiat and Giday spent eight months clearing out the space before they could even start working on opening Waziema. It might not have taken that long, but it appears Mrs. Robinson was a bit of a hoarder.

"Mrs. Robinson wanted to go through everything, so she just sat there reading things. She had to decide which things to keep and which to sell," Nebiat said.

Considering the space had been boarded up for 20 years, it was in surprisingly good shape. Other than redoing the floor, adding some soundproofing, and fixing a bit of water damage, they didn't have to do much else to the place. And as an added bonus, when they peeled off the wallpaper, they found the velvet you see there today. It's rumored to be from 1947.

The many lives of 543 Divisadero.

543 Divisadero has had a lot of interesting lives. I once again enlisted the help of the ever-incredible Pam Larson, a local history sleuth who previously worked at SF Heritage. While it's certainly possible that the building existed before 1908, Pam couldn't find any evidence of its existence before that date. Below are the many lives of 543 Divisadero:

- 1908-1914 — A ladies' tailor and habit maker shop owned by Max Weinstein. In 1914, he moved the business a few blocks away to 809 Divisadero.

- 1915-1919 — A bazaar/notions shop owned by Bartholomew Marino.

- 1920 — An art shop owned by Frank D. Mathewson.

- 1923-1928 — Beck Bros. Painters owned by Henry T. Beck and George T. Beck.

- 1930 — A restaurant owned by Ernest Simoni.

- 1931-1959 — Barney's Cafe & Pizzeria owned by Bartholomew R. Lazzareschi (sure were a lot of Bartholomews involved in the place's history).

- 1959-1977 — Club Morocco owned by John Robinson and Josephine Pierce.

- 1978-1980 — Duffies Cocktail Lounge owned by James McDuffy.

- 1981-1998 — Vacant.

- 1999-2024 — Club Waziema owned by Nebiat Tesfazgi and Giday Beshue.

Considering that 543 Divisadero was Barney's Cafe & Pizzeria for 28 years, I would love to know more about the place and what went on there. But alas, it's probably lost to the sands of time.

Luckily, though, we do know quite a bit about Club Morocco, and it is incredible.

In the time between World War II and the Urban Renewal of the '60s and '70s, Divisadero, Fillmore Street, and other stretches of the Western Addition were considered the "Harlem of the West" because of the rich and thriving Black culture that flourished there. When the Robinsons opened Club Morocco in 1959, it was just one of many jazz clubs that lined Divisadero. Places like the Both/And Club and the Half Note regularly featured legends like Miles Davis, Ike & Tina Turner, Thelonious Monk, Big Mama Thornton, Dexter Gordon, and more.

Club Morocco — whose name was inspired by the time Mr. Robinson spent in North Africa during WWII — had no shortage of legends who tread the boards as well. Billie Holiday, B.B. King, James Brown, and Marvin Gaye all played at Club Morocco.

The elevated area you now see in the back room was once the stage, and it was bigger back then. In fact, the entire club was. According to this 2013 interview with Nebiat, there was a second entrance in the back that wrapped around where Popeyes is now. This made the club horseshoe-shaped, which gave it the nickname "the Horseshoe." LarryBobSF on Flickr has this photo from 2004 showing the former second entrance, with the shape of a horseshoe around it, on Hayes Street, next door to Popeyes. According to Nebiat, Club Morocco also had a pizza oven, which I'm guessing was left over from the Barney's Cafe & Pizzeria days (shout-out to Bartholomew!).

Alas, all good things come to an end, and by the late '70s, the combination of Urban Renewal and the fact that the scene had moved to the Upper Haight led to Club Morocco shutting down.

Waziema's next chapters.

Anyone who has spent more than a night or two at Club Waziema can tell you that Nebiat has a distinctly warm, motherly vibe. Considering how many regulars give her hugs when they see her, she's like the dive bar mom of Divisadero, which works out well, considering drunk people are basically giant toddlers. But the familial feeling extends beyond just the clientele. Nebiat's whole household has worked at Waziema at some point.

Over the past 25 years, Giday would often work at the bar when not at his regular job as a nurse (Nebiat also worked as an RN before opening Waziema). While retired these days, he still runs the sound for the DJs on the weekends. All three of their kids have also worked at Waziema while in college, and the youngest still does on the weekends. The kids are also helping keep the musical legacy alive. Nebiat and Giday's daughter, artist Rewina Beshue, is friends with Chaz Bear from Toro y Moi, and he DJ'd four different benefit shows for Waziema in recent years.

With fundraisers in mind, we talk about the future of Waziema. Despite being a legacy business, the bar's prospects are uncertain.

When the Robinsons died, they left the building in a trust, 50% to their son and 50% to their grandchildren. When the son died during the COVID-19 pandemic, his widow took over his share of the trust and has made it clear to Nebiat that after the lease is up in three and a half years, she wants Waziema out unless they're willing to pay a much higher rate — possibly $15,000 to $17,000 a month.

Supervisor Dean Preston is a big supporter of Club Waziema and, according to Nebiat, has said his office will help as much as it can when the time comes. She also thinks the neighborhood will step in and help petition the landlord since so many local organizations use Waziema as a meeting place, free of charge.

"But I'm 64," Nebiat tells me. "I don't know if I want to continue after that."

As we wrapped up our conversation, I promised to lead the charge of getting the word out if it looked like Club Waziema was going to close. On my way out, though, I had one more question: I wanted to know what Waziema meant.

"It means 'eve,' like the night before a holiday," Nebiat explained, which was kind of perfect. Whenever you hang out at Club Waziema, it always feels like there's time for one more drink and that tomorrow isn't too big of a deal anyway. Or at least it does for me.

SUTTER STATION: WHERE NO FUCKS ARE GIVEN
San Francisco Bay Guardian; 2014

Sutter Station doesn't give a fuck. In fact, it has been steadfastly sitting on Market Street, not giving fucks since 1969. That's before BART existed, before *Tales of the City* came out, and before the Beatles broke up. The United States was still tangled up in the Vietnam War when Sutter Station first opened its doors to show San Franciscans what not giving a fuck looked like.

Sutter Station is a weird and wild place. And I don't mean weird like "Ooh, look at him, he's walking down the street in a tutu." And I don't mean wild like a bunch of drunk bros screaming WOOO when their friend takes a shot. I mean weird in a disconcerting way and wild in the sense that you may genuinely get your ass kicked for acting stupid. Sutter Station is a working-class bar that somehow still thrives in the heart of downtown San Francisco, where Budweiser is always $3 and sometimes people get physically tossed out the back door. They generally deserve it, too.

There's a legend about Sutter Station. There was once a lingerie show there. That's it. That's the whole legend. Stepping inside the joint, you can tell that's enough. Sutter Station is like if a Tenderloin dive bar walked over to the Financial District for a change of scenery and decided to stay. Have you ever sat down in a bar in the TL and said, "Gee, I wish there was a lingerie show here." That's my point. Some legends are legends for a reason.

Sutter Station isn't all hard motherfuckers though, as the week draws on, the crowd gets pretty diverse. People who say they "work in the FiDi" pop in for happy hour beverages, filling some of the tables with women in pencil skirts and men with their shirts tucked in. Both genders wear North Face fleeces for some reason. You do actually see some of these same people during other hours as well. Sometimes the ones with drinking problems dip in for a liquid lunch where they know none of their colleagues will find them, while others hang out far after happy hour, drunkenly making friends with people they will ignore when they pass them on the street the next day. Sutter Station attracts all kinds for different reasons. It attracts me because of the free pizza they offer on Fridays.

As real bars keep disappearing, only to be replaced by more and more craft cocktail joints, the importance of spots like Sutter Station grows. Bars are supposed to be where you unwind, have a drink, and let the day slide off you. They are to make merriment, make friends, make lovers, and make amends. I like a really nice cocktail just as much as anyone, but even more so, I like just having a drink and seeing what happens from there. The beauty of Sutter Station is that literally anything can happen from there. As real bars continue to disappear in San Francisco, I can't help but give a fuck. Luckily, Sutter Station doesn't.

SAN FRANCISCO NEEDS TOSCA MORE THAN TOSCA NEEDS SAN FRANCISCO
7x7; 2012

> Tosca has been bought & sold a number of times since this piece was published in 2012. I popped in recently and they'd even gotten rid of the beautiful old giant espresso machines mentioned in this story. That said, I'm glad this 100+ year old place remains, even if it's now a fancy restaurant and not a divey bar with fading stars in its eyes.

Ever since I heard that Tosca was served an eviction notice, I've been thinking a lot about a few lines in "Gobstopper (Remix)"—a track from Richie Cunning's *Late Night Special* mixtape that goes:

> It's kinda sad when I'm in my city walking around/and all the places I grew up in they knocking them down/So they can build a new scraper with a million dollar sky view/and fill it with people who don't love the city like I do.

Those lines really resonate with me and should for pretty much anyone who's spent a reasonable amount of time loving and living in San Francisco. I didn't grow up in SF like Richie did, but I've been here for a decade and have lived most of my adult life in this city. There have been a lot of battles recently to save local institutions, some of which the good guys won (The Tonga Room) and some of which were lost to greedy landlords who could give a damn if San Francisco just became one giant mayonnaise mall (The Gold Dust Lounge). Sometimes it seems like they're trying to sell the San Francisco out from under San Francisco.

Combined with Specs' and Vesuvio, Tosca is part of what I call the Holy Trinity of SF bars. They offer a glimpse into the San Francisco that was, a bit of the magic that reminds us why San Francisco is so special. I don't recall when I first visited Tosca, but I've been going there for at least a decade. Walking in, it's hard not to be impressed by the length of the bar, the ancient paintings on the walls, the opera music swimming from the jukebox, or the giant vintage espresso machine that looks like it belongs on some kind of steam-powered fictional airship. If it's your first time in Tosca, you ask the bowtie-wearing bartender about the chocolaty drinks lined up on the counter and find out that they're House Cappuccinos, made of hot cocoa and brandy. And you realize what people who've been visiting Tosca for the past 92 years already know, there's almost nothing better to fight off the cold San Francisco fog than one of those Cappuccinos.

Tosca also boasts a devoted clientele of famous people, complementing its famous drink. Both Francis Ford Coppola and Sean Penn are known to frequent Tosca's exclusive backroom, which was supposedly a favorite drinking spot of Hunter S. Thompson, and just a few years ago, Pulitzer Prize-winning poet Gary Snyder had a book release/reading there. Hell, I even took a piss next to Baron Davis once in the men's room.

But having famous patrons doesn't really matter. What matters is this: San Francisco needs Tosca more than Tosca needs San Francisco. In a time where San Francisco was just declared the most expensive city in the US, and The City's artists and working-class people are being quickly replaced by boy-faced millionaires who care more about reaching their IPO than creating A-R-T, places like Tosca allow us to romanticize this beautiful city. They allow us to remember that this city was built on gold dust and denim, union organizers and poets. They allow us to remember that, for much of its history, San Francisco has been a place to fit in if you didn't fit in anywhere else. What's important about Tosca is that its sheer existence reminds us that San Francisco is not like everywhere else.

In the article I read about Tosca's eviction, it mentions that the landlord, strip club magnate Roger Forbes, is trying to work out a deal to keep Tosca there and not replace it with a titty bar. I hope for the sake of San Francisco that it's true and that the good guys come out on top. If not, perhaps we could petition Francis Ford Coppola or Sean Penn to purchase it.

P.S. RIP The Purple Onion.

DAMN, I MISS INDIE MART AT THEE PARKSIDE
San Francisco Bay Guardian; 2014

I've fallen in love many times at Thee Parkside. Okay, that's a gross exaggeration. I've fallen into moderate, short-term infatuation many times at Thee Parkside.

For years, it was home to Indie Mart, the DIY, rock-n-roll, block party Kelly Malone and Co. used to throw. Scores of local artists and designers would set up booths along Wisconsin Street, selling all the strange and beautiful things they created, while grimy-looking bands played ear-splitting music inside.

The parade of manic pixie dream girls was unnerving. They had no real place in society and only belonged as unblemished ideals in my mind. Some would float into town for the weekend and set up shop, only to disappear as soon as Indie Mart shut down. Others would flit from booth to booth, trying on each other's wares and complimenting each other's outfits. All of them pretty much sold the exact same shit, not that it mattered to me, they were all so lovely to look at and really only brought things to sell to each other anyway.

Thee Parkside is way more than just for day-long block parties full of whimsically dressed Amelies, though. It's a semi-legendary dive bar famed for its out-of-the-way location and its kick-ass live shows. Any night of the week, you can see a variety of punk, metal, or country bands playing their hearts out on that tiny stage in that perfectly dingy barroom.

It's also known for a fabulous kitchen that turns well-executed dishes like *bahn mi* and Cuban sandwiches into perfect bar food. If you haven't been before, the Original Famous Twang Sundays are a great introduction to Thee Parkside life. Where else in The City can you hear country and bluegrass at an all-ages venue with a back patio for free? I think that's what Sundays were invented for.

Despite these great things that happen at Thee Parkside, it's still all those Indie Mart afternoons that most poignantly stick out in my mind. Maybe that's just because, for many San Francisco's doers and makers, Indie Mart was a place where we found a community of like-minded bad asses. Dozens of people who were tinkering with wonderful things all throughout the Bay Area suddenly had a place to coalesce, sharing and selling what they made.

Sculptors, screen printers, and jewelry designers set up shop next to each other while vintage clothes were hawked down the way and carpenters displayed their crafts. People who may never have encountered each other otherwise were now meeting and forging relationships that would lead to marriages, babies, collaborations, and successful businesses. A diaspora of creative people now had a base, a community, and a way to show the world what they were up to. It was, honestly and truly, with all earnestness, magical. And Thee Parkside allowed that to happen.

Like all great scenes, Indie Mart came and left just like a goddamn fireball. One day, it jumped from being a small thing in Kelly Malone's backyard to a block party at Thee Parkside. It burned hot and heavy for a few years, and then suddenly it was done. But what it left in its wake was a slew of creators who now had the confidence and contacts to make a business out of what was previously just a hobby. And of course, Thee Parkside is still around too.

Every time I pass by, I think, maybe I should get some people together and throw one more big block party for old times' sake. And then I say nah and stop in for a Cuban sandwich and a cheap drink instead.

SUPERB MARTINIS AND A SHOT OF NOSTALGIA AT AUB ZAM ZAM
7x7; 2014

While my Week Nighter Column Began as a Weekly Nightlife Column, it Quickly Became a Vehicle for me to Lament the Heartbreak I Felt as SF Rapidly Changed Before my Eyes.

Aub Zam Zam was the Second to Last one I wrote Before 7x7 Ended the Column and out of total Coincidence, it Put A Perfect Bow on the Project.

When I started this column over two years ago, I meant for it to be what it says in the intro. I told myself and my editor that I'd be doing things like talking about the most creative cocktails and the best happy hours in the city. Then I realized that I find that shit abysmally boring, and decided to do what I do best: tell stories about the places and people that make my life amazing, the ones who make San Francisco one of the most phenomenal cities in the world.

By coincidence, The Weeknighter started around the same time the populace fully realized how out of control things were getting here. The city that so many of us had left our hearts in was suddenly leaving us behind. Like fickle Aztec gods, human hearts were no longer enough to appease the hills and buildings and fog and landlords we all lived amongst, between the ocean and the bay. So, from the outset, this column became, in its own way, a reverie or a meditation on what it meant to be in love with a place that was rapidly changing while so many people wanted it to stay the same.

The Weeknighter also became a way for me to exorcise some of the demons of my sticky and complicated personal life. I started the column around the same time I was ending a relationship of over five years. The words I wrote were always a series of little love poems to San Francisco. They just happened to be filtered through the din and dimness of bars on weeknights. And in these poems, the daily tragedies and triumphs of my life spread out across the digital page. Heartbreak, lust, love, and friendship were stirred and shaken with barstools and benches, drunks, and neon signs. All of it topped off with nostalgia, sometimes even for the times we're living through right now.

And in a way, Aub Zam Zam is the sum of all of this. Opened in 1941, Zam Zam has always been a place of nostalgia. I don't know if the original owner ever visited the Middle East or North Africa, but the official name of the joint was Persian Aub Zam Zam, and it looks straight out of the set of Casablanca. A rounded art deco bar takes up most of the front room, while the oil painting behind the bar depicts the mythological love story of King Khosrow and Princess Shirin. Even when it was built, it was reminiscent of a different time and place, and that feeling has never left.

There's a lot of mythology around Zam Zam and Bruno, the cat who owned it for 50 years until he died in 2000. The way the story goes is that if Bruno didn't like your attitude or the way you looked, he'd kick you out and tell you to go drink at the Gold Cane. It seems more people got kicked out than were allowed to drink, so the ones who managed to make it past Bruno's misanthropy cherished Zam Zam as a personal safe haven and shrine. And it's still a place to go to if you like a little abuse; my buddy Joe works there, and you can tell that while he loves being a bartender, he doesn't necessarily like people. Someone's gotta keep it cranky at Zam Zam, and Joe does so beautifully.

The Weeknighter is supposed to be a bar column, and Aub Zam Zam is a bar. That doesn't mean I really care about the happy hour specials or what the best cocktails are. What I care about is that no matter what San Francisco is becoming, Zam Zam will always be a place beyond time, where nostalgia is the floater poured on top of every drink. It's perfect for a drink with friends or for moping by yourself. It's perfect for a first date or for a tipple on the way to your anniversary dinner. And it's perfect for writing little love poems for the people and the city that sometimes break your heart.

I know I said I don't care what the best cocktails are, but get a martini anyway. They are superb.

ALL OF US WRITERS KNOW EACH OTHER. AT LEAST IN SAN FRANCISCO
7x7; 2013

I'm working on a screenplay based on this piece. If you're some Hollywood cat and wanna make it with me, holler!!

We all know each other. We call ourselves things like bloggers, columnists, reporters, and journalists. Personally, I don't think of myself as a journalist; journalists have to deal with the truth, and the truth is often ugly. I just wanna tell stories, so I call myself a writer. All of us writers know each other at least in San Francisco.

Most of us were there a month or so back at the opening of Hard Water. In fact, that's where most of us always are: Openings for bars or restaurants or art galleries or concert halls. We go for the free booze and the free food because we get invited and because, while we have the power to absolutely make or break your fucking business by simply typing our fingers, most of us can barely pay our bills.

This is what Carolyn and I were talking about while I shoveled delicious bits of deep-fried alligator and pork belly into my mouth.

No One Ever Fell In Love At A Poetry Reading At A Startup

Many of the usuals were there: Marcia from Tablehopper, John from Chow, Caitlin from the SF Bay Guardian. We all congratulated Allie for taking over as editor for Eater, since Carolyn had moved over to San Francisco Magazine.

Most were there to actually do their job: Take photos, scribble notes, ask questions, and ultimately write something about Charles Phan's latest venture, which is a New Orleans-style whiskey joint on the Embarcadero. I was there to do what I always do: eat and drink the free stuff, flirt, network, and jot down random thoughts in case I ended up writing about the place.

Starkly decorated with mostly concrete, marble, and whiskey bottles, Hard Water is a tiny spot with limited seating, but plenty of room to stand, nibble, and drink. Carolyn and I were tucked into the corner by the shellfish, waiting for oysters to come around and drinking exquisite drinks with names like Dixie Cocktail and Cocktail à la Louisiane. We were debating the merits of this weird lifestyle we lead. On one hand, it's amazing; we get to be creative and use our brains and words to introduce people to things they wouldn't have known about otherwise. Plus, there's the free shit thrown our way by those simply hoping that we'll mention their place/product/concept in our writing somewhere. And sometimes we're able to create things that truly and honestly touch people, so much so that they search us out or email us just to say so.

But then there's the other side, the part of the equation that sometimes keeps us up at night with frets like *How will I pay rent this month? And how the fuck will I ever be able to retire when the only thing I know about a 401k is that I don't have one?*

Hard Water is incredibly well done. The drinks are perfect, the food is fresh and flavorful, and if it proves successful, San Franciscans are gonna love standing in line forever just to continue standing while they eat and drink inside. But it's also the kind of place that I probably would never have been able to go to if I didn't live the weird lifestyle that I do. All of us writers know each other.

We see each other at all the openings and media events, clinking drinks and laughing as we taste whatever it is that we're supposed to be tasting. And then, when the drinks have kicked in and the talk gets serious or honest or both, we admit to each other how often we wonder what the fuck we're doing with our lives. Luckily, we almost unanimously come up with the same answer: I don't really know, but I can't imagine doing anything else.

FOGGED IN AT 620 JONES
San Francisco Bay Guardian; 2014

We decided to walk around the Tenderloin instead of going through it. I had my computer, Gene had his bike, and Sabrina had a bag of things I'm sure she didn't want taken from her as well. We were coming from my weekly Wednesday gig at Monarch, where I do a coloring book happy hour.

"It's very San Francisco out," I said as we came up Taylor and saw the fog sliding its fingers down the sides of Nob Hill's buildings. "I love summer in San Francisco," I mused. "Me too," Sabrina said, "I hate when people bitch about it. It's part of San Francisco, and loving it is part of being a San Franciscan."

As we got to the entrance of 620 Jones, the three of us landed on something we felt was important at the moment, that before this current gold rush, it was San Francisco's summers that weeded out who would stay and who would go. You couldn't take the mist and the fog? Then you got the fuck out of town. That fog is our inheritance and our merit badge, and such a part of The City that you have to love it to live here.

Walking out onto the patio at Jones, we were surprised to find no heat lamps. The entirety of the joint's drinkers were crammed into the little sidebar adjacent to the patio, and as we sat down at the short end of the bar, the three of us gave each other a knowing glance. It said: How many of these people are experiencing their first San Francisco summer? How many would be considering packing up and heading back to wherever they're from if they weren't here for the gold rush? How many are living in apartments recently vacated by people whose love for the fog, and all it represents, just wasn't enough to be able to keep them here?

Gene tipped the barman with a two-dollar bill. "Oh wow," the bartender said, "you're still doing that after all this time?" Gene told us he'd met him years before, during the first dot-com boom, when the guy tended bar at 111 Minna. "Back then, Minna was just a small one-room space, not like it is now, Gene explained. "And I remember being there and learning for the first time how badly cocaine got on top of some people when these two girls, up from LA, were offering to blow people for blow." As I looked around the room at all the pretty and well-dressed people, I wondered what they'd all be willing to do to get something they really wanted. I wondered the same thing about myself. What was I willing to do to stay in San Francisco if push came to shove and shove came to eviction?

Across the bar, I noticed a friend who was obviously on a date and even more obviously drunk. "Hey, look who it is," I said to Sabrina, who was also friends with the girl. Our conversation shifted to the fact that another integral part of living here is being okay with your past.

"You can't burn bridges," Gene said, "since you're bound to run into that person on a barstool sometime soon." To which I replied, "If you burnt San Francisco's bridges, all we'd be left with was the Peninsula..." The joke hit all three of us harder than expected. We looked around, looked at each other, and then left the bar. We felt more at home amid the fog anyway.

THE FIRST TIME I WENT TO COLUMBUS CAFÉ WAS WITH A CON ARTIST NAMED NELSON
7x7; 2014

The first time I went to Columbus Café was with a con artist named Nelson. Well, at least that's what he said his name was. I guess I'll never really know his real name, not that it matters. It was also around this same time that I became Broke-Ass Stuart. It was the early 2000s, I was 22 and working at Z. Cioccolato, a candy store down the street and around the corner from Columbus Café. It was here that I conceived the idea for the first *Broke-Ass Stuart's Guide to Living Cheaply in San Francisco* zine, the little 30-page pamphlet that launched my life in such a bizarre direction. Nelson was my manager at the candy store, and one night after rotating the taffy, wrapping up the fudge, counting the register, sweeping the floor, and locking up, we went to Columbus Café.

Alfonso came with us. He and Nelson were co-assistant managers or some shit like that, and on the walk over, he told me, "Yeah, it's been a while since we went to Columbus Café. A few months back, Nelson and I were about to get in a fight with some douchebags when all of a sudden, he reached down and pulled a gun out of his boot and started waving it around. The place went crazy, and we ran out of there. I haven't been back since. He's a good guy, though, he just gets a little crazy when he drinks." I soon found out that Alfonso also got a little crazy when he drank; they'd both been in the military, and it seemed every third time I went out drinking with the two of them, there was a point in the night where a fight almost happened. Luckily, Nelson had stopped carrying his gun by the time I started working at the candy store.

Walking into Columbus Café that first time, I realized that my relationship with it would be a lot like my relationship with Nelson and Alfonso. It would be a lot of fun, but there would also always be the possibility of things very quickly getting out of hand. That's just how Columbus Café was, and still is, really. The bartenders have incredibly heavy hands, and the drinks are cheap, so drunkenness comes on fast and hard. Plus, they have the best happy hour in the city: for every drink you buy, they give you a token so you can redeem a free drink next time. The tokens don't expire. Back then, you could redeem those tokens at any hour, whereas now you can only redeem them during happy hour. Either that or the bartenders just liked us since we spent so much time there. Bars are a lot like people in the sense that sometimes you can understand everything about them from the first second you meet. I could tell I was gonna love the Columbus Café.

First opened in 1936 to serve the many longshoremen who were in San Francisco at the time, Columbus Café has always been a working-class bar with a devoted clientele. While in recent years San Francisco has dramatically shifted from blue collar towards...um, Google collar (have they invented that yet?), Columbus Café still manages to attract people that span the entire range of the socioeconomic spectrum. I've sat at that bar under the neon beer signs, sports gear, and nautical memorabilia, tipping back pints with everyone from Hell's Angels to tourists and from plumbers to whatever you call those slick fucks who work in finance. There are usually a few woooo girls chirping out their mating call by the jukebox while someone is getting taken to town on the pool table. Columbus Café can be everything to everyone, so long as you like bars that are divey, dark, and don't take shit from anyone.

One day, a few months after I started working at Z. Cioccolato, Nelson completely disappeared, and when he did, he took a lot of people's money with him. It wasn't until then that any of us realized everything he said was total bullshit. His whole background, all his stories, and even his name. Apparently, he'd stolen the identity of the real Nelson from a guy he bunked with in the military (I guess at least that part was true). Besides making off with money from the shop, he'd also "borrowed" money from pretty much everyone he knew besides me; I didn't have any to lend him. I never saw Nelson again, and a little while later, I moved on from slinging candy and became a waiter at Pasta Pomodoro down the street. While I'll never know who Nelson really was, I'm eternally thankful that he turned me on to Columbus Café. Well, that and the fact that I never let him borrow any money.

THE TENDERLOIN DIVE BAR THAT ENCAPSULATES SAN FRANCISCO HISTORY
SFGate; 2024

"When I started working here, we had one bartender who was a former empress of the Imperial Council of San Francisco named Mae," Joe Mattheisen, manager of Aunt Charlie's Lounge, tells me. "She had a glass eye, and she'd roll it down the bar saying, 'looking at you', or drop it in somebody's drink."

That's the type of wild story I expected to hear when I asked Mattheisen for a wild story while sitting in the Turk Street bar's tiny upstairs office, surrounded by office clutter and drag queen paraphernalia like wigs and sequins.

Despite the many transformations San Francisco and the Tenderloin have gone through since the bar opened its doors in 1987, Aunt Charlie's really hasn't changed much at all. It's still a tiny, campy, sliver of a dive, where the floor is carpeted, the walls are lined with mirrors, and a giant neon "Aunt Charlie's" sits above the bar. People from all parts of the gender spectrum feel comfortable here, making it always a pretty mixed crowd.

Donna Personna shines during one of her acts in The Hot Boxxx Girls show at Aunt Charlie's Lounge in San Francisco's Tenderloin District on Friday night, Oct. 4, 2024. But any visitors expecting something elegant will be sorely disappointed. I mean it is home to the Hot Boxxx Girls, the most deliciously lowbrow drag show in town (I once saw a transgender performer do her act topless with just tiny pieces of wet bar napkin covering her nipples). The performers don't even have a backstage; it's more of a storage area with a board laid over the trash cans so people can sit. Which is to say, Aunt Charlie's is absolutely perfect.

The birth of a drag destination.

"Bill bought this one in 1987," Mattheisen explains as he tells me about the bar's ownership.

The Bill in question is William "Bill" Erkelens. When he bought the bar in 1987, the Tenderloin still had tons of gay bars, and Erkelens already owned a few of them, including the New Bell Saloon, the *P.S. Bar and Restaurant, and the Railway Express Saloon. These days, Aunt Charlie's is the last queer bar in the Tenderloin.

Sadly, Erkelens died in a boating accident on May 19, so when I walked into Aunt Charlie's the other week to interview Mattheisen, there was one of those yellow "Public Notice of Application Ownership Change" signs posted out front. Erkelens' wife, Marie Roehm, now has control of the bar, but the Roehm-Erkelens family trust will eventually become the owner of it.

"Wait," I interrupt Mattheisen as he's explaining this, "there's a straight couple who owns the bar?"

"Well ..." Mattheisen says with a smirk, "not exactly straight."

In fact, that's part of the reason Aunt Charlie's has drag shows today. In 1998, Erkelens and Roehm's youngest kid went off to college, and Erkelens planned on spending more time at the bar.

"Bill's a crossdresser," Mattheisen tells me. "He decided that if he wanted to come into his own bar on Friday or Saturday night, he was not going to be the only person in here in a dress. So, he started the drag shows."

Another thing that led to Aunt Charlie's having drag shows was illegal gambling ... or at least the cessation of it.

Before 1998, quite a few Tenderloin bars and restaurants had poker machines in them, Mattheisen says. The story goes that a man lost his whole paycheck on the poker machines at the old Polk Street bar N'Touch. When his wife went in and demanded it back, the bar basically told her to kick rocks, so she went to the authorities. After years of looking the other way, the police raided dozens of locations,

No One Ever Fell In Love At A Poetry Reading At A Startup

including Aunt Charlie's and Erkelens' other bars.

"And so, they seized everything out of the safe, and the money, and that was his fine," Mattheisen says regarding Erkelens' punishment. "His stipulation was that if he ever got busted again for gambling — whether it's dice, football pools, anything like that — he would be hit with a racketeering charge."

To make up for the loss of gamblers, Erkelens had to start bringing in bigger crowds, so he turned to drag queens ... obviously. Specifically, he turned to Vicki Marlane. Marlane was already well known in the community, so they let her pick the talent and concept. This led to an incredibly fruitful partnership; Vicki Marlane ran the drag shows from 1998 until she died in 2011. Then, in 2014, the city changed the name of the stretch of Turk Street that runs in front of Aunt Charlie's to Vicki Mar Lane. It was the first street in SF to be named after a transgender person.

I interviewed Marlane in 2010 shortly before she died for the travel TV show "Young, Broke & Beautiful," which I co-created and hosted on IFC.

"I started out in the carnival in the '50s," Vicki Marlane told me as we sat "backstage" at Aunt Charlie's.

"When we were allowed, I was a hoochie coochie dancer," Marlane continued, "When it wasn't allowed, I would do the sideshow. I was the third and fourth legs for the lady with four legs, I was the alligator skin girl, I was the girl in the iron lung ..."

It's interesting watching that sizzle reel now because so much has changed in San Francisco since we shot it. With appearances from Marlane (who passed away in 2011), former poet laureate Jack Hirschman (who passed away in 2021), and the Bohemian Carnival (which hasn't happened in SF since 2016), it's like a time capsule of a wild and magical San Francisco right before the 2010s tech boom blew it all to smithereens.

But, luckily, Aunt Charlie's is still around and has expanded its programming over the years, often letting community members throw their own events there. Bus Station John (whose moniker is even more worthy of a snicker than Broke-Ass Stuart) has been throwing the dance party Tubesteak Connection for 20 years. It currently happens on the last Thursday of the month. Other events like Angels (a drag show and dance party on second Tuesdays) and Climax (a first Thursday dance party) fill out the calendar.

Mattheisen has been the manager of Aunt Charlie's since 1997 and is a veteran of gay bars in SF, LA, and Phoenix since the early '70s. He's also a veteran of the armed services who did three tours of Vietnam before landing in LA in 1972, where he began bartending at a gay bar named the Outcast.

"When I'm done here, I'm done," Mattheisen tells me, meaning that he plans on working at Aunt Charlie's until he can't work any longer. "I don't really need to be working right now because I have my military disability, I have my Social Security, I could live nicely just on that."

That sentiment of love and loyalty toward Aunt Charlie's seems to be quite common for the people who work there. Jose, the daytime bartender, started in the early 2000s. A bartender named Bob Dougherty worked behind the stick until he was 92 years old. Speaking about Dougherty in a 2015 SFGATE article by Esther Mobley, a customer named Kyle Quinn said, "He moves at a glacial pace and is really hard of hearing, but is so dedicated to his job."

But who the hell is Aunt Charlie? I'm so glad you asked!

Charlie's many lives.

When Erkelens bought the place in 1987, Charles "Chuck" Hemphling had already been working for him at his various bars for about 20 years.

"So, he named it after Chuck," Mattheisen elucidates. "The auntie comes in because in the early '80s this whole area was ..." Mattheisen pauses, searching for a delicate way to put this, "... hustlers. And Chuck was an auntie to many of the boys and girls."

Erkelens not only named the bar after Hemphling, he also installed Aunt Charlie as the manager, from when the bar opened until 1997, when he moved back to his original home, Alabama. He passed away there in 2012.

Before it was Aunt Charlie's, 133 Turk St. was another gay bar called Queen Mary's Pub, owned by Rodger Hall, the original

No One Ever Fell In Love At A Poetry Reading At A Startup

proprietor of the recently shuttered Gangway. In fact, Chuck Hemphling worked there way back in the day. And it seems to have been a bar for most of its life.

To find out the rest of the building's history, I once again enlisted the help of the ever-incredible Pam Larson, a local history sleuth who previously worked at SF Heritage. She wasn't able to find anything before the 1930s, which she found odd since the building is older than that, but here's what Pam discovered:

- 1935: A chemical wholesale store owned by Carl W. Krause. I mean, that's halfway to being a bar, right?

- 1936: Ace Printing Company owned by Oliver D. Olinger. I wonder if people called him Oli Oli.

- 1941: A restaurant owned by John Messer.

- 1943: A bar called Rourke & Perry owned by William J. Rourke and Harry Perry. It's listed as "Liquors/Bar," which means it also likely sold bottles to go as well.

- 1945: The Trap owned by William J. Rourke and Harry Perry. Also, a "Liquors/Bar" situation.

- 1948: Pat & Charley owned by Patrene King and Charles Grelss. Same deal.

- 1951: Mitch's Club, owned by Mitchell Abdo and Rodger K. Winslow

- 1955: Mitch's Cocktail Lounge, owned by Mitchell Abdo and Rodger K. Winslow

- 1978: Queen Mary's Pub owned by Rodger Hall and Joe Roland.

- 1987: Aunt Charlie's Lounge.

It's very likely that either or both iterations of Mitch's were also gay bars, considering that, during Mitch's run, the Tenderloin was full of gay bars frequented by queer soldiers and merchant marines who decided to stay in SF after the war. And we can't forget that the Compton's Cafeteria riot happened virtually across the street from Mitch's in 1966. The iconic drag performer Donna Personna, who performs at Aunt Charlie's most weekends, used to hang out at Compton's Cafeteria in the 1960s and was a consultant for an immersive theater reenactment of the riot that is expected to come out soon.

Aunt Charlie's forever.

While Aunt Charlie's hasn't changed too much over the years, it seems the Tenderloin has. First and foremost, all the other queer bars are gone; Aunt Charlie's is the last one in the TL. This is staggering because, at its peak, there were probably nearly 20. Mattheisen chalks this up to the mainstreaming of the acceptance of queer people and culture. Now that queer people feel safe in nearly all bars in San Francisco, there isn't the same demand. The other way the Tenderloin has changed is its drug of choice.

"When I first started," Mattheisen explains, "it was basically drunks on the street. Now, it's no longer drunks, it's the drugs on the street. It gets a little weirder with people tweaking out. There's a difference between a stumbling drunk and somebody screaming on drugs."

While that didn't seem to have too much of an impact on Aunt Charlie's business, the pandemic did.

"Since the pandemic, downtown is closed," Mattheisen tells me. "All my retail customers are gone. ... I had a lot of waiters who'd come in, but restaurants have been closing."

Things got so dire during the pandemic that Aunt Charlie's was in danger of closing. When it got really tough, Myles Cooper, who throws the High Fantasy disco and drag party on Tuesdays, joined with some other folks and started a GoFundMe for the bar. Aunt Charlie's is so loved by so many people that within a week, they surpassed their goal of $100,000, the bar was saved, and it remains ... absolutely perfect.

No One Ever Fell In Love At A Poetry Reading At A Startup

EVERYBODY NEEDS ADVICE SOMETIMES, EXCEPT MAYBE THE BARTENDER AT MR. BING'S
7x7; 2013

> Bing's is no longer a Chinese bar. It's an Irish bar now. They smartly got rid of the odd Horseshoe bar that took up way too much room. The new clientele is far better looking, but infinitely less bizarre. I wonder if that old bartender is still alive.

I've seen it with my own eyes. The man is more than a man, he's a titan, an iron-livered superhero, an unshakable pillar of stamina. I've never in my life seen someone drink like this. I wish I knew his name, but around the people I know, he's just referred to as, "Oh, THAT bartender. That dude can drink!" I've been there in Mr. Bing's while the regulars slam their gambling dice onto the bar, WHACK! and the tourists peer in the windows, not realizing the marvel their eyes just gazed upon. What makes the bartender in question such a fine specimen of nightlife humanity? Nearly every time someone buys a shot, he does one with them. And it's often from the same bottle as the customer, which means he's not just drinking colored water, so it appears like he's drinking. He's actually going round for round with the entire bar! And he's unflappable; never a slurred word, never even a slight lean. Some might worry that this is acute alcoholism and that if he stops drinking, he will surely die. To this I say nay. We may never see someone like this again in our lifetimes. If he stopped, maybe a little bit of us would die too.

Crouched on a corner where North Beach kisses Chinatown (while the Financial District watches from down the street), Mr. Bing's is the kind of dive bar where literally anything can happen. You're just as likely to get weeping drunk with an old Chinese man and share stories with each other about heartbreak and failure as you are to stumble into what you think may end up a one-night stand, but instead becomes your one true love. It's not that magic happens at Mr. Bing's.

No, it's that life happens there. Weird characters drift through as if it were a port city. Some come for a night and fill the jukebox with all the right songs, and tell all the right jokes, and buy all your friends drinks, and then disappear, never to step foot in Mr. Bing's again. Others get stuck there, and you wonder where the line is drawn, whether they are a part of Mr. Bing's or if Mr. Bing's has become a part of them. It doesn't really matter anyway, generally speaking. Mr. Bing's is like a virgin, it's doesn't give a fuck.

Part of this dive's allure is that it's kind of a weird-looking place. Because of the building's odd shape, the bar shoots out into the middle of the room at an angle, taking up most of the space. There are strange things like a cut-out circle in the ceiling and a possible out-of-use ticket window or coat check in the corner, hinting mysteriously towards Mr. Bing's past. When you've had enough rounds with the bartender, you begin to think there's a metaphor in the way the bar looks, some kind of life lesson, but you're not quite sure what. And you never really figure it out.

One night, I sat at the bar and ended up talking to a young drug dealer who couldn't have been older than 22. He wasn't selling at the bar (that shit wouldn't fly), but before he even began bragging about banging the strippers on Broadway and being their coke dealer, I knew what his profession was. Sometimes you can just tell. I wanted to say to him that I'd met him before. That I'd known lots of versions of him throughout the years, and that flaunting your dealings and flashing your wad will only get you killed or put in jail. But I didn't say anything about it, because those words didn't affect any of the previous versions I knew either. That's just the kind of place Mr. Bing's is, sometimes you sit next to a firefighter or waitress or stockbroker or a doctor. Sometimes you sit next to a dumb kid who you hope hasn't caught a bullet yet. Sometimes you're the one giving the blurry advice, sometimes you're the one who needs it. Everybody needs advice sometimes, except maybe the bartender.

What advice do you give a man who's better at drinking than you'll be at anything in your life?

No One Ever Fell In Love At A Poetry Reading At A Startup

IN A SEA OF SF CLOSURES, A BELOVED BAR TURNS 130
SFGate; 2023

I recently found myself at the Little Shamrock on LSD... for the second time. It's not really anything I've ever set out to do, but after a long day traipsing and tripping through Golden Gate Park, it's just kinda one of those things that happens.

Yes, San Francisco is known around the world as a psychedelics and weed town, but really, at its core, this is a drinking town. And people have been drinking at the Little Shamrock in the Inner Sunset for a very long time. In fact, it might be the oldest bar in continual use (meaning using the same name) in San Francisco, but that's a point of contention among historians and drunks alike. What can't be argued: This iconic gem of an Irish pub turns 130 this weekend. They're celebrating with an anniversary and Halloween party at 1 p.m. on Oct. 28 at 807 Lincoln Way. Expect to find split pea soup from a Victorian recipe discovered in the walls during construction a few years back.

"If I wanted to be a stickler, I could be like, yeah, we're the oldest bar in San Francisco," owner and absolutely hilarious character, Tavahn Ghazi, tells me over the phone. "The Saloon [in North Beach] did burn down [in the 1906 earthquake and fire], so the Saloon is 1907. We're 1893. But at what point do we stop the whole 'who came first' thing and just say, 'Look, we all live in this beautiful city, and we're all doing our best.'

You don't need to be on acid to tell that the Little Shamrock is doing its best as the perfect neighborhood dive bar. Tiffany-style lamps dangle from the ceiling, illuminating the room, while stained glass and historical ephemera line the walls. The tables and chairs look like they came from a combination of garage sales and antique stores, giving the feel of a dowdy Victorian parlor, while groups of people play board games, drink booze, and cheer for whatever Bay Area team is on the TV. There's even an entire darts room in the back. While they do have carpet (you know how I feel about carpet in a bar), it's made up for by the fact that they have a clock that's stood still since the temblor of 1906. Walking into the Little Shamrock, you get the vibe that the bar has been around for a long time and has seen a lot.

One of the upsides of having a bar that's a contender for the oldest bar in San Francisco is that it comes with just as much lore as it does history, and often it's hard to tell them apart.

According to some great history dug up by the Western Neighborhoods Project, while the bar claims it was originally opened on Oct. 28, 1893, by Antone Herzo, "to serve the thirsty workmen who were creating the Midwinter Fair in Golden Gate Park," the project says, it may have actually been opened by his widow, Julia. Traditionally, it's thought that Julia then married a man named J.P. Quigley, who put his name on the bar, as evidenced by some historic photos, and they eventually owned three bars throughout SF's west side.

"One piece of lore that I happen to love is that a woman started the bar, and she had to pretend to be a man," Tavahn tells me gleefully. "Her name was Julia Herzo, her maiden name was Julia Quigley, but she married this guy named Anton Herzo, and when he died, she pretended to be J.P. Quigley."

While this story is certainly a possibility, it's hard to parse lore from truth since there really aren't that many records of the west side at that time. "We were like the third water account in the area, after the Sutros," Tavahn explains. "There were very few buildings on the whole west side of the city. Just a bunch of sand dunes with this Irish bar in the middle."

And with this in mind, it makes sense why there aren't many records of what the Little Shamrock was doing during Prohibition. Considering how sparsely populated the Sunset was, it may have been able to slip beneath the radar. There is some evidence that the Little Shamrock and other saloons flew under the radar by operating as soft-drink parlors that served the stronger stuff in the back.

As the Western Neighborhoods Project points out, though, the later years of the Little Shamrock are easier to pin down.

Tony Herzo Jr. took the helm when his mom, Julia, passed away. He married his sweetheart, Charlotte, and they had two kids. A lot of their business came from the fact that numerous sports events were held across the street in Golden Gate Park, and that made people thirsty. They also did well when the 49ers played in Kezar Stadium. People who had to park near the Little Shamrock to go to a game would stop by for a tipple or triple on the way to and from the stadium, or a scoop of warm beans, free of charge. Apparently, even

No One Ever Fell In Love At A Poetry Reading At A Startup

back then, it was a shot-and-a-beer kind of place where fancy cocktails were looked down upon.

In 1969, Tony sold the Little Shamrock to an Irishman named Enda Barkley, who would famously shout at the end of each night, "All right, you bunch of bloody lushes... Last call for alcohol — it's motel time!"

And then on June 16, 1974, Tavahn's dad, Saeed Ghazi, bought the bar. It was actually the day Tavahn's older brother was born.

Saeed Ghazi moved to the United States in 1964 from his native Iran, and on this fateful day, 10 years later, his life would be irrevocably changed ...twice. His wife had just given birth to his first child at St. Mary's Medical Center, across the park, and Saeed was on his way home to shower and change clothes. "It's kinda the lore of the bar," Tavahn explains. "He saw a parking spot right in front of the Shamrock and said, 'F—k it, I'm popping in for a quick little celebratory drink.'"

While there, Saeed overheard "this beautiful little old Irishman named Enda" talking about how he was gonna sell the bar, but the guy who wanted to buy it wanted to change things, and it was breaking his heart. "And my dad, in his thick accent, was like, 'Nope, I'm getting you a f—king bunch of cash from strange, hairy-knuckled Persian men, and we're gonna buy this thing tomorrow.' And the guy was like, 'Prove it.' And my dad did. It's been 50 years."

While Tavahn took the bar over from his dad in 2003, he grew up in and around the Little Shamrock. When asked about the darts room in the back, he told me they built it because his dad loved darts, but also, "When I was a kid, there used to be arcade games in the back room like Ms. Pac-Man and Arkanoid." He also shared a story from his youth about how his dad helped broker a deal between an Armenian man and a Turkish man to sell a sandwich shop next to the Shamrock, which he noted is a significant event given the history between the two countries. "That was a wild time for me as a kid, where I was like, looking at everyone coming together, just getting the sandwiches done."

One of the most remarkable stories Tavahn told me about his memories growing up around the bar was that his dad befriended a number of the homeless folks who lived in Golden Gate Park and would hire them to work at the bar, and sometimes let them live there. And over the years, a few of them died while working behind the stick. "Okay, so when G died, I remember that because I got pulled out of school and had to go help pull him out of there. I was like 8 years old."

Surprisingly, Tavahn says the place isn't haunted ... that he knows of. "I'm sure others may have their own things to say. I've spent many very late hours in there in prime haunt hours with nary a visit. Practically taunting them at times."

While there's an incredibly loyal regular crowd — Val, one such regular, has been drinking on the same stool for 60 years — and a good chunk of the area considers the Little Shamrock the neighborhood's living room, there's a specific group of people who visit the bar surprisingly often: fans of the crime thriller novelist John Lescroart.

Since my Kindle is linked to both my dad's and mom's accounts, I can read the books they download. My dad reads a lot of crime thrillers, so I recently decided to check out the work of Lescroart. I found that Dismas Hardy, the main character in Lescroart's most popular series, is part-owner of the bar in the books. It was a delight to be reading one of the novels and suddenly find a bar that I'd been to oodles of times (including on acid) was an integral part of the series. There's even a framed and autographed picture of Lescroart on the wall.

So, I of course asked Tavahn how often people come to the bar and gush about its connection to Lescroart, to which he responded, "People come in and ask about him multiple times a day." I guess this makes sense considering the author has sold over 12 million books.

Beyond having a devoted customer base, the Little Shamrock also has a loyal staff. "I've got the same people working in there for 15 years. One of them, my manager Bob, has been there for 20 years, and she's the best. When we had our last press photo, it was her, my dad, and me. She's part of the family for sure."

After learning the fun history and great stories, I had one last question that had been bugging me for years. What was the deal with the bathroom whose hallway was extremely long, whether you were on acid or not?

"It's a grandfathered-in, ADA thing that my dad had to include when he added the dart room in the back. So now it's like a strange little thing, like, how many idiots can we fit in there? And what are we going to talk about when we get in there?"

The Little Shamrock has all the bits that make a great dive bar. A long history, wild stories, a quirky owner, a famous novelist, and weird s—t that can only be explained by the fact that it has always been there. I mean, where else would you want to end up after doing acid all day in Golden Gate Park?

WARMING UP AT THE FIRESIDE BAR
San Francisco Bay Guardian; 2014

The Noah mentioned in this piece is the same Noah who I wrote "Poem For Noah Tao" about, which also appears in this book. I'm not sure if I ever did get around to visiting him at the Fireside. Damn, I miss that dude.

There's something romantic about San Francisco's summertime fog. Those damp and chilly nights belong only to us, and the atmosphere they create is what dreams are made of. While the rest of the country simultaneously shares the same experience of panting and sweltering, we bundle up in scarves and coats and hoodies and boots just to run to the store. Maybe that's the real reason San Francisco feels like a bubble. Maybe it's not just that we're this bedrock of progressiveness and technological innovation. Maybe it's that, like living inside a shaken snow globe, our lives are defined by the fact that the rest of the world is obscured from us by the mists floating in the air.

I've been telling Noah for a while that I'm gonna visit him at the Fireside Bar. We used to work together on Thursday nights at the Golden Gate Tap Room until we stopped, and I've been meaning to catch up with him during one of his shifts at the Fireside. Situated at the corner of Seventh and Irving, the Fireside may be the perfect neighborhood bar. It's got a dive bar feel without being rundown and smelly, the drinks are stiff and cheap, and the regulars are friendly enough. But most importantly, it's got a motherfucking fireplace.

Imagine this: You've decided to get out of your regular routine and go explore somewhere else. Maybe you wandered around Golden Gate Park or decided to check out the Inner Sunset. Or you just walked to the end of Upper Haight and decided to keep on going into the unknown. It's July in San Francisco, and the sun is starting to go down, and you've been wandering around all day with someone who makes you feel all warm and gooey inside. "Let's grab a drink", one of you says as your feet start to hurt and your mouth feels parched, and the top of the ear where you just kissed your special person is cold to the touch. And then you see the Fireside Bar. While San Francisco summers have been around far longer than the Fireside, it's weird to imagine one without the other. You think about this as the two of you order drinks before sitting down to make love-eyes at each other near the fireplace.

I first moved to San Francisco in the summertime, and considering I lived in the Upper Haight, the fog was like a visitor who showed up towards the end of each day. My friend Maria lived just a block away, so one night we got drunk at her place and decided to go on an adventure. I grabbed my skateboard, she put on her roller skates, and we headed west to explore parts of SF neither of us was familiar with. Cutting through the fog and the shadows of UCSF, we eventually found our way to the Fireside, where we stopped for drinks and so Maria could clean up the scrapes she received from falling repeatedly on her skates. We got warm by the fire and then managed to get our drunk asses back to our respective homes without either of us cracking our heads open. It was a romantic night, not in a sexual way, but in a way where we both knew we were two people falling in love with San Francisco and its foggy ways.

I think it's time I finally get my shit together and go visit Noah. Maybe I need a little fog and the Fireside to remind me of all the reasons I fell in love with this city in the first place.

No One Ever Fell In Love At A Poetry Reading At A Startup

THIS HAUNTED SCOTTISH CASTLE IN THE TENDERLOIN IS ONE OF SAN FRANCISCO'S MOST UNIQUE DIVE BARS
SFGate; 2022

"I actually got stood up here one time," I tell Tay Kim as I sip a drink at the long old bar inside Edinburgh Castle. Scottish flags dangle from the ceiling and year-round Christmas lights twinkle, while Kim stands behind the bar and we trade stories about our decades-long histories at this fabled Tenderloin dive bar.

Even though it's been 17 years and I'm now married, I still remember that indie rock party from 2005 where a girl I had a huge crush on didn't show up, or even bother to leave a message on my Motorola Razr. It's probably not the first forlorn love story Kim has heard, considering he's been behind the stick at Edinburgh Castle for nearly 30 years. But his history with the place goes even further back than that.

When he was 10 years old, long before he bought the place or even worked there, Kim once peeked his head into Edinburgh Castle, thought it was ominous and weird, and decided he wanted nothing to do with the place. He had recently moved to the Tenderloin from Korea and had probably never seen a cavernous dive bar meant to feel like the love child of a Scottish castle and a pub. They didn't have anything like it back in Korea, but hell, there wasn't even anything else like it in San Francisco.

The Castle was opened on New Year's in 1960 — in what was most likely an old auto garage — by a pair of Scotsmen named Douglas Kirk and Robert Johnson. The bar took its theme very seriously. Actual medieval weapons adorned the walls, which must've been bolted down tightly because anyone who's spent enough time in bars knows that booze and battle axes are a dangerous combination. To this day, a caber — one of the tree trunk-type things people toss in Scottish Highland Games — is still fastened to a wall near the pool table.

And like so many other San Francisco institutions, it has a haunted past, of course. Kim shared a story with me about a late-night incident where he went upstairs to flip a light switch and the spot he was standing in shook like a major earthquake, though nothing else in the building moved. One of the bartenders saw it happen.

Photo by Kevin Kelleher & Emily Trinh

But Kim isn't the only one who experienced weird things at the bar — many past barkeeps have told him stories about seeing things move by themselves that shouldn't and noticed strange dark shadows creep through their peripheral vision late at night.

But after a 30-year-plus run — which included a residency by a cageless parrot named Winston who spent years flying around the bar stealing quarters and hating bagpipes — The Castle closed in the early '90s. Six months later, Kim's cousins bought the bar in 1994.

At age 24, Kim had just gotten back from traveling and needed a job, so his cousins hired him as a waiter. "When I first showed up, I thought, 'Oh no, not this bar,'" he laughs, recounting the story of when he first saw the place at 10 years old. The thought that he'd now be working at the bar that gave him the willies all those years ago has a funny irony to it.

"We were the only bar in the neighborhood like this," Kim explains as he hands me another drink. "Back then, everything else around here was either a Korean dive or a gay bar, so we were different."

Kim was considering going to art school, but when he found out his cousin was trying to sell the Castle, he figured an opportunity like this wouldn't come up again. So, in 1999 at age 29, he became the owner of the most famous castle in San Francisco, where you can buy a Tecate and a shot for seven bucks.

No One Ever Fell In Love At A Poetry Reading At A Startup

I have a lot of fantastic stories about Edinburgh Castle from my 20s as well. When I started hanging out there in the early 2000s, it was known around the city as a spot for young hipsters to knock back cheap drinks and hopefully meet someone sexy at one of the bar's many diverse events. There were raves, "Star Trek" nights, pub quizzes, a Robert Burns poetry night, a swearing festival, and even a haggis celebration. My favorite was a party called 1964, where the DJs only played '60s soul music and we all danced so hard we sweated through our clothes.

It was a regular stop on pub crawls I used to host, because it was one of the few SF bars large enough to accommodate a school bus full of 40 weirdos. And the small front room with the piano was one of the first places someone recognized me for my writing and bought me a drink because of it, which was one of the coolest things that had happened to me at the time and is seared into my memory. I'd always wondered what the hell that small room with the graffiti-painted piano and empty kegs was originally for, and Kim finally supplied the answer.

"It was originally a Scottish gift shop," Kim explains, "but has since been used as a number of things, like an art gallery, a chill out room, a keg room, and a make out room."

During the 1990s and early 2000s, Edinburgh Castle made an unlikely transition from a 3000-square-foot dive bar popular with Scottish, English, and Northern Irish expats to one of San Francisco's literary hubs. And most of that had to do with the bar manager, Alan Black.

Originally from Scotland and having been involved with the literary scene there, Black brought his love of words and books with him when he started at the bar alongside Kim in 1994. He also brought a connection to a then-up-and-coming writer named Irvine Welsh, who in 1995 was touring behind his new book of stories called "The Acid House." Welsh did a reading at the Castle's hidden upstairs stage, and according to an SFGATE article from 2002, "A new chapter in the pub's history has begun, and everyone there knows it."

Before "Trainspotting" became a hit movie based on Welsh's book of the same name, Edinburgh Castle had the exclusive rights to produce the play. They did this for four straight months, selling out every night. Kim even helped do some of the set design.

"Too bad there were no cellphones back then," Kim laments. "I think there's a VHS recording of it somewhere, but I don't know where exactly." Despite the play's success, they ended it after four months, "out of respect for Irvine."

Shepherded along by Alan Black, many other great people and things came out of Edinburgh Castle's literary scene. Well-known writers like Po Bronson, Noah Hawley, and Mary Roach would do readings there. San Francisco's famous Litquake literary festival was conceived over pints by Jane Ganahl and Jack Boulware. And in 2005, Black teamed up with writer Luke James and former bartender Sean O'Melveny to put out "Public House," an anthology of spoken word, short fiction, and poetry works from the Edinburgh Castle's writing scene.

But Edinburgh Castle's relationship with the arts didn't stop with the written or spoken word. They used to throw small 50-person concerts in the hidden upstairs room where local bands like Train and Two Gallants had their early shows. The tiny space is still used for comedy and theater. And scenes from the movies *So I Married an Axe Murderer* and *Venom* were shot in the bar. Kim loves to tell the story of the band The Killers trying to cut the line, and him saying no. Everyone is treated equally at Edinburgh Castle, even rock stars.

Things are a bit slower than in the 2000s' salad days, unfortunately. The pandemic was "depressing and shocking" for Kim and the Castle since they were closed for a year and a half. And even though they are back open, business is a quarter of what it was in the "before times." Sadly, even Alan Black had to leave and now tends bar at Specs' in North Beach. One of the only things that keeps the Castle alive is the fact that Kim bought the building back in 2010.

In fact, Kim has been considering selling the place, and there are some interested parties. However, according to Kim, one of the stipulations is that they must preserve the property's connection to the history of Edinburgh Castle, given its landmark status.

"So, what would you do if you sold the place?" I asked Kim as things were wrapping up. "Would you finally go to art school?"

He laughed and said no, but he would love to buy some property in the East Bay and do some farming and metalworking, which sounds pretty badass.

Luckily for all of us, though, neither Kim nor Edinburgh Castle are going anywhere at the moment. So, you should think of it as your duty to pop by for a pint or two and bring a couple dozen friends. The drinks are still cheap, the vibe is still perfect, and if you're really nice, Kim might even tell you a real-life ghost story.

POP'S SPARKS DEBATE OVER THE TERM 'DIVE BAR'
SFGate; 2023

"I know it's splitting hairs, but if you call Pop's a dive bar, it's kind of an insult to dive bars," Tom Tierney tells me over the phone. We're discussing the watering hole he's been co-owner of since 2014, a place with a long legacy stretching all the way back to 1937. "Because dive bars have their own place in San Francisco and America," he continues, "I consider ourselves a neighborhood bar."

What exactly is a dive bar? As someone who has spent a good chunk of his 20-year career writing about them, I don't think I can accurately tell you. Even the Wikipedia definition of it is wishy-washy. Just like explaining the meaning of "cool," it's impossible to define what a dive bar is unequivocally. You just kind of know one when you see it.

So then, what's the difference between a dive bar and a neighborhood bar? Well, I guess that just depends on the neighborhood. And in San Francisco, that can mean everything.

Pop's in the aughts.

The first time I went to Pop's was probably in 2004 or 2005. A few of us were walking down Valencia, trying to figure out which Mission bar to spend our pitiful earnings in when my friend said, "I know! Let's go to Pop's! It's really divey and really cheap, and they kinda don't give a f—k about anything." At that point, the rest of us hadn't heard of it, but it sounded exactly like the kind of place we loved, so we tromped down 24th Street, past the *panaderías*, laundromats, storefront churches, jewelry stores, and nail salons.

We were a group of college kids and recent graduates, primarily white, with some Black and Asian members. The Mission was cheap, central, warm (for San Francisco), and full of bars and taquerias. And even though it was largely still a Latino neighborhood, it was also our new neighborhood. And we loved it. It felt, to us, like there was a beautiful blend of cultures happening all in one place.

At the time, we were too young, or too naive, or we just didn't have the framework to realize we were spurring something that would alter the Mission forever. We were the harbingers of gentrification. The word wasn't part of our lexicon yet — that would happen a few years later. But being young kids, who could often afford a little more, we pushed up the rents and kicked off what would ultimately lead to the Mission changing very quickly, with the percentage of Latino residents falling from 50.1% to 34.7% between 2000 and 2020.

But none of that was even remotely in our minds as we walked into Pop's for the first time that night. It was just as my friend described it: divey and super cheap, and nobody in fact seemed to give any fucks. It was also loud and smelled bad, and it was full of skaters, graffiti writers, and people who grew up in the area. It was a quintessential dive bar. And a neighborhood one too, I guess. It was perfect.

That night, my girlfriend at the time and I popped into the photo booth and found a wallet with $1,000 in it. We walked around the bar trying to match the driver's license to a face in the crowd. Once we found him, he was the kind of relieved you get when you realize you have just narrowly averted a serious calamity. Apparently, it was all his money for rent and bills for the month — back then, it would've easily covered rent on my huge $700 room — and so he bought us a drink to say thank you and welcomed us to his favorite bar.

It's been many people's favorite bar over the years, and while they've cleaned it up a bit since the rip-roaring days of the 2000s — mostly just hanging up cool historical s—t and getting rid of that awful smell — Pop's is still a fantastic bar in one of the best neighborhoods in the world. And I argue it's still a dive, too.

Decades of drinks.

These days, the bar is owned by Tom Tierney and Michael Kraus. (You might remember them from my article on Madrone.) But there have been many different owners over the years, and each brought their own personality to the bar.

"My favorite owner is Jack O'Connor," Tierney explains. I can almost hear him smiling through the telephone. "He was part of the beatnik scene. And what I really liked about him is that he was a gambler. He was a drinker. He was a World War II vet. And he was a well-respected cat in that environment, and so I really love talking about him."

When Tierney and Krouse started digging into the history of the bar, it first seemed that Pop's Bar was opened in 1947 by World War II gunner Jack O'Connor, returning home from the South Pacific. The story was that his father helped him open the bar, hence the name Pop's. But they were eventually proved wrong.

One day, a man named Brian Saxsenmeier strolled into the bar and told the folks there that his grandfather, Carl Joseph Saxsenmeier, AKA Pops, was the real Pops. After a records search, this story was found to be true, so the timeline of the bar was bumped back a decade. At this moment, it appears the bar was opened by Saxsenmeier in 1937. Before 1937, rumor has it that he ran a business named the Clubhouse and was a bootlegger during Prohibition.

The reason I say "at this moment" is because there always seems to be more to learn about the bar's past. As Tierney says, "Someone could walk into my store tomorrow and give me a lot more history." As it stands, this is what they know about the history of the bar's ownership and locations. Much of this info came from the Legacy Business application, which got approved in September 2022:

- **1937:** Pop's Club House opened at 2820 or 2830 24th St. Carl Joseph Saxsenmeier, AKA Pops, was the founder of the bar.

- **1941:** Pop's Club House was sold to Jack Pryal.

- **1947-1951:** Jerry O'Connor (the second "Pops") and Jack O'Connor (his son) owned the bar. Jack got married, sold the bar, and then got divorced before opening the New Hearth (now known as The Hearth) at 4701 Geary Blvd.

- **1951-1957:** Charlie Leahy was the owner of Pop's Club House. He sold the bar after marrying the daughter of the owners of St. Francis Fountain.

- **1958-1967:** There were three owners of Pop's Club House during this time: Buff "Red" Volkmeir, Walt Brennan (granduncle of Gavin Newsom), and Albert Beurgelson. Brennan would host baseball fans before and after the SF Seals games that took place at the 16th Street and Potrero stadium, where a Safeway now stands.

- **1967**: Bob and Connie Griffin, along with Jacqueline Griffin, became the owners.

- **1970**: The Griffins moved Pop's Club House down the block to its current location at 2800 24th St. and renamed it "Pop's Bar." They brought the classic neon sign with them.

- **1982-1985**: The Castillo Family took over ownership of Pop's Bar.

- **1985-1994**: Bradlee J. Fitzgerald was the owner of the business. He was a biker, and rumor has it they had a firing range on the inside and used to shoot into hay bales.

- **1994-2003**: Frances Prieto was the owner, and the bar mainly served the Latino community.

- **2003-2014**: Malia Spanyol and Harmony Urmston owned Pop's Bar. It catered to lesbians, skaters, graffiti writers, and punks ... among others.

- **2014**: Tom Tierney and Michael Krouse became owners.

The Pops of today.

"But who does Pop's cater to today?" I asked Tierney.

"We have everything, every walk of life. It really depends on what time of the day you show up," he explains. "We've got doctors and nurses and blue-collar workers at 6 a.m. Same thing for happy hour. We've got electricians, plumbers, lawyers, graffiti artists, and service industry people. You can throw a dart and hit almost any career, and I bet they show up in my bar."

There's a good reason why so many doctors and nurses end up at Pop's at 6 a.m. San Francisco General Hospital is just a few blocks away, and those getting off the graveyard shift often want a drink. Realizing this, the Pop's team rather cleverly decided to begin opening at the buttcrack of dawn back in 2015. The change has been a serious contributor to the financial success of the business.

As someone who has bartender'd in SF for a decade, that sounds like a hellish shift to me, but there's a scratch for every itch. "The early-morning bartender is a specific kind of bartender," Tierney elaborates. "The people working the morning shifts are people who want to work them. They like the morning time. They like the vibe."

No One Ever Fell In Love At A Poetry Reading At A Startup

But even that absurdly early shift was impacted by the pandemic. Luckily, Pop's has been slowly rebuilding its morning-time clientele. And like so many other bar owners I've talked to in this column, Tierney chalks up the bar's survival through the worst of it to its customers.

"We would be nothing without our loyal customer base," he makes plain. "Because it's been around for such a long time, Pop's has special meaning to a lot of people. And I think because of that, people really supported us when we were doing our outdoor drinks and a drink window."

Tierney does have a take on the pandemic I haven't heard yet, though — "I will say this: The pandemic was awful, but I had a really good time trying to help save the business. All you could really do was throw things against the wall to see if they worked. It was kind of freeing in a way."

I guess there's a silver lining to every neon sign.

A GUY NAMED "JERRY THE SWAMPER" ONCE LIVED IN A CRAWL SPACE IN THE HIGH TIDE
7x7; 2012

Sadly, The High Tide And its incredible Neon Sign Are Now Gone. I think it's A Halal Grocery Now, Which is Easily the Healthiest thing to Ever Happen there. I wonder what Happened to the topless painting of Richie Cunning's Grandma

The big neon sign at the corner of Geary and Jones is a beacon of beauty on a dark Tenderloin night. I'd say it draws me like a moth to flame, but actually it draws me like a drunk to a dive bar. A tilting martini glass sits atop the words High Tide Cocktails, poetically mimicking the lushes inside who are themselves tilting on barstools, spilling their guts to anyone who will listen. This is my kind of bar.

Just the other night, I was in the High Tide waiting for my friend Kristin to show up. The only thing that had changed about the place since I lived up the street from it 8 years ago was that they recently got an internet jukebox. A guy in his late 50s was trying to impress the youngish female Asian bartenders by telling them that he was gonna play "Gangnam Style." They begged him not to. He did it anyway. Earlier, I had asked one of the barkeeps why they got rid of the old jukebox. She said that the internet jukebox was better because you could have any song you wanted. Once "Gangnam Style" came through the speakers, I looked at her and said, "I bet you wish you had the old jukebox now." I know I did.

Non-internet jukeboxes are important because they allow a bar to curate the feeling of the place. Before they put in the current abomination, the previous box even had local hip-hop genius Richie Cunning's masterpiece *Night Train* in it. This was great not only because it's one of the best albums about San Francisco in years, but also because both Richie's father and grandfather used to own the High Tide. If you look behind the bar, nestled amongst the dozens of signed $1 bills that are stapled to the ceiling and the walls, there's a painting of a young topless woman with a great rack. That woman was Richie's grandmother! My favorite story Richie told me about the bar, though, is that there used to be a guy called Jerry the Swamper who lived in a crawl space in the men's bathroom during the day, and "swamped the bar" (cleaned up all the wet messes) at night. Jerry the Swamper is no longer in residence at the High Tide, but that's not to say it isn't full of characters.

The High Tide's clientele is as diverse as any bar you can find in SF. Its denizens include hipsters, recently off work Salvadoran cooks, white dudes in button-downs, international people from the nearby hostels, and local Tenderloin weirdos who're slowly but surely giving their lives over to the bottle. It's the kind of place that you pop into for a game of pool and a beer and end up closing the bar down with people you've just met and who've told you life stories too fantastic not to be true. Despite the martini glass on the neon sign outside, I'd be surprised if anyone ever actually ordered a martini in there.

The Tenderloin is a weird place. More and more, brilliant and beautiful bars are opening that serve precious cocktails seemingly derived from alchemy. This juxtaposed with the crackheads and junkies that flit about outside like emaciated velociraptors, illustrates the many imbalances that San Francisco represents. At the High Tide, nobody gives a fuck about any of that shit. They just wanna have some

No One Ever Fell In Love At A Poetry Reading At A Startup

drinks, play some pool, and bump "Gangnam Style" on the jukebox.

This one's for Jerry the Swamper.

CRABS, COMMUNISTS, AND COPS: THE STORY OF SPECS'
The Bold Italic; 2012

I'm sitting across from Richard "Specs" Simmons in his apartment near Fisherman's Wharf. Books, photos, papers, power tools, and the paraphernalia of a life well-lived are stacked and strewn in a manner to leave routes big enough for Spec's to get his scooter through. We're at the countertop in his kitchen, me asking questions, him giving slow, raspy answers peppered with curse words and wit. While his 83-year-old body is in revolt from Parkinson's or some similarly fucked up disease, Spec's mind and tongue are still incredibly sharp, especially when talking about his bar. "In over 40 years, I never called the cops. Not once," he tells me, his

Boston accent coming through, "but I used to have a card game with some of [the cops] at Tosca. One time, one of them says to me about my bar, 'That place is full of Communists and faggots,' and I say, 'Yup.' I never trusted cops."

Photo by Myleen Hollero, courtesy of The Bold Italic by GrowSF

Stuart Schuffman

The bar in question is officially called Specs' Twelve Adler Museum Cafe, but everyone just calls it Specs'. I don't recall precisely when I first discovered the joint, but I've been a regular ever since. To the uninitiated, I describe visiting Specs' as like walking into a Tom Waits song. It's probably my favorite bar in the world, one of the only places on Earth where you can have an 85-year-old Beat poet sitting on your left and a hot young thing on your right. It's also the place where I often take a first date. I figure if the girl doesn't like Spec's (the bar), it's probably not gonna work out between us.

Certain wild plants secrete oils meant to keep predators from eating them, and Spec's has a similar defense mechanism; it exudes an authenticity which repels douchebags even on the worst Saturday nights. The bar looks and feels like it's sweating out the ghosts of the Barbary Coast. The walls, the back bar, the ceiling, and even the counter space are covered in bric-a-brac. With just a quick look around the room, you'll take in 19th-century scrimshaw, a staged fight between a taxidermied mongoose and cobra, photos of San Francisco burning down in 1906, tribal masks, antique signs, ancient Buddha statues, and flags from around the world. And this is just a small sampling of the wonderful oddities and curiosities that live here. When I asked Spec's if he had a favorite piece, he mentioned a few things and then told me about the little cast iron inkwell that looks like a crab. It was the first thing he put in the back bar to remind him of the girl who brought him to North Beach from Santa Monica. "She ended up kidnapping and savaging me. It was fucking lovely. She lived up here, and she left me with crabs. Since she hung out in 12 Adler, which was a woman's gay bar then, I put this crab in the back-bar in her honor when I bought the place 15 years later."

Barfly view.

Specs originally came to San Francisco from Boston in 1948 in connection with some left-wing "political crap." Then they headed down to Los Angeles for a year, where there was more opportunity in his trade, metalworking. A year later, he came back up here looking for his lady of crustaceans. Though he never found her, he did find a job cooking and bartending at Vesuvio for a year before going back into metalworking for 15 years.

No One Ever Fell In Love At A Poetry Reading At A Startup

Photo by Myleen Hollero, courtesy of The Bold Italic by GrowSF

Specs tells me all this and then goes silent for a moment, as if collecting his thoughts and cursing his body at the same time. He continues, "By that time, North Beach turned into this big topless thing. There were only a few spots for locals to hang out. I was sick of swinging a hammer, and I figured, maybe I'd find a joint. Eventually, we located 12 Adler, and we've been there ever since. That was 1968."

When the bar opened, San Francisco's waterfront was still a bustling place, and North Beach was, if not the heart of the city's Bohemia, certainly its liver. So, Spec's clientele consisted of a mix of stevedores, seamen, union organizers, artists, poets, musicians, and strippers (the girls from the strip club upstairs would use a staircase that's now closed up to patronize the bar's bathrooms). Many of the clientele had FBI files on them, including Spec's, who told me about a paper calling him a "clear and present danger to the United States" due to his involvement in left-wing politics in the '40s and '50s.

While the dock work long ago moved to the East Bay, taking its workers with it, Specs' still attracts artists, writers, and musicians. San Francisco's Poet Laureate, Jack Hirschman, holds court at the bar Wednesday evenings. On most nights, you can find someone making art at one of the back tables, while others busk outside the bar's doors.

Time in a bottle.

There's another pause in Specs' storytelling, "Damn medication..." he mutters, voice husky with the frustration of a man dismayed by the weakness of his formerly strong body. He recovers and finishes the thought with one of the finest deadpans I've ever seen, "...it fucks up my drinking" and then continues. "This used to be the strongest union town in the country. Now, I've got about the only union bar left. All my employees are covered with medial and all that.

The Republicans have been trying to kill fucking unions, and it started with that air traffic controller strike. Regan, that slimy cocksucker, he broke them."

We go on to discuss the famous writers and artists who have spent their days and nights in the bar, people getting 86'd from Vesuvio, Specs' role in almost writing the "M.T.A" song, all the changes to San Francisco that he has witnessed, and a hundred other priceless stories that that won't fit with my word count (you'll have to find me and ask me about them). When I get up to leave, my mind is buzzing with local folklore and my iPhone recorder is brimming with the insight and shit-talking wisdom that only a smart-ass Pinko, who's been bartending in San Francisco since 1948, can impart.

A few nights later, I'm at Specs' 12 Adler Museum and Cafe, drinking, flipping through the postcards that sit on the bar, and shooting some shit with the bartender. When I mention to him that I recently interviewed Spec's Simmons for this piece, the old timer on the barstool next to mine looks over and says, "Oh yeah, what kinds of lies did he tell you?" Then he smiles and tells me he's been drinking at Specs' for over 30 years, and that he loves Simmons immensely. "He's a strong, honest, and fair man," the regular says, "Don't make a caricature of him."

I hope I haven't.

No One Ever Fell In Love At A Poetry Reading At A Startup

PIER 23 CAFE IS THE PERFECT PLACE TO AWKWARDLY DANCE WITH TOURISTS
7x7; 2014

Things can get weird at Pier 23. It sometimes seems like all the forces in the universe collide there, creating a perfect storm that embodies what San Francisco should be to those outside looking in. It's a seafood joint on the Embarcadero, with live music, a full bar, plenty of tourists, and a good amount of locals. Red-faced yahoos, drunk on margaritas and tourism, dance in ways they maybe wouldn't at home, while dining families look on. People let it all hang out because this is San Francisco, they tell themselves; this is what you do. And they're right, this is what you do in San Francisco, and nobody busts anyone's balls too hard because we've all had a few too many margaritas as well.

Every time I go to Pier 23, I forget that I know half the staff from various eras of my decade-plus in San Francisco. It's always a pleasant surprise and one that reminds me that, when you've lived here long enough, no place is safe from running into your friends...for better or for worse. I guess that just depends on the margaritas, though. Those fuckers can be deadly.

I wish I were a tourist and could stumble upon Pier 23 with fresh eyes. It's the kind of place that's far enough away from the freak show of Fisherman's Wharf that those who find it accidentally think they've found a San Francisco secret. And maybe they have. When they get back to wherever the hell they're from and they tell their friends about the night they wandered off just to see what they'd find, they'll say they found the real San Francisco. They'll marvel at the diversity of the crowd and how everyone seemed to get along. *It's not like this back where I'm from*; they'll confess to someone sitting next to them at the bar. This person will probably look different from them or be of a different sexual orientation. This might be the interaction that sends our hero home with the realization that people are people, no matter what their skin tone is or what gender gets their sexy parts all tingly. And the last thought before the awkward dancing begins is *Fuck man, what's in these margaritas?*

God bless that awkward drunk dancing. At the end of the day, it's what really makes us human. You think this as you watch all that's going on inside through the window behind the bar. You're on the back patio, by the railing, finishing a drink, smelling the salt water, and wondering if it's okay to smoke. It's not, but you do it anyway, until someone asks you to put it out. The food smells good, real good, but you're lost in contemplation, wondering what the waterfront was really like back in the days when it was teeming with stevedores and workmen.

And that's Pier 23. A great place to be on a sunny day and an even better place to be on a weird weeknight. Go for the margaritas and stay for the company. Who knows, maybe it will be you who walks away from the experience with your mind blown, thinking, "I didn't know people who didn't live in San Francisco could be so cool." People are people, especially when they awkwardly dance.

DISCUSSING PETER PAN SYNDROME AT EL RIO
7x7; 2012

I Actually did the most grown up thing ever at El Rio... I got Married there!! Well Had own Wedding party there At Least. But there was still Peter Pan Vibes: Everyone wore weird costumes and took lots of mushrooms and molly.

I was leaning against the bar, checking out a pretty blonde girl who looked like she took a wrong turn out of her front door in the Marina and somehow ended up in the Outer Mission. She was very obviously bored watching her bro-ish boyfriend and his friends play shuffleboard. "When did all the nermals start finding their way to El Rio?" I turned and asked my friends, Kathy and Christine. I was drunk enough to think that calling them "nermals" instead of "normals" was funny.

"I was just thinking the same thing," said Kathy, "But then I looked down at what I'm wearing and realized that I look like a normal person too." I appraised my own outfit: Cowboy boots, jeans, a blue shirt open enough to show some chest hair, and a black velvet coat. Sure, I'd just come from a date that I'd wanted to look spiffy for, but still, I looked pretty normal, too.

No One Ever Fell In Love At A Poetry Reading At A Startup

"Wait, fuck," I said, "when did we become normals?" Kathy mentioned it might just come with getting older, to which I responded, "No one really gets older in San Francisco." The girls rolled their eyes at this, and Christine said, "Well, the dudes certainly act like they don't get older." I guess she had a point.

I looked around the main bar room. The DJ was spinning a Madonna jam while gay boys in neon with funny haircuts made out in line for the bathroom. A drag queen sashayed by us on her way to the big and busy backyard, and a hipster boy in a mustache bought his black clad girlfriend a PBR. Nobody around us seemed to notice that we looked like "nermals." And that's the brilliance of El Rio. Everyone is welcome.

I first heard about El Rio while researching my San Francisco book. Someone had pointed out to me that they offer free oysters during Friday happy hour, and that on Mondays, PBR is $1 and well drinks are $2. I, of course, checked it out and have been in love with the bar ever since. Every night of the week, something excellent is going down at El Rio. Whether it's the Red Hots Burlesque show in the side room on Wednesdays, Ben Fong-Torres and Los Train Wreck playing their monthly Tuesday Open Mic Jam, or the wildly insane Hard French parties in the backyard on Saturday afternoons, El Rio is always buzzing with something exciting.

This particular evening was a Monday night, and it was one of those strange, almost balmy ones that we've had a lot of this summer. People were out in droves, so we grabbed our $2 well drinks and headed outside to El Rio's finest feature, the backyard. It was packed as expected, and while the crowd of people bopped and swayed to the individual conversations each of them were having, the three of us perched up on the wooden patio just under the giant painting of Carmen Miranda. Christine was talking about wanting to move from San Francisco back to Louisiana. She's in her 30s and has been in SF for nearly a decade. When I asked her why she wanted to move, she said she wanted to be somewhere where she could meet a guy who actually wanted to settle down. She's tired of Peter Pans and Lost Boys and guys who don't want to commit to anything.

"Yeah," I said, realizing that I'm a Lost Boy myself, "you're totally gonna miss San Francisco though." She nodded in agreement, and Kathy asked her what she's gonna miss the most.

Stuart Schuffman

Christine looked around at all of the beautiful weirdos and nermals and queers and straights grooving with each other in El Rio's bustling backyard and said "this."

BENDER'S BELONGS IN THE SAN FRANCISCO DIVE BAR HALL OF FAME
SFGate; 2022

I'm not sure how long it had been since I'd set foot in Bender's — you lose track of time during a pandemic — but after far too long, I was finally there to see Richie Cunning perform at a Noise Pop happy hour. Almost immediately after grabbing a drink, I was stopped in my tracks by something that made me gulp with both cheerful admiration and wistful nostalgia.

Sitting on the back wall below a collection of pool tournament trophies and above a Kiss band-themed pinball machine, I saw the famous sign that used to adorn the outside of legendary San Francisco dive bar Lucky 13.

After several years and announcements warning us of its impending doom, the bar finally shut down in December 2020, and now the sign with that ornery, hissing cat had taken its rightful place on its rightful wall.

The walls of Bender's are somewhere between a graveyard and a hall of fame. Covered in the signs of dearly departed San Francisco businesses, walking into the bar almost feels like a shrine to a city fading into the rear view mirror.

That is, until you hear the loud rock 'n' roll and notice the shot glasses clanking on the bar as people throw back Jameson and Fernet. It's then that you realize this is not a shrine at all. It's a kick-ass dive bar with a storied history. And you discover that the intersection of a graveyard and a hall of fame is a wall of infamy, and Bender's is nothing if not infamous.

I mean, what else would you call a bar that had a weekly special called Tequila Terror Tuesdays, had to stop allowing Jell-O wrestling for insurance purposes, and was once firebombed? What else would you call a place where bikers, bloggers, and techies drink elbow to elbow while munching on tater tots and nodding vigorously to Motörhead blaring from the speakers? What else, if not infamous,

No One Ever Fell In Love At A Poetry Reading At A Startup

would you call a bar whose proprietor is a gravelly voiced veteran barman who goes by Johnny Motherf—king Davis?

"We did Jell-O wrestling for our anniversary party for about the first eight years until the insurance company got wind of that," Johnny tells me as we sit at the bar inside Bender's one afternoon in March. "They tried to increase our insurance by $100,000 for Jell-O wrestling one day a year. So, we had to put an end to that."

Hanging with Johnny is always a treat because you are guaranteed to hear at least one story that makes you say, "Oh damn!" and given that Bender's is approaching its 20th year in business, many of them take place in this bar.

"We had a good one for Noise Pop," he smiles, recalling the show, "Lost Puppy Forever played, and their drummer sports a full furry puppy dog outfit while smashing it on the drums."

Sounds about right.

Bender's has been a lot of things to a lot of people. Back during the explosion of hyperlocal blogs during the 2000s/2010s, the barroom served as a haunt for the folks who ran sites like Mission Mission, Uptown Almanac, SFist, and, of course, my site, BrokeAssStuart.com. We'd even have "official" drink-ups where scribblers from all kinds of publications would get together to kibitz over cheap booze and sometimes make out with each other. We'd often joke that if someone dropped a bomb on Bender's during one of these nights, 90% of all the snark in San Francisco would be wiped out.

Tragically, the idea of Bender's being destroyed wasn't actually too far-fetched. In 2003, Johnny opened the bar with his buddies Liam, Kevin, and Dion. Three years later, an arsonist firebombed the place for reasons no one quite knows. But that didn't stop them from realizing their dream, and 18 months later, they reopened a better, badder, louder Bender's.

In fact, Bender's role as the sign sanctuary for SF's shuttered businesses began after the fire. During the period when they were rebuilding, Leather Tongue Video, the Mission video store specializing in strange and hard-to-find movies, shut down. "I would be coming down here to work on Bender's every day," Johnny explains, "and see that huge Leather Tongue sign on the wall of the building and just think to myself, somebody's going to come along and paint that white one day, someday it's going to be painted over." So, the Bender's crew reached out to the owner of Leather Tongue and the artist who painted the sign, offering a good home for the well-known piece of SF ephemera.

Among the many signs from closed SF businesses are the Lusty Lady (the only co-op strip club in America), Cheap Thrills (a kitschy Haight Street gift shop), and Mission Records (the long-shuttered punk rock record store). And unfortunately, the pandemic has brought them even more treasures to adorn the walls with: "It's sad. We've acquired a lot of new items since the start of the pandemic. In fact, we had so many things offered to us that we had to turn some down."

The fact that a place that houses so many SF memories is still alive and kicking is a special kind of blessing.

"We've been burned down once. We've been shuttered twice [because of COVID lockdowns]. And we're still here." Johnny then sighs, "We survived COVID, we made it this far, but things have been nothing but difficult."

Thinking the initial lockdown wouldn't be very long, the guys dipped into their savings to fix things around the bar while they were temporarily closed. The closure lasted for a whole year, forcing them to take out substantial loans to stay afloat. But Johnny is optimistic at the moment, since restrictions are lifting and most San Franciscans are vaccinated and boosted.

When I asked him to describe the crowd at Bender's, he said, "Wow, no one has asked me that before. I guess it's rock 'n' roll fixed gear motorcycle neighborhood Mission rats," he says while laughing. "You know, you can sit down next to a lawyer who's sitting next to a plumber who's sitting next to a bike messenger, who's now a blogger, who's sitting next to an author. And they'll all be having a great conversation."

But as the city has changed over the years, the crowd has slowly changed as well. Other than that, there's only been one real significant change at Bender's since the pandemic: after nearly two decades, they finally take cards!

"The world has shifted on its axis, and Bender's now takes cards.

No One Ever Fell In Love At A Poetry Reading At A Startup

Yeah, it's a new world here, folks. It's been kind of wild. So, you've got to give us dinosaur bartenders a little breathing room when we're clearing your tabs on your card."

BOW BOW COCKTAIL LOUNGE: WHERE GETTING WEIRD WAS INVENTED
7x7; 2013

MAMA CANDY HAS Retired But this is still A great PlAce to get Weird

There's an incredible song that Johnny Cash recorded on the first of his *American Recordings* albums called "The Beast in Me." The first stanza goes:
> The beast in me
> Is caged by frail and fragile bars
> Restless by day
> And by night rants and rages at the stars
> God help the beast in me

I think we can all relate to that on some level. There's a bit of each of us that has to be restrained just so that we can be participatory members in society. Anyone who has spent an evening in Bow Bow Cocktail Lounge knows what it's like to have those frail and fragile bears fall apart. Invariably, the Beast gets out, and it's usually Mama Candy's fault.

Dimly lit and supremely divey, Bow Bow has decorations. That is to say, I'm pretty sure there are decorative things on the walls, I just don't know what they are. It's impossible to walk out of there with all your faculties firing properly. By the time you're about to call it a night and do the responsible thing of going home and getting into bed, Mama Candy doesn't let you leave. She pours you a free shot and says, "How about some Chinese whiskey?" and you say, "Ok Mama Candy, just one," and the next thing you know, you've had four more and your arms are around complete strangers, belting out the *bum bum bums* of "Sweet Caroline."

Yes, Bow Bow has karaoke too. But there's no stage, or spotlights, or even a KJ. There's just a big TV at the end of the bar playing weird videos, like people sailing remote-controlled boats, and other random things that have no relation to the song being played. That's how the fuck Bow Bow rolls. Half the songs in their karaoke book are in Cantonese, and the ones that are in English are poorly categorized.

Does Mama Candy care? Fuck no! She won't even let you sing karaoke if you're just drinking water; you at least have to buy a soda, and even then, she gives you a little bit of the stink eye. That's because Mama Candy wants you to be the full you, the you that yells the lyrics to "Hot for Teacher" at the top of your lungs (even though you have a microphone), attempting to take off articles of your friends' clothing. Things happen at Bow Bow that shouldn't ever be mentioned again; The Beast comes out, and Mama Candy eggs you on without even offering to be your confessor. She doesn't want to hear your shit; she just wants you to work through it...in front of everyone.

If you were to say that Bow Bow is the kind of San Francisco establishment that is imbued with magic, I'd agree with you, but qualify that it is black magic. It's the kind of powerful necromancy that you're not sure any place should be allowed to contain. Big, tough men enter, hopped up on beer and adrenaline after seeing a Giants game, and leave wearing pantyhose on their heads like a hat. Quiet, sheepish people enter, looking to be a voyeur, and end up exorcising their demons while singing "Girls Just Wanna Have Fun" under the harsh glare of a row of swimming baby ducks on the TV screen. I often say things at the start of a night like "Let's get weird." Bow Bow Cocktail Lounge invented getting fucking weird. Which is, of course, why I love it.

God help The Beast in me.

No One Ever Fell In Love At A Poetry Reading At A Startup

DOC'S CLOCK REMINDS ME OF THE MISSION I MOVED INTO IN 2004
7x7; 2012

I walked into Doc's Clock and everyone cheered. I knew they liked me there, but not enough for that kind of salutation. Looking down past where the bar ends, I saw the cluster of people gathered around the shuffleboard table and realized my arrival wasn't as momentous as I'd thought; someone had just out-shuffled someone else. Given that it was late on a Wednesday, it was a local crowd. All walks of life were represented, like some kind of Mission United Nations. Old man drunks, heavily tattooed pin-ups, skinny boys in skinny jeans, new-to-the-neighborhood start-uppers, off-work Salvadorean cooks, and a couple of working girls getting a drink in before heading back to Capp Street. This was the Mission that I loved. It felt like the one I moved into in 2004, in that time between the bust of the dot-com bubble that whizzed around the city like a balloon with the air let out, and whatever the fuck the historians are gonna call this thing we're living through right now.

Doc's Clock is like that, though. The closest to that world embodied by Valencia, with its glut of great restaurants and well-thought-out boutiques, comes to infiltrating Doc's when the restaurant employees from the surrounding eateries stop through for their post-shift drinks. I settled into a barstool between an old guy muttering into his whiskey and a lesbian couple deep into working out some shit about their relationship. The darker-haired of the two Carries who work there came up and poured me a shot of Jameson. "Stuart! Long time no see! Let me buy you a shot."

Doc's used to be a regular spot for me when I lived just a few blocks away, but since moving in January, I haven't been able to give it the love and attention our relationship needs. One of the deep-in-conversation lesbians was saying her girlfriend was doing the same thing to her. It's hard to foresee where life's currents are gonna drag us. "Yeah, sorry, Carrie. Now that I live on the other side of the Mission, I'm just not over here that much anymore, but I miss you all." I told her as she poured me another. Despite being one of the most dog-friendly bars in SF, Doc's was canine-less that night. The second Carrie usually brings her rescued Greyhound, and other patrons bring their furry pals as well. Doc's Clock is also proudly one of San Francisco's greenest bars. They've been certified as such, and signs around the bar confirm this. But those aren't my reasons for going there.

I go to Doc's Clock because of the great people who work there. I go because the drinks are stiff and cheap. I go because they have board games and shuffleboard. I go because it reminds me of my younger days and that other Mission that I loved so much. But mainly I go because their neon sign that says, "Cocktail Time" once said "Cock Time", and that's just fucking hilarious.

HOW A WESTERN ADDITION PHARMACY BECAME ONE OF SF'S MOST CHERISHED PARTY BARS
SFGate; 2022

Photo by Kevin Kelleher & Emily Trinh

"Hey! I had sex in that pantry!"

That's what I said to Madrone Art Bar owner Spike Krouse, grinning as we passed through the kitchen of his apartment, which is connected by a secret staircase that leads to the venue he owns downstairs.

This was not the first time I've bragged to Krouse about my lustful dalliance in his larder, but it is probably the first time I've seen this place since the licentious act occurred at a Halloween party in 2006. Back then, the apartment was full of rambunctious 20-somethings who threw raucous parties and staged naked photo shoots (not necessarily at the same time, but really, anything is possible).

Settling down over some mezcal at his living room table, we begin to chat about the much-adored downstairs bar that Krouse has helmed since 2008. While there, I can't stop myself from marveling at what a difference 16 years and some semi-responsible grown-ups can do to a place.

What I foggily remember as the type of giant, quirky, San Francisco Victorian party house that always had at least a couple of guys living on the couch is now, quite literally, the kind of giant, quirky, San Francisco Victorian that everyone who's ever moved to this city has always dreamed of living in. Besides the fact that it has *a freaking secret staircase*, wonderful artwork of all kinds fills the odd nooks and crannies that can only exist in a sprawling Queen Anne built in 1888. And oh, the many lives this building has led since then.

From Western Addition pharmacy to Divisadero dive.

During the eleventy-hundred times I've been to Madrone, I couldn't help but notice the lovely mosaic inlay at the front door that said "Green's Pharmacy," so I asked Krouse if he knew the back story of the place. While he gave me a good rundown of it, he did me one better by showing me the book *Historic Houses of Alamo Square* by Joseph B. Pecora, which includes the following history of the building.

500-502 Divisadero was constructed in 1888 by architect Samuel Newsom (a distant relative of Gov. Gavin Newsom). The building's original owner was a Gold Rush pioneer named Theodore Green, who opened Green's Pharmacy downstairs with his chemist son Franklin, while he and his wife Phebe resided in the flat above.

By 1896, both Theodore and Phebe had died, and Franklin took over management of the pharmacy for the next 40 years, renting out the upstairs apartment to doctors and druggists. He was apparently a busy guy because during this time he also worked as a coroner, a toxicologist, and the dean of the School of Pharmacy at the UC Medical Center on Parnassus (now UCSF).

When Franklin died in 1944, Herman Lincoln — who had been employed at the pharmacy — bought the building and carried on the Green's Pharmacy name. When Lincoln died in 1955, the building changed hands once more before being sold in 1982, at which point Green's Pharmacy had been dispensing drugs to denizens of the

Western Addition for 93 years.

In her Hoodline article about the building, R.A. Schuetz furthers the story of 500-502 Divisadero, noting that the building served as a Mr. Falafel, a sandwich shop called SUAD, and eventually became a symbol of Divisadero's fight against formula retail when Burger King unsuccessfully tried to take over the building.

And that's when Madrone sauntered onto the scene.

The birth of an art bar.

When Leila Fakouri opened Madrone Lounge in 2004, there really wasn't anything like it in the neighborhood. This was back when Divisadero got pretty sleepy after sunset, before real estate agents christened the area "NoPa." The opening of a bar with rotating arts shows and nightly DJs reinvigorated the nightlife. And they had some pretty great stuff, including a weekly Tuesday night party called Change the Beat that featured local turntable heroes like Gaslamp Killer (who moved to LA in 2006), Mophono, and Citizen Ten.

Even though I've been drinking at Madrone since it opened in 2004, it wasn't until I was sitting at the upstairs living room table last week — learning the building's history and taking in all the accumulated art, that I finally, fully, understood the magnitude of f— king dopeness that is Madrone Art Bar.

Madrone isn't just a funky bar with sweet tunes and well-curated things on the walls. It's the perfect embodiment of what happens when art, nightlife, and community get infused with the ineffable spirit that, even today, makes San Francisco special. And a major reason for that is Spike Krouse himself.

After decades of creating art (he went to the San Francisco Art Institute) and working in San Francisco bars like Tony Nik's and the Boom Boom Room, Krouse was looking for a way to fuse his two worlds into a creative community space. It just so happened that Fakouri was trying to sell Madrone, so in 2008, they made the hand-off, Madrone Lounge became Madrone Art Bar, and Krouse has been curating the vibes both upstairs and down ever since.

That's because while he doesn't own the building, he did take over the lease of both the bar and the apartment above it at the same time. "When I bought the bar," Krouse tells me, "I kept the people who were living in the apartment, and then I just kind of slowly waited until they moved out. And then once they all moved out, I just moved myself and my family in and cleaned it up."

While Madrone probably didn't need the same level of cleaning up that the apartment did, Krouse imbued his own sensibilities into the bar. Phenomenal pieces of art like the assault rifle wrapped in Burberry and gold made by Peter Gronquist were added to the permanent collection, while rotating art shows transformed the interior. "My favorites are ones that are installation-based and changed the feeling of the bar," Krouse explains. "Like this guy, Sam Mell covered the entire wall in a grid with blue tape. The way it transformed the room was fascinating." The giant window facing Divisadero also became a space for installations so that art could be shared with the community outside the bar.

Under Krouse's management, the programming at Madrone took on a more robust life as well. Starting in 2009, Motown on Mondays turned one of the deadest nights of the week into one of the hottest parties in San Francisco and has since spread to over 45 cities around the globe. Other events like Fringe (one of SF's first indie rock parties) and the various fetes thrown by DJ Sonny Phono helped turn Madrone into one of the venues where you were guaranteed to have a blast every time you went.

But with an eye on creating community, Spike set out to make Madrone different from all the other DJ bars out there. For as long as anyone can remember, the Bay Area soul/jazz/funk hero Oscar Myers has had a Tuesday gig. Midweek has always featured a variety of live music, ranging from open mics to jazz trios.

Krouse explained that the midweek bands aren't as financially successful as DJ nights, but booking live funk and jazz has more to do with honoring the history of the neighborhood. Anyone who was here 20 years ago remembers that the Western Addition used to be a predominantly Black neighborhood. And boy, is that not the case now.

To exemplify this, Spike told me the following story: One of his regulars is a Black woman in her 60s whose partner was the only white person in their building when they moved in many years ago. These days, it's the opposite; the neighborhood has changed so much that she's now the only Black person in that building.

The funkiest lemonade stand in San Francisco.

Aside from the changing demographics of Western Addition, the most seismic shift to Madrone's business model took place during the early days of the pandemic. Before parklets sprang up everywhere and bars were limited to selling to-go drinks, lemonade stand-style, it was the community Krouse built at Madrone that kept the place going.

One customer in particular would come by every day and always tip $100. When Krouse asked him why he was doing it, the guy said he had always loved the space. Although his life had changed, and he no longer came as often, he still loved what the bar provided.

Krouse elaborated on that theme.

"Having a business that's been here for so long, people have memories of what it means to them. That's what made me realize how much the place means to people. Besides it being my business, it's theirs too. In a way, I've got a better bar than I did before the pandemic."

I'm not sure if Franklin Green would have any idea what you were talking about if you explained that his pharmacy would one day be a bar that, as Madrone's website states, is also "a constantly changing site-specific installation art environment where two and three-dimensional works, multi-media, and performance are combined to form an aesthetic constellation that affects attendees' perceptions from the moment they enter the place."

But considering he ran a business integral to the Western Addition neighborhood for more than 40 years, he would certainly understand that which drives Spike Krouse's vision: community.

TOP OF THE MARK: WHERE ALL OF SF'S GHOSTS STILL LIVE
7x7; 2012

When you've lived in San Francisco long enough, your personal history becomes a residue on every block you pass. Over there is the restaurant you worked in when you first moved to The City. Around the corner is the bar you spent too much time in back when you had extra time to spend. Across the way is the house you lived in in your early 20s, when the things you thought were important were the things you couldn't give a shit about now. Storefronts and businesses come and go in this town, but your experiences and memories attach themselves to places like ghosts that haunt only you.

A couple of months ago, I was at the Top of the Mark with Becca and Lindsay, talking about the different lifetimes we've each seen while living in San Francisco. It seemed rather appropriate considering that the Top of the Mark was opened in 1939 and has probably seen more lifetimes than just about any place in The City. Officially, we were there because the PR company they work for represents the Top of the Mark and wanted me to write about it. This happens a lot; I write about some places, and others I don't. Regardless, I make it a rule never to pass up booze and food when it's offered to me. We discussed work-related topics for the appropriate amount of time before sharing our personal stories.

The last time I'd been at the Top of the Mark was for an ex-girlfriend's birthday. I'd taken her there after we'd seen one of Bob Marley's many children at The Fillmore. Before that, I'd really only been there during their exquisite Sunday brunch. This was an anniversary tradition with another girlfriend I had. These were my ghosts, my personal history left as a residue in this rooftop bar at the Mark Hopkins Hotel. Becca and Lindsay offered up their own stories, and we talked, ate, and drank while a few drunk old men looked out the window longingly, probably thinking about their own past lifetimes. Tourists snapped photos of themselves making funny faces in front of the world-class view, not realizing they were leaving their own historical residue amongst the decades of ghosts that already inhabit the place.

It was a Monday night and even though there was no live jazz like there is Wednesday through Friday, the atmosphere was still sultry and sophisticated. In a town where most millionaires dress in hoodies and jeans, the Top of the Mark feels like a throwback to old money and elegance, while still being accessible to the rest of us. At one point, I walked around enjoying the view and looking at photos of the Top of the Mark throughout the years. Apparently, it was customary during World War II for GIs to have one last drink and take in the view before shipping off. The northwest corner was even called the "Weeper's Corner" because the soldiers' sweethearts would watch with tears and running mascara as the ships departed the bay carrying the young men off to war.

But there was no weeping this night. Instead, we were celebrating our histories, telling stories, and talking optimistically about our futures. We all had great things on the horizon, especially Lindsay, who informed us about her recent engagement. We drank and offered cheers to Lindsay and her future husband, adding one more layer of historical residue to a classic establishment that already has plenty and will receive much more.

TALKING OPEN RELATIONSHIPS & STRONG BOOZE AT COMSTOCK SALOON
7x7; 2013

The line "Who uses a bar review to talk about lost love and regret anyways" originally linked to my piece about falling in love at the Lone Palm, that is also in this book. This was definitely written during the period where I was using bars as a vehicle to write about my messy sex/love life.

The first time I went to Comstock Saloon was with a woman I wasn't dating. My girlfriend at the time was out of town, and we were trying out being in an open relationship. It was our weird way of slowly letting go. Relationships are the hardest ships to keep afloat, and ours, which had always been so buoyant, was sinking.

We'd been with each other for five years—those important years that come after the formative ones, the ones that make up the second half of your 20s. The ones where, when you look back, you realize you were fumbling towards adulthood, and up until then, we were doing so together.

We didn't fully capsize until at least six months later, but by opening up our relationship, we were readying the lifeboats, testing the waters, and seeing how much it would hurt to be set adrift at sea alone.

No One Ever Fell In Love At A Poetry Reading At A Startup

I had forgotten about that first visit to Comstock until this morning, when I sat down to write this piece. Up until yesterday, when I revisited the bar and restaurant, my strongest memory of the place was running into my cousin Judith while I was there on a Grouper date. I chuckled at the thought that, in San Francisco, it would've been totally possible to be set up on a blind, group, internet date with your own cousin. Luckily, I wasn't, but it certainly didn't surprise me that I ran into her. Because of the size and nature of this city, San Francisco forces you to both keep your nose clean and own up to your shit; no matter what, you're guaranteed to see someone you know. So, the first thing I did when I saw Judith was admit that I was on a random, blind, group internet date. She responded, "Of course you are."

Whether you're attempting an open relationship or going on a blind, group date, Comstock is pretty much a perfect location. It's a nod towards the Barbary Coast, that time and place in San Francisco history to which the "anything is possible, and everything goes" mentality that so thoroughly permeates the Bay Area's culture can be traced back. Comstock nails the feeling of a turn-of-the-century saloon: The mahogany bar is twenty feet long and 100-plus years old, ancient knick-knacks dot the space's interior, and there's a gas fireplace for people to warm up next to on cold and foggy SF summer nights. There's even a little trough under the bar; some say it was so patrons could relieve themselves without having to get up from their stools, while others say it was there to make swamping the place easier after closing.

The same amount of thought has been paid to the details of the space as to the menu. The cocktails are all classic, pre-Prohibition concoctions, and all the food is the chef's modern take on recipes he finds in turn-of-the-century cookbooks. Comstock Saloon is the closest you're gonna get to being in the Barbary Coast without using a time machine. Hell, they even claim Emperor Norton as their patron saint.

Speaking of patron saints: Saint Francis is the patron saint of animals and ecology, so it's kinda perfect that our city is named after him. It's almost like the Spanish were telling the future when they gave this place its name. He's also the patron saint of stowaways. I'm tempted to use that as a way to tie this whole piece together by referencing whatever things were lost, like stowaways, with the sinking of the ship in the first paragraph of this piece. But I won't. Who uses a bar review to talk about lost love and regret anyway?

DELIRIUM HAD THE WORST DIVE BAR BATHROOM IN SAN FRANCISCO. IT'S FINALLY BEEN FIXED.
SFGate; 2022

In the 2000s and early 2010s, if you had tattoos or brightly colored hair or tight jeans or stark eye makeup or facial piercings or liked loud rock 'n' roll or whiny emo music, chances are you spent some Friday and Saturday nights at Delirium in the Mission. The drinks were hella cheap, the music was rowdy, the backroom was full of dancers and cigarette smokers, and, most importantly, people were beautiful. In the days before Tinder and Bumble, people met each other in bars, and there was no better pickup joint for the skinny-jeaned, asymmetrical banged, fingerless-gloved hipsterati of San Francisco than Delirium.

"I once made out with a Republican on your pool table," I tell current owner Angelo Basso as I point across the room to the felt-covered scene of my crime. It's a Thursday morning in December, my birthday actually, and Basso and I are sitting at a table behind the short end of the bar while I interview him about his family's drinkery. "I'm pretty sure we drank until last call, then afterwards partied at some weird warehouse space until the sun came up. I never saw or heard from her again," I continue to regale him.

Smirkingly, Basso responds, "Sounds about right."

The reason I'm at this closed bar at 9:30 a.m. on the morning of my birthday is that something momentous has happened to Delirium: They redid the bathroom!

For years, the bathroom at Delirium was the kind of dank and fetid hellhole that only immunologists and dive bar patrons will ever fully appreciate. Potently foul-mouthed graffiti covered nearly an inch of the wall; there were many nights (including the one where I took the most ignoble shit of my entire life) where the door was missing from the toilet stall, and the entire chamber smelled like the drainage pipes were, at best, on furlough.

If you ever touched a single surface in that bathroom, chances are you didn't actually need a COVID vaccine; your body's immune system was already superheroic.

No One Ever Fell In Love At A Poetry Reading At A Startup

Photo by Kevin Kelleher & Emily Trinh

The thing about that bathroom, though, is that its repugnance only made it more glorious. My friends and their friends, along with their other friends and those people's frenemies, and almost everyone we knew, were 20-something hipsters who somehow figured that the grimier a place was, the better. And we weren't exactly wrong. We frequented dive bars all over the Mission — all over town, really — but none of them felt as divey as Delirium, and as such, none of them had as much as much vivacity and tumult either. The neon sign that says "Service for the Sick" can attest to that.

Yes, dear reader, I was just as flabbergasted as you are now when, one night in 2020, I popped by and saw the facelift—so floored actually that I tweeted, Facebooked, and Instagrammed about it multiple times. The responses to this tweet were just as shocked as you and I.

Given the historic nature of this revelation, it was only fair that I checked in with the bar to learn what other things I'd missed, especially considering that this year is Delirium's 20th anniversary.

In his early 30s, Angelo Basso is a friendly, kinda shy guy who was born and raised in Noe Valley. Not only is he a third-generation San Franciscan, but he's also a third-generation barman. His family has owned bars in San Francisco since his grandfather Dado opened the House of Chips at 18th Avenue and Geary in 1948. Since then, the

Basso clan, including Angelo's father Wayne and older brother Tommy, has owned nearly a dozen bars throughout the city. Up until recently, that included Noe's Cantina at Church and 24th Street and Lister Bar (formerly Park 77) in Parkmerced. But given the vagaries of changing San Francisco and then the pandemic, Delirium is the only horse currently in their stable.

While Angelo has been running Delirium for the past five years, the spot was opened by Wayne and Tommy in 2002. Previously, it had been an even divier bar called the Albion, which I know because on the wall they have a 2003 award from the SF Bay Guardian for the "Best Makeover Without Ruining a Good Spot." Angelo was only in middle school then, but his family brought him into the business as soon as they could. "I kind of started learning the stuff at 16," Angelo tells me. "My dad would take me to help him close to see what he did."

At 21, he started bar-backing at Delirium and shortly thereafter met his wife while working. "She was sitting right here," Angelo points to the barstool next to us. "I was working, and she was having a drink." They've been together over 10 years now and have a daughter, adding a fourth generation of San Franciscans to the Basso lineage.

But apparently, meeting hotties at Delirium isn't what it used to be. Like nearly every bar in California, the pandemic has really screwed up business. While I haven't personally spent much time at Delirium in recent years, it was still apparently a pickup joint up until COVID dashed normalcy to hell. They still had dancing in the backroom seven nights a week, and that combined with ridiculously cheap prices ($2 Tecates, a shot and a beer for $7) kept Delirium bopping.

Luckily, the Bassos bought the building that houses Delirium about three years ago, so they didn't have to worry so much about going out of business, but as Basso told me, "We're surviving, we're not doing bad. We're not thriving anymore. But we're not sinking." As the omicron variant surges, that's unfortunately as much as one can ask for.

While dancing is currently only happening on weekends now and the bar is rarely packed elbow to asshole these days, there are things in the works to bring Delirium back to its (not quite) resplendent glory. Longtime bartender Sheau-Wha Mau has taken on the role of events coordinator, planning new nights of activities like karaoke, and booking DJs that will help bring folks back in. The good news is that the bar is still open seven days a week, even on holidays.

"I'm just trying to keep the old dive bar idea alive," Basso tells me. "Everyone else is changing. I think all the new-age San Franciscans want high-end cocktails or to stay home, Netflix and chill, and Uber their liquor. Many places have to upgrade for them to come in, but I want to keep an old vibe."

For those who spent their glorious salad days drinking, dancing, and kissing under Delirium's dim lights, it's refreshing to know that, unlike the rest of San Francisco, not much has changed at Delirium ... other than fixing up their bathroom, of course! They even put in new drainage!

"Lots of people said they were amazed by the new bathroom," Basso wryly shakes his head. "I was kind of trying to keep it painted and clean, [since] I thought people would leave it alone. I thought if you keep it nice, no one will touch it, but it's not true."

Just before I left Delirium, I peeked into the lavatory to see if it still had that astonishing fresh new sheen I'd seen in 2020. Of course, the graffiti was already steadily creeping back, but at least the place smelled better.

You can help keep Delirium delirious! Pop by and have a few drinks. Who knows, you might just meet the next love of your life, or at least the love of your night.

VESUVIO: ATTRACTING WEIRD MOTHERFUCKERS SINCE 1948
7x7; 2013

North Beach has a certain magic to it. The neon lights and the strip show barkers blend with the San Francisco night and the smell of garlic, creating something old school and current, ancient and timely. On the right evening, with the right amount of intoxicants, you can almost believe for a second that you're part of something bigger than you are; that you're continuing in the steps of the art and writing and culture and madness that San Francisco has always seemed to represent.

If you can ignore the groups of lads driven mad by lap dances, you can land yourself in what I call the Holy Trinity of SF bars:

Spec's, Tosca, and Vesuvio. I've already written about the first two, so it's only fair that Vesuvio gets its turn.

Walking into Vesuvio, it's impossible to miss the influence that the Beats had on the place. Pictures of Kerouac, Ginsburg, Cassady, and more sit nestled between the art and ephemera that cover the walls. Bob Dylan is smoking with Gregory Corso. Charles Bukowski is being a dirty old man. This isn't just some bullshit put up to rope in tourists for a San Francisco shake down, though. Vesuvio is just doing what it does best: being a dope bar. Opened in 1948, it's been attracting weird motherfuckers since before the Beats even existed and still does long after they've been gone. That said, its ties to that movement are inextricable.

One of the most quintessential San Francisco experiences is buying a book at City Lights, going next door to Vesuvio, finding a spot upstairs in the window, and reading it while you have a drink. There's something romantic about the notion that isn't there? And that's precisely what makes Vesuvio important. In a city that is currently trying to decide whether to hide from its past or run from its future, Vesuvio reminds us that the previously mentioned art, writing, culture, and madness are more critical to San Francisco's identity than any tech boom will ever be. There's not enough venture capital in the world to fund an app that William S. Burroughs hung out at. No one ever fell in love at a poetry reading at a startup incubator.

The earliest you can buy alcohol in San Francisco is 6 a.m., and Vesuvio is one of the few bars that opens at that time. The 6 a.m. crowd is a mixture of people getting off the graveyard shift, travelers not adjusted to the time zone, and, of course, the drunks who need to get their fix. Come to Vesuvio at 6 p.m. and you'll find the same kind of people, though. International accents mingle in the air with jazz music, and the guy sitting next to you at the bar might be a millionaire or a bum. You never really know. Not that it matters anyway, he's guaranteed to tell you a good story if you let him.

I'm sure Vesuvio has a happy hour. And it probably has nightly drink specials too. I've never bothered to find out. But I can tell you that the bartenders are equally sweet and surly, the drinks are stiff, the customers are fascinating, the art is interesting, and the vibe is somewhere between an old man dive bar and a Parisian cafe. As far as

No One Ever Fell In Love At A Poetry Reading At A Startup

I'm concerned, that's worth more than all the tech stock in Silicon Valley. If you want me, I'll be upstairs in the window reading a book.

YES, WE DID AT THE BROKEN RECORD
7x7; 2012

I call Guy Fieri a douchebag in this piece and I'd like to say I no longer think he is one. Sure his schtick is a bit cheesy, but after the way he raised millions for all the kitchen staff who couldn't get government money during the pandemic, he's a hero in my book.

As the cab pulled up to the curb in front of the Broken Record, the bar exploded in ecstatic cheers. Krista looked at me as we exited the vehicle and said, "Oh my god, I think we won." This was election day 2008, and the results from California had just come in. Barack Obama had been elected the 44th President of the United States. We'd been hopping all over town, trying to find a viewing party to watch the election results, and after waiting in line at Mezzanine for far too long, we hailed a cab and headed out to the Broken Record. All of our friends were there anyway.

Walking into the bar the night of November 4th, the crowd was abuzz with whiskey and optimism. People were hugging the shit out of each other and buying rounds of drinks. I got a text from my mom, who was in the hospital, that said, "Yes, We Did!" It was the same chant that was echoing through the streets of San Francisco from Hunter's Point to Pacific Heights. The text message brought me to tears.

For those who live in the Excelsior, the Broken Record is an anchor of awesome in a sea of not much else going on. For many, it is the only nightlife option out there. For those who don't live in the Excelsior, the Broken Record is cool enough to inspire us to sail our little ships in its direction, even if that means a long, late-night adventure on the high seas of San Francisco mass transit. Besides having great prices and a legendary whiskey collection of 300+ bottles (that includes whiskey on tap), the Record is equally famous for its kitchen. What other dive bar can you get lobster mac & cheese and duck confit potato skins? It's so well regarded that Guy Fieri featured it on his show *Diners, Drive-Ins, and Dives*. Even if Fieri is a total douchebag, at least he's got good taste.

I've been a fan of the Broken Record for a long time, even before it was featured on the Food Network. Since it first opened its doors in 2007, I've been making the trek to visit it. From having it as a stop on one of my yearly pub crawls to simply going out there for a change of scenery, the Broken Record has always proven to be filled with a friendly clientele, great bartenders, and a healthy amount of beer pong. I even had my 30th birthday at the Broken Record, which proved disastrous. There's a photo floating around out there of me slumped down in a chair next to a Christmas tree, passed out with my hat over my face. My only real recollection of the night was the flashing lights of the Disco Cab that ferried me home. Like any good bar, the Broken Record accepts you for who you are at your very best and your very worst.

That night in November 2008, we were all at our very best. We were drunk not just on whiskey and beer, but on promise, on a new beginning, on what we thought was the kind of change some people wait their whole lives for. I kissed Krista and hugged my best friends, and we howled and screamed and danced in the streets, and I realized that there was no better place to be on that fateful Tuesday night than at the Broken Record. Maybe I'll be there on election night this year, too.

SAN FRANCISCO'S STRANGEST DIVE BAR HAS AN EXPLOSIVE INSPIRATION
SFGate; 2024

Back in my early 20s, I had a girlfriend who went to USF, and I'd often stay in the dorms with her. We were always in search of what we felt was the real San Francisco, so we'd make the short trek from campus to the Lower Haight and bask in the weirdness and cheap beers that abounded within the walls of Noc Noc. While there, I'd often run into one of my favorite San Franciscans of all time.

Just when I was hitting the point of being too drunk, I'd hear, "Tamales!" and look up to see Virginia Ramos, aka the Tamale Lady, rolling in with her coolers full of corn husk-wrapped salvation. While the tamales cost a few bucks, the hugs and advice were free. God damn, I miss that woman.

Walking into Noc Noc, the first thing you notice is that it's not like other bars. Colored lights illuminate glass fixtures that look like they are oozing from the ceiling. Odd shapes and patterns are painted on the walls, but also jut off them, giving the walls texture and extra peculiarity. Strangely shaped, hand-painted chairs that sit around the bar look like random boards that were found and decorated by Basquiat on a bender. The DJ booth is hidden in a wall like some kind of audiophile's sepulcher. The whole vibe feels like it was designed by Otho, the interior designer from Beetlejuice. And I mean that as the highest form of compliment.

Yes, Noc Noc holds a very special place in my heart. The same goes for many San Franciscans. But it wasn't until I sat down with the bar's owner, Rahmat Shirakhon, that I learned its fascinating history.

"Noc Noc is short for Nocturnal Nocturne," Shirakhon tells me as we sit at one of the bar's tables a few weeks back. "Nocturne means music for the night, and nocturnal, of course, is people who stay up late."

Crashing on Haight street.

In essence, Noc Noc was opened as a place for people to come at night and listen to good music. While Shirakhon has been the steward of this dusky wonderland since 1991, he's not the one who founded it. That credit goes to Ernest Takai and his business partner, Michiko, in 1986. Takai is the mad genius who conceived of and built out Noc Noc.

"His idea was like a plane that crashed in the ocean," Shirakhon explains. Pointing to various objects jutting from the walls or ceiling, he says, "See this here? That's an airplane. This is a bomb from a B-52. And at the end of the hallway, you might see the controller from a B-52." Takai definitely took some creative license with this theme, considering I've been drinking at Noc Noc intermittently for over 20 years and just now am realizing the design inspiration.

Most importantly, though, Takai wanted Noc Noc to be a bit of a mystery, the kind of place where those who knew it loved it, and everyone else had no idea it existed.

It's almost comical to think there was a time in San Francisco when a bar could survive with such an elusive business model or that anything could, in fact, stay a secret. But that was a very different era.

"It was really, really shady," Shirakhon explains while discussing what the neighborhood was like when he took over in the early '90s: "At the time, I had eight employees and seven of us, including myself, were mugged on the street in one year." (Personally, I blame Chesa Boudin.)

According to Shirakhon, when Noc Noc opened in 1986, it was the only bar in the Lower Haight. Toronado opened a year later, and within a few years, Mad Dog in the Fog (now Woods), Midtown (now Molotov's), and Café International opened. The Peacock Lounge was there, but it has always been a private event space.

The many lives of Noc Noc.

But what was in the space before it was Noc Noc, I wondered, and Shirakhon offered a surprising answer: a water bar. Well, at least half of it was.

"They had like 48 different types of water at the time and lasted less than 48 days," he tells me. "They were way ahead of their time."

The water bar only took up half of the space that Noc Noc now occupies. If your back is to the front door, the left side of the venue is where Noc Noc originally opened. It was so small that the DJ booth was located in what is now essentially a broom closet. The bathroom was outside, behind the building, in what amounted to little more than an outhouse. According to Shirakhon, this space was a clothing shop before Takai and Michiko took over. They opened up the second side of Noc Noc in 1988.

To find out the rest of the history of 557 Haight Street, I once again enlisted the help of the ever-incredible Pam Larson, a local history sleuth who previously worked at SF Heritage.

•1929-1931: A tailor shop owned by David Roberts, who lived around the corner at 245 Fillmore

•1932-1933: Haight Malt Co., owned by Abbot Stokes

•1937-1939: Bell Cleaners & Dryers, which was part of a chain of stores

No One Ever Fell In Love At A Poetry Reading At A Startup

throughout SF with other locations at 2443 Fillmore, 1044 Hyde, 4495 Mission, 1220 Polk, and 1012 Taraval

- 1940-1943: Post Office Station 16 (I'm curious as to why it was only a post office for three years).

- 1944: A flower shop owned by Louis Cimina, who lived down the block at 538 Haight St.

- 1945-1952: Another florist named Preston's, owned by William Preston

- 1953-1957: Yet another flower shop named Colonial Florist, owned by Mrs. Carrie Abshire, who passed ownership to Irving L. & Carrie Huges in 1954, then Dorthy A. Lowry in 1955

- 1957: Colonial Florist, owned by Dorthy A. Lowry

- 1958-1960: Vacant. After 14 years and five different people trying, it seems someone finally got wise to the fact that this place just wasn't meant to be a flower shop.

- 1961: A mysterious shop named Ketch All, owned by Joan Paxton

- 1962-1981: Jack's Shoe Shine Parlor, owned by Jack Jackson

- 1982: Flying A Art owned by Glenn Grafelman. It doubled as Grafelman's painting studio.

- 1986: It becomes the weird wonderland that is Noc Noc.

Considering we don't have any documentation of what was there between Flying A Art and Noc Noc, it's fairly safe to assume it was the clothing store Shirakhon mentioned.

With help from Larson, I was able to get hold of Glenn Grafelman, whose painting studio was Flying A Art. He's now an artist working in Minneapolis and New York and was able to give some great insight into what the neighborhood was like in the 1980s.

"The Haight-Fillmore, during the early 1980s, was home to many artists. Several of the storefronts were art studios and galleries," he said. "We organized an annual event, the Haight-Fillmore Open Studios, which helped create an upbeat community vibe — the new Haight-Fillmore Whole Food Company and Henrietta's [the area's first gay bar] brought stabilization and revitalization to the neighborhood. A positive growing artist enclave north of Market Street."

The strangest little DJ booth in town.

Besides being loved for its wild interior, Takai wanted the bar to be known for its musical flavor. According to an old quote on the "About Us" section of Noc Noc's website, Takai claimed the club helped pioneer quite a few genres of music.

"We are the first place to play industrial, ambient, dance, acid jazz in San Francisco next to The Quake radio station back in those days...I remember people didn't like to hear our music back then," it read. "They thought it was strange. So I must play the new music for nocturnal people that they will love to listen to 15 years from now...and now everyone loves it!"

Another thing that Takai infused into the bar's DNA was the love of his country's most famous drink: sake. Since the California Department of Alcoholic Beverage Control would only grant him a beer and wine license, Takai leaned into it, making sake one of the featured offerings at the bar. And that tradition continues today: Noc Noc still doesn't serve liquor and has a robust sake menu. They've also always been about high-quality beer and not the macrobrews that come out of places like Milwaukee. A sign behind the bar says, "No Bud, No Coors, No PBR." Under Shirakhon's guidance, Belgian beer has become Noc Noc's specialty, and they have a nice selection of sours. Considering they are located next to Toronado, the best beer bar in SF, Noc Noc can't afford a weak selection. Between bottles and drafts, they now have around 50 beers to choose from.

While Shirakhon has kept the look of the bar almost exactly as Takai designed it, there has been one massive, illuminating change: the addition of windows.

The big front windows that you see today weren't always there. Instead, the bar had an even darker, even more cave-like vibe. Then, about 12 years ago, while Shirakhon was visiting his native Iran, his son Samson, who worked with Shirakhon at the time, had the windows installed.

"I came back and said, 'Oh, my God, the wall is gone. The windows are here.... Sam, what have you done?'" Shirakhon says. But Samson's instincts proved to be right. Now, when they open the bar each day, the first three places that are usually taken are right there in the front windows. And it helped business pick up since more people realized there was a bar there.

The origins of a dive.

During our conversation, a thought kept bugging me: How does an immigrant from Iran — one who happens to have degrees in both electrical engineering and accounting — end up buying a beer and sake bar from a mad genius Japanese artist?

"I came to this country in 1974 from Iran," Shirakhon tells me. "I was working in restaurants and had done everything from dishwashing, busboy, waiter, manager, all the way up. And I wanted to open a restaurant."

When a broker told him there was a bar for sale in the Lower Haight, Shirakhon and his wife decided to check it out. Even though the neighborhood felt shady to them, they explored the space anyway and were blown away by the interior. When they asked about the restaurant part of the business, the bartender pointed to a blackboard that said, "Ham Sandwich. Cheese Sandwich. Ham and Cheese Sandwich. And Nachos." Right then, Shirakhon decided to ditch the restaurant idea and go into the bar business. As soon as he took over, the blackboard came down. He's been a barman ever since.

"I'm never gonna retire," he laughs and points to a spot behind us. "See this area right here? That's my tombstone."

But where is Ernest now? After opening Noc Noc, he did the interior of nearby Zip Zap Hair. Then, he went on to open a Noc Noc in Seattle and Los Angeles, but neither of them still exists. These days, he's back in Japan, hopefully making completely bananas interiors.

Luckily, Noc Noc in SF is still kicking. Surviving in this city for over 30 years has taught them that sometimes you have to pivot. Lately, they've been having more private and semi-private parties. A private party is over 40 people, with no minimum spend, and costs $100 for weekdays and $150 for weekends, while a semi-private party is under 40 people, with no minimum spend or rental fee required.

Noc Noc is such an ideal San Francisco bar, and it gladdens my heart to learn that it has an equally perfect San Francisco story. Just don't say "Beetlejuice" three times in a row while in there because you never know what might happen.

Let's Get Weird

(Lifestyle)

What can I say? My life is strange and beautiful. This chapter is full of stories that make all the other bullshit in life worth it. I have so many other stories that would be perfect for this chapter, but I haven't written them down yet. Maybe I'll get to them when I finally write my memoirs. The title just comes from one of my favorite sayings ever, "Let's Get Weird!"

THE IMPORTANCE OF BEING EARNESTLY COSTUMED WHILE YOU PARTY
Fest 300; 2013

There's a photo of me floating around out there that virtually guarantees that I can never run for public office (Note: this was obviously written way before I ran for mayor). In it, I'm clearly intoxicated and wearing Mickey Mouse ears and a pink leotard. One of my eyes is going the wrong way while the other has that red Terminator thing going on, and I'm holding a large bottle of Puerto Rican scotch named Black Cock. Yes, Black Cock.

Included in my cohort that night were a 1940s mobster, a flight attendant, Holly Golightly, and Jesus. It was Halloween 2008, and like people all over the country, we'd been waiting all year for the chance to put on costumes, drink unfortunate amounts of alcohol, behave irresponsibly, and laugh giddily at the wonderful getups we saw people vamping in the streets. For a night, we got to be someone other than ourselves, even if that person had absolutely no affiliation with the costumes we were wearing.

And in a way, that's what makes the act of wearing a costume so magical. The costume is transformative. It can be spiritual or playful, sexy or sedate. In San Francisco, we revel in the chance to dress up. Seeing as each year there's some new event added to the calendar for which we're expected to wear weird shit and dance in the streets, any respectable San Franciscan has a costume box in their domicile. It's part of our culture. We use costumes as a way to express the parts of ourselves that don't normally get to sing.

Getting dressed up in silly outfits and merrymaking through the city is obviously not just a Bay Area thing; people celebrate in various ways in every corner of the world and have been doing so since the first time humankind had enough extra material to own more than just one loincloth. From ancient shamanistic rituals, where holy men and women would wear sacred outfits while communing with the

Let's Get Weird

gods, to modern-day shit-show bacchanalia like Mardi Gras or Carnival, costumery is an intrinsic part of giving oneself to the celebration. It's about being part of something bigger, a collective tremor that vibrates until the lines between reality and make-believe become momentarily fuzzy. Suddenly, you're part of something bigger than yourself; whether dancing for deities, scaring away spirits, or just joining the crowd, the act of participating makes anything seem possible.

Think about the last time you dressed up, whether it was for a costume party, Halloween, Burning Man, *Dia de Los Muertos*, or even Prom. Now remember the feeling you had while getting ready: the excitement, the nervousness, the anticipation of what the evening may hold for you, and the joy of recounting previous nights where you put your grown-up self to bed early and let your kid self stay out all night long. This is all part of the transformation, part of the letting go. You're beginning to build towards being some strange fucking creature that looks and sounds like you, but is someone completely different. Tonight, you will be Cleopatra, or Oscar the Grouch, or some odd amalgamation of the random shit you found in your closet. Tonight, you will be a sexy nurse, or a fireman, or some beautifully plumed demigod who dances with others in choreographed routines through the streets of Rio. Tonight, you will be you, but not you, but completely you, and no one can say a damn thing about it. Wearing a costume is all about saying "yes", even if there wasn't a question asked.

And then it's over. You danced and sweated and hugged. You ate, laughed, and met new friends. You fell in love with someone dressed as Little Red Riding Hood as she passed through the other side of the crowd, even though you never got a chance to talk to her. You met a man dressed as some green sparkly thing, and you went home with him, the sad knowledge that tomorrow, when you wake up, he will once again just be a man. Even when the fervor and fever and feel-good all dies down, and you take off your make-up and outfit and get into bed, you're still in costume. It's not until you wake up the next day and smile, thinking about all the inexplicable magic that happened the night before, that you're back to being regular you. Unfortunately, when you're doing that long, hungover, morning-after-getting-laid trudge home, you're back to being regular you, too, even if you're still all dressed up.

INDIAN SUMMER IN THE CITY
SF Sounds; 2013

Some brilliant bastard called this time of year "San Francisco's High Holidays". I wish I could remember who it was, but I did tell him I was gonna steal it, so at least I'm keeping my word.

These couple of months between Burning Man and Halloween are the closest thing to magic many of us will ever know.

Starting with Burning Man, you're either out howling at the universe through a bacchanalia of massive art projects, mind-bending drugs, and casual sex, or you're celebrating that all those motherfuckers are out of town, by finally eating brunch at Zazie without waiting in line for two hours. The Burners drag their dust-covered butts and psychedelically splattered brains back into The City, and for a couple of weeks, hugs last just a little longer than usual, and people seem so much more earnest. It's like the rapture of the playa manages to rub off on the rest of us for a little while... then again, that could just be dust.

While the rest of the Northern Hemisphere is blowing sad kisses to their shorts and sundresses while mournfully closing the drawers their summer clothes live in, San Franciscans are taking off as much clothing as possible and running outside. The jury is still out on whether "Indian Summer" is racist or not, but for this brief period, San Franciscans are too busy frolicking to figure out if they should be offended. The jury itself is halfway to Baker Beach as we speak, excited for some nude sunbathing.

It was particularly hot at this year's Folsom Street Fair. Clocking in somewhere around 90 degrees, oodles of dominatrices hung up their whips for the day, complaining the sun was doing all the work for them. Somebody better call their union rep. The Furries had it pretty rough, too, as litters of them dropped to the ground, passing out from heat exhaustion and dehydration. Onlookers weren't sure if it was all part of some new role-playing. Regardless, the day was splendid and reminded so many of us that part of what makes San Francisco special is seeing two men dressed as firefighters blowing each other in the street. To everyone who attends Folsom every year: god bless your perverted little hearts. At some point amid all the frolicking and buggering, Fleet Week arrives on the scene, haircut all high and tight, ready to make it rain in North Beach strip clubs like it was a goddamn hurricane. The streets of The Castro run wild with seamen, and the Blue Angels screech through the sky, scaring the bejesus out of every fury creature for a hundred miles. If animals were able to keep calendars, this would be the time of year they'd save up all their vacation days for. I imagine plenty of battle veterans aren't too keen on it either.

That's one of the many reasons I miss the Power to the Peaceful Festival. Anchored on the other end of our Frisco summer than Fleet Week, it was a free one-day festival that usually started with yoga with Michael Franti, which led to speeches by folks like Angela Davis, and then music by people like Ziggy Marley. It's where teenagers from Walnut Creek first learned about the Prison Industrial Complex because of a pamphlet they were given, and where the American Communist Party and the American Socialist Party weren't allowed to have booths next to each other due to all their glaring.

Luckily, Hardly Strictly Bluegrass is still around and is probably the most incredible free concert in the world. Three full days of world-class music and large enough crowds to give even the most serene person a mild panic attack. It must be the only place ever where you can probably sell more Xanax than MDMA... actually, that does sound like a rather lovely combination.

As if all this wasn't enough to make you believe in magic, every other October, the San Francisco Giants go to the playoffs and win the World Series. With all the black and orange being worn, it's hard to tell if someone is a Giants fan, a Halloween enthusiast, or both. If it's an even-numbered year, nearly all of San Francisco is drunk for the entirety of October. This means lots of babies are born the following July, and lots of bartenders know what it feels like to make fuck you money, even if it's just for one month every two years.

These months really are San Francisco's High Holidays, and the frenetic energy that surrounds everything during this time orgasms with the costumed revelry that is Halloween. And then San Francisco rolls over, falling fast asleep, with dreams full of fog, and if we're lucky, lots of rain too.

I TOOK ACID AND WALKED THE ENTIRETY OF GOLDEN GATE PARK
The Bold Italic; 2021

I really love LSD! It's my favorite drug by far. I recommend everyone taking psychedelics and walking all of Golden Gate Park at least once. Well, almost everyone...

[handwritten drawing of two stick figures among trees, labeled: "You and me on acid in Golden Gate Park"]

Kayla, Alex, and I were standing in front of the Rideout Fountain in Golden Gate Park's Music Concourse as the world vibrated around us. Children chased each other screaming, teenagers canoodled on park benches, dogs wore tuxedos for their people's wedding photos, tourist families scuttled between museums, and we stood there absolutely peaking on acid, giggling at the absurd statue in the middle of the fountain.

"It has like...the body of a man, the paws of a jungle cat, the face of a panther, but then big-ass saber-tooth tiger teeth. And why is it fighting a very surprised-looking snake?" Alex told us. "Apparently, the sculptor set out to make a mountain lion, but had never seen one, so made this instead."

We were only a couple of hours into our long, hilarious, LSD odyssey through Golden Gate Park, and this hideous fountain was just one of the many mysteries we'd discover that day.

* * * *

I'd been wanting to ramble the entirety of the park, from the Panhandle to the beach, tripping balls — ever since my friend Josiah had mentioned it being one of his favorite things to do a few years back. And now, on this strangely foggy, humid, and warm September day, the game was finally afoot.

We met at the William McKinley statue at the tip of the Panhandle at noon, and each put a gel tab of lysergic acid diethylamide (LSD) under our tongues. The goal was to make it to Ocean Beach for the sunset at 7:15. In normal circumstances, the four-mile walk would only take about an hour and a half, but with the grass breathing and the leaves shimmering in wild shapes, the real question was if we'd make it at all.

Acid is a hell of a drug. It can make you feel euphoric, see colors and patterns much more intensely, hallucinate things, and roll on the ground laughing at the stupidest shit. And since I didn't know how hard I was gonna trip, I tried to dress incognito. (It would be kinda weird to have someone stop and want to take a pic with me if I was seeing trails everywhere).

Wearing a ballcap and a hoodie, I thought I wouldn't be as recognizable, but of course, as we made it to the Conservatory of Flowers, the guy checking vax and ID cards said, "I thought it was you!" and my cover was blown. I probably should've worn a MAGA hat or something, but I didn't want to give everyone a bad trip.

We meandered, and the acid started to come on right about when we entered the Conservatory of Flowers. The only thing I've never really enjoyed about psychedelics is the body high. It makes me feel like I can't get physically comfortable, and can give me mild anxiety. Considering how hot and humid it already was outside, entering the tropical environs of the Conservatory gave me an almost freak-out moment. But looking at all the strange and bulbous plants that hung like fuzzy alien sex organs helped a lot. The real key to getting over the body high, though, was getting a few drinks in me, so we hopped outside the park to what felt like the hinterland of Richmond to find some beer and White Claws.

It was at this point that things got weird. For some reason (read: drugs), we didn't think to look at Google Maps for a liquor store until we'd been wandering for ten minutes. "Are we in the Excelsior?" Kayla asked.

"No love, we're still in the Richmond," I said, "but also, I'm not really sure I'm feeling anything yet. Are you all?"

They were definitely feeling it, and I was too — I just didn't realize it yet. I even considered taking another half a tab, but am REALLY glad I didn't.

After lumbering into Denhard's Market on 10th Avenue to grab drinks, we knew it was time to get out of the concrete weirdness and get back to the more vibrant green weirdness of Golden Gate Park.

Which is how we ended up at the Rideout Fountain. The White Claws had taken the edge off my trip, and we were sitting on a bench in the Music Concourse cackling about the things we thought we saw, but were probably mis-seeing. "I'm pretty sure that's an entire choir sitting on that bench practicing."

No, dear reader, it was not. I think it was people just having lunch.

Alex got up for a closer look at the statue.

"I just looked at that fountain up close," he said. "Some fountains are meant to be admired from afar."

And we soon found out he was entirely correct.

A strange thing that happens when you're on psychedelics is that bizarre phenomena inexplicably occur. For example, the last time I did acid was up in the Santa Cruz mountains at a friend's wedding (this kind of thing was encouraged, and about 20 of us took it). At one point, someone came over and said, "Hey, come check this out! There's a zebra next door!" There were, in fact, two zebras...and a bunch of peacocks, emus, and other unexpected animals. Apparently, the neighbor rescues them and has something like 27 species.

While this kind of stuff doesn't seem to happen when you're just going through regular life, it often does while on mind-altering substances. It was at this point, at the peak of our trip, that we decided we needed to venture further into the park. We still had about 40 blocks to go.

* * * *

Continuing west, we skirted the Botanical Garden, marveling at all the humans cramming in for the Flower Pianos. I don't know about you, but psychedelics make me extra mischievous, so when we saw a place in the fence where it would be easy to hop, we almost did. Then one of us realized that the festival was free to S.F. residents anyway, so what was the fun of crashing something that we were invited to?

Skipping Stow Lake — because "Whoa... there are so many people," and having no desire to climb Strawberry Hill because "Fuck climbing hills right now" — we found ourselves at 19th Avenue, once again looking for booze.

If zigzagging through the sleepy Richmond felt a little eerie, coming out onto 19th Ave. felt like Carmageddon. Acid tunes up your

Let's Get Weird

senses, so you're more sensitive to sights, sounds, and ambient feelings. But we had The Thirst! Thus, we trudged on.

And that's when everything got really weird.

Walking out of the liquor store that we finally found around 19th and Kirkham, we came across a true oddity: a duck in a diaper. He was straight up chilling on the sidewalk, like "What, you don't have ducks in diapers in your neighborhood?"

I turned to the lady loitering outside the store and said, "Is that really there? I mean I'm on acid, but I'm not that high."

The duck wasn't alone, though. Her owner was there too, wearing a shirt with a duck on it. I guess some folks are dog people, some are cat people, and apparently, others are duck people.

"Why does that kind of shit only happen when you're on drugs?" I asked.

"What are you talking about? You just saw a guy walking a chicken on a leash in the Tenderloin like a month ago," Kayla reminded me.

I like doing psychedelics outside. I like looking at the magnificence of nature, ruminating on concepts I haven't had time to concentrate on, and having the ability to roam around. And San Francisco is a fantastic place to do this. There are nearly 250 parks in San Francisco, considering the federal, state, and city levels. And each one has something different to explore. That said, Golden Gate Park is probably the most interesting. Sure, Dolores Park is a great place to buy drugs, but maybe not the best place to take them.

Escaping the concrete jungle and re-entering the Eden that is Golden Gate Park, we eventually made it to Hellman Hollow, where finally, thankfully, we were not the most fucked-up people around. We grabbed a seat on the grass and watched a bunch of college kids play a very competitive game of Sloshball, by which I mean, a race to the bottom of sobriety.

From there, we bumbled by the Polo Fields, which were somehow covered in thousands of birds...at least we were pretty sure they were. Then our titanic meandering and staring led us accidentally to stand directly in the way of a Frisbee-golf tournament.

Somewhere along the way, Kayla had decided that we weren't leaving until we saw the bison. We managed to go the long way and stumbled upon a part of the park I didn't even know existed.

* * * *

The Golden Gate Park Dog Training Area is like the Chase Center of dog parks. Under normal circumstances, Kayla and I sometimes find ourselves the creeps who hang out at dog parks unaccompanied by a furry friend, but this was something different. Dozens of dogs chased each other, shitting everywhere. We sat down to rest our legs, choosing a bench that seemed to have a great view. Unfortunately, it was just on the other side of the fence from where every dog within a 10-mile radius must come to shit. There was so much shit, in fact, that we decided the bison pen must smell better.

I can now report that the bison are underwhelming even when you're on acid — but we did get to see a hawk swoop down and snatch a mouse straight out of the bison paddock. We cheered that hawk on like fucking psychopaths.

We trudged on like champions and found a little lake none of us had ever been to. To be honest, I don't even know if I could find it again. We immediately came across a few families of raccoons and thus named the place Raccoon Lagoon. The little bandits were obviously used to people because they were playing up their cuteness, but we still didn't trust them. The journey continued.

By now, we were five or six hours into our expedition. Our legs were tired, and our sides hurt from laughing, but we could not stop. Even though it had been incredibly foggy and humid all day, we could feel the ocean getting closer by the salinity in the air. Plus, we'd just stumbled upon Chaparral Ranch, so we got to murmur endearing things to the horses we found there. That is, until we noticed there were other people around and realized how weird we were being.

Stumbling through the underbrush, we exited the shrubbery into civilization...or whatever you'd call several dozen teenagers playing soccer while grown-ass adults yell crazy shit at them. The Beach Chalet Fields meant we were almost at the Beach Chalet, which, in turn, meant we were almost at the beach. We had an hour or so before sunset when we stopped at the Park Chalet for a bite and a beer. Sitting there, snickering about all the ridiculousness of the day, we acknowledged that a) we were indeed still relatively high and b) we had one last thing to do.

Let's Get Weird

* * * *

I'd love to tell you that the sunset was magnificent. That my LSD vision helped emblazon the luminous sky to bring me tears of joy and beauty. But it would be a lie. We couldn't see shit. There essentially was no sunset. It might honestly be one of the thickest fogs I've ever seen. The sky went from hazy grey flannel to hazy black bed sheets. Not an ounce of color in the sky. But that's OK because what we encountered was even more fascinating.

Standing on the sidewalk above the beach, peering at the dozens of bonfires dotting the Great Nothing ahead of us, we learned what teenagers do for fun in San Francisco. There were literally hundreds of them clumped together on the beach like penguins clustering together for warmth. That is, if penguins gossiped loudly and snuck sips of booze from under their hoodies. As we approached the wall above the sand, three teenage boys furtively shoved bottles under their garments and shuffled away from us because to them, we probably looked like narcs. Little did they know!

"This is awesome," I told Alex and Kayla. "It reminds me of growing up in San Diego. This is exactly what we did as teenagers." And I dwelt upon the circle of life. In the semi-near future, some of these youngsters would be embarking on their own voyages of psychedelic discovery.

I wondered how many of them would inherit the tradition of the Grand Tour (a term I just made up) of taking acid and rambling through Golden Gate Park.

Then again, I also wonder, after reading this article, how many of you might also do the same.

THE GOLDEN AGE OF LAZINESS
San Francisco Examiner; 2018

We're living in the Golden Age of Laziness.

A legendary epoch of sloth. A shining era of indolence. This stage in history will go down as the moment when it was decided that we, as a society, just couldn't be bothered to put on pants anymore. And to be honest, it's rather glorious.

There's a new saying: "Netflix and Chill." It's when you invite someone over to watch Netflix and then, you know, fiddle with each others special parts. Well, I have my own version of this. It's called "Netflix and Cheese," and it's just me sitting around in my underwear, eating fancy cheese, and watching my stories. The wildest part is that I don't even have to get dressed to buy the cheese!

If I'm willing to pay the fees — which is usually only when I'm really hungover — I can use apps like Instacart, TaskRabbit, and Postmates to have that chunk of Truffle Tremor delivered right to my door from Rainbow Grocery. And you know I'm not putting on pants to answer the door.

Part of living in San Francisco is that we've got the pleasure — earnestly or sarcastically, depending on how you look at it — of being the guinea pigs for all of the new technology-driven services that emerge. We get front-row seats to witness the vagaries of free-market capitalism happen at hyper speed.

Remember when Uber and Lyft had to compete with Sidecar and Summon? Or when Sprig, Munchery, Spoonrocket, and whatever other silly-named companies were all vying to be the one that would deliver freshly made lunch directly to our faces? One of the unexpected outcomes of this most recent tech boom is that, within just a few years, we've become remarkably accustomed to having nearly anything we want arrive at our doors at incredible speeds. And while it's making everything far more convenient, it's also making us assholes.

I'm not saying the breakdown of patience and courtesy is entirely because we can have chimichangas, lube, and Q-tips delivered at any hour of the day. But it's certainly making people more self-centered and weakening our social skills.

I bartend once a week, and one of my roommates owns a bar. A few weeks ago, the two of us and some other friends were sitting around late at night discussing how much ruder people have become: I could be head-down, obviously in the midst of making a drink for a customer, and someone will come right up and start ordering from me as if I'd looked them in the eye and asked what they wanted. Similarly, if I pass someone up because they're twiddling with their phone, they'll get cranky that I served a ready customer instead of waiting patiently for them to stop taking selfies. Worst of all, people say "please" and "thank you" less than ever before.

Let's Get Weird

I see the worst manifestations of it in folks who work at big tech companies; I know because their clothes say the name of their employer, and they're often drinking on the company card. And if I worked someplace where all my meals were taken care of and I could just take a yoga class and drop off my laundry, I'd probably subconsciously get used to the idea that the world was set up to make things very convenient for me.

The issue arises when they leave the bubble and interact with people who don't exist in that world. It's a kind of cognitive dissonance: "What do you mean I have to wait for other people to be served before I can have the thing that I want?"

None of us realizes we're doing this until it's pointed out. If someone barks a drink order at me, and I say, "What's the magic word?" in response, more often than not, they realize they're being rude and sheepishly apologize.

"Oh, wow. I'm so sorry. Can I please have an IPA?"

I'm plenty guilty of this ridiculousness, too. I've huffed in annoyance that a Lyft Line wasn't going to show up for 9 minutes, only to be reminded of how long it used to take for taxis to show up when we had to call dispatch.

We're all spoiled by the conveniences of living in San Francisco. While there are bigger conversations that need to be had about the ethics surrounding these conveniences — like how the people doing the delivering aren't getting enough labor protections, and how we should also be supporting small local businesses — we also have to remember how good we have it. Just because you can now get Taqueria Cancun delivered to your house doesn't mean you should forget how to be courteous and kind when you order in person.

P.S. "Netflix and Cheese" is not an exaggeration. I live on the third floor of my building and often don't have time to put on clothes before running down to answer my door.

One time, I ran down in my underwear, and the UPS guy lit up and said, "Hey! You're Broke-Ass!" Makes me wonder what pictures he's seen of me.

Stuart Schuffman

YEARNING FOR BURNING MAN
San Francisco Examiner; 2016

It's always about this time of year that I start to have dreams about Burning Man. They rarely make any sense, but generally all have the same theme: I'm trying to get there, but it's always either too late or I can't get in.

I guess that's not surprising. For most of August, as I see so many of my friends preparing for the annual desert pilgrimage, I feel the same way in my waking hours as well. All year long, I'm like, "Psshhh, Burning Man is too much of a hassle." As it gets nearer, I begin thinking about all the weird magic I'm missing. It's a strange, dust-covered FOMO that blinks, shines, and glimmers in my mind's eye.

I went to Burning Man in 2004, and it blew my fucking mind. Like, top-of-my-skull-still-flapping-in-the-wind-a-month-later kind of mind blown. It was only about 30,000 people back then — half of what it is now — and I went with an itty-bitty camp that consisted of just me and a couple. I spent most of that week alone in the desert, biking between massive pieces of art, dancing to loud beats, meeting beautiful weirdos, and seeing things that, up until then, I didn't know existed. Without realizing it then, it was my last hurrah before the internet went from a tool that slept in a desktop in my room to a monster that lived in my pocket and ran my life. It was probably that way for most of us.

I remember the night after I came back from Black Rock City. I went to a USF party with Tia, my girlfriend at the time, who hadn't gone to Burning Man with me. I came in with the angel-headed swagger of being emotionally covered in Playa dust and regaled Tia and her friends about this incredible experience in the desert. I went on about how nobody used money, people gave gifts to strangers, everyone was mainly naked and beautiful, and all anybody wanted to do was share.

I'd felt nearly the entire range of human emotions while out in the desert, and all I could do was extol the virtues of this insane alternate universe that only existed for one week a year.

I haven't been back since.

It's not like I haven't wanted to go back — my desire to go back is particularly thirsty right now — it just seems like there is always something else to do each year instead. For example, last year I was running for mayor, and afterwards I went to Mexico City. This year, I'm going to Shanghai. I can't afford to go to Black Rock City on top of all the other places I want to go each year. So, I always end up choosing another stamp in my passport over another trip to what nearly amounts to outer space.

And the reports each year make me wonder if I'd even find the same transcendence now that I did in 2004. With millionaire private yurt complexes and P. Diddy sightings, it seems like the openness and possibility of absolute wonder might have diminished. Then again, so many of my weirdo friends still go back each year, which means the magic must still be out there somewhere.

Part of me hopes a free ticket and camping situation drops in my lap, making it so that I almost can't say no to Burning Man. But the other part of me doesn't want to tarnish the memories I made all those years ago.

A NAUGHTY PARTY REMAINS PURE SF
San Francisco Examiner; 2018

I don't go to Folsom Street Fair; it comes to me. And if I'm lucky, it doesn't come on me.

Since I live on Folsom Street, I make a point of not drinking too much the night before the festival. That's because, at 10 am, the bass from the speakers outside makes my room sound like I'm in the middle of a rave.

Kayla and I tried to watch Netflix that morning, but we had to put on the subtitles because we couldn't hear the words.

Despite my apartment getting the Manuel Noriega treatment during the event this past weekend, I love the fair.

It's this weird, wonderful day that reminds me of the city I fell in love with. The San Francisco I moved to in 2002 was full of freaks and oddities, people who found refuge in SF because they didn't fit in anywhere else. And Folsom Street Fair is kinda like homecoming for many of those folks.

This naughty, bawdy, tawdry party is billed as the world's biggest leather event, but that really doesn't do it justice. Folsom goes way beyond leather. Any kink you can imagine – and some you've never even fathomed – can be found strutting in its finest and filthiest regalia for all to see. In fact, the participants really want you to see them; that's part of the fun.

Walking through the festival, you'll see people dressed in latex dog outfits playing on their hands and knees in a pen, people bound, gagged, and whipped in front of cheering onlookers, people in gimp suits being led on leashes, and dicks. So many dicks.....well, you know what I mean, it's a panoply of dicks.

Yes, there are many reasons I love the Folsom Street Fair, but one of my favorites is that it would be complicated to make this a corporate event. I've written before about how shamefully corporate Pride has gotten. How sadly ironic it is to see companies like Walmart, which pay their employees terribly, march in the Pride parade sandwiched between two labor unions. But thankfully, I don't see major corporate advertisers paying to be part of the Folsom Street Fair anytime soon. That said, I'd love to sit in on the meeting where the marketing team pitches the idea to the executives.

If there's one thing that's reaffirmed for me each year, it's how hopelessly straight and vanilla I am. But that's ok too, Folsom Street Fair accepts you for who you are. You can tell I've been in San Francisco for too long because the only thing that grossed me out was seeing a woman dancing barefoot on Folsom Street. I mean, that's just disgusting.

As San Francisco becomes more mainstream, Folsom Street Fair becomes even more important. Even if it makes my apartment an impossible place to sleep for one day a year, it's totally worth it. I wouldn't want to live in a San Francisco that didn't have the Folsom Street Fair.

Would you?

STRANGE BEDFELLOWS
San Francisco Examiner; 2018

"Free food makes strange bedfellows."

That's what I said to Examiner columnist Joe Fitz as we stood on the crowded Ellis Street sidewalk on Tuesday.

"Free booze, too," he replied with a clink of his beer to my wine glass.

Let's Get Weird

"That's the new saying, then," I smiled. "Free food and free booze make strange bedfellows."

Nowhere is this more evident than the luncheon at John's Grill that's thrown by John Konstin and Willie Brown every election day.

I was first indoctrinated into this wonderfully strange event when I ran for mayor in 2015. Here's the event history, according to legendary press agent Lee Houskeeper (who is also a co-host along with Alex Clemens):

> *The San Francisco Election Day Luncheon was created in the 1980s by restaurateur/Commissioner Angelo Quaranta and lawyer/lobbyist Bob McCarthy, who co-hosted it each year at Quaranta's Allegro Restaurant at 1701 Jones Street in Russian Hill. The Luncheon was intentionally created to stand apart from the many other political events that transpired in the heat of active political campaigns. Rather than being partisan and focused on supporting one candidate or initiative or another, it was a celebration akin to Switzerland: it was open to all those who worked in politics in San Francisco, regardless of their political orientation.*

The tradition was discontinued sometime in the 2000s. Then, in 2015, Brown and Konstin revived it at Konstin's famous restaurant.

By the time I arrived on Tuesday, a line had already formed. Brown had invited all of San Francisco in his "Willie's World" column in the Chronicle, so other than a handful of early arriving politicos, the line was mostly made up of people who came for the free food ...which was half the reason I was there, too.

When I arrived, Housekeeper saw me in line and beckoned me past the velvet rope.

"This is Broke-Ass Stuart, our token communist," he said, introducing me to KTVU reporter Elissa Harrington.

"Socialist, actually," I replied before he wandered off to introduce other random people.

It's actually something Lee loves to do, especially if he's introducing people who come from very opposite ends of the political spectrum.

The first year I attended, Lee said, "I've got someone you should meet." He walked me over to a big guy with grey hair and said, "Ron Conway, this is Broke-Ass Stuart. You two should get a photo together."

I was wearing my "Beat Ed Lee" shirt, but since my jacket was buttoned, Conway hadn't noticed it. Right before the picture was snapped, I unbuttoned my coat

Photo by Lee Houskeeper

next to the evil billionaire who bankrolled Lee's mayoral campaign. The shit-eating grin on my face shows what a priceless moment it was.

That's what the luncheon is all about — priceless weird moments that would never happen anywhere else, all collected at one restaurant, huddled around pasta, chicken, wine, and beer. You have elected officials, candidates, lobbyists, nonprofit workers, journalists, activists, freeloaders, and maybe even an occasional Republican, and everyone is rubbing elbows and making nice. You might legitimately be having a bite and a drink with someone you said nasty things about on the internet just days before. The whole thing is surreal.

Considering the hundreds of people who come and go throughout the afternoon, the luncheon must be an incredibly expensive event to host. Konstin must spend thousands each time he throws it — and this year there are two elections!

Since Willie is the one who invited everyone — he wrote, "I host, John pays" — I asked someone familiar with the event why Willie doesn't help foot the bill, especially since he's probably one of the wealthiest people at the event. The answer was also priceless: "Because Willie is one of the cheapest people I know."

Taking a page from Willie's book, I, too, am going to invite the whole city to a party I'm not paying for. Come to John's Grill on Election Day in November for a bite, a drink, and some unexpected new friends because free food and free booze make strange bedfellows.

ENJOYING THE WEIRDNESS OF SAN FRANCISCO THAT REMAINS
San Francisco Examiner; 2019

The instructions were to meet some "distributors of magic" at the corner of Hayes and Shrader. Saturday night was chilly, so we stopped by a liquor store for a little Jameson to warm our bones.

By the time we got to the location, a crowd had begun to form. We quickly found our magic distributor and made the secret signal, a pantomime of looking through binoculars. We were then handed a blank piece of paper with a little baggy of trinkets and were told something like "Sometimes it takes a different kind of light to see properly."

Opening it, I took out a small black LED light and connected it to the watch battery that was also in the baggie. Suddenly, the blank piece of paper was illuminated with a map.

The Night Owl Ceremony had begun.

These are the kinds of unexpected adventures that made me first fall in love with San Francisco. In 2004, I moved into a Victorian house on 1907 Golden Gate Avenue. At the time, I didn't know much about it, other than it was a sprawling, funky old house, and the rent was cheap. I quickly learned that my new home was legendary. For over 20 years, it had been a den of artists, weirdos, and creativity. When the decision was made to move Burning Man from Baker Beach to the Black Rock Desert, it was done in the living room of 1907, and in the years before I lived there, it functioned as a de facto clubhouse for a group of free spirits called the Cacophony Society.

I'd never heard of the Cacophony Society before I moved in, but Miss P Segal, head mischief maker of the house, regaled me with stories of their wondrous pranks, hijinks, and happenings. They included the creation of Burning Man, Fight Club, Survival Research Laboratories, The Billboard Liberation Front, and Santa Con, among other things. I had somehow Craigslisted myself into an alchemic Arcadia and had managed to tap directly into the vein of what made

San Francisco weird and wonderful.

Then we got Ellis-Acted, and 1907 Golden Gate's 20-plus-year run came to an end. Even though I only resided there for six months, I created Broke-Ass Stuart while living there. BAS was the last bit of magic to germinate in that house before it became just another high-priced single-family home.

Luckily, what began there never really went away. The offbeat things that started at 1907 have spread around the world like a blown dandelion, and not even the crushing cultural slaughter caused by the tech boom and the affordable housing crisis can take that away. That's part of what Saturday night was all about.

Following our secret map, the Night Owl Ceremony led us through a series of one-night, unsanctioned installations and performances throughout Golden Gate Park, each one teasing our senses in different ways. At the first stop on the journey, they asked us to eat the miracle fruit berry that was also in the baggie. After doing so, they gave us lemons and limes to taste, and we marveled at how the miracle berry had suddenly made them sweet.

In spirit, the event was a direct descendant of the Cacophony Society shenanigans. Other strange, immersive events happen in The City. There's the Lost Horizon Night Market (a random meet-up of giant moving trucks where inside each truck a different interactive activity is happening, like a birthday party or bowling) and another event that I am not even allowed to name (odd, enchanting, underground parties in places we really shouldn't be at). But these are by special invitation only, and most people rarely hear about them because they carry a strict no social media policy.

The Night Owl Ceremony was different. It was open to everyone, including children and dogs, and was even featured on SF FunCheap. It was part of Immersive Design Week, a week-long decentralized festival featuring everything from escape rooms to augmented reality walking tours to immersive theater experiences.

What makes events like the Night Owl Ceremony special is that they allow us to venture into something that is so desperately missing from life in the 21st century: mystery and a sense of wonder. When you have a machine in your pocket that can answer any question, the enigma quickly disappears. The Night Owl Ceremony gave people the

Let's Get Weird

chance to say "yes" to something without being certain of what lay ahead. And in 2019, that might be one of the rarest treats there is.

SHIBARI AND TEA
San Francisco Examiner; 2017

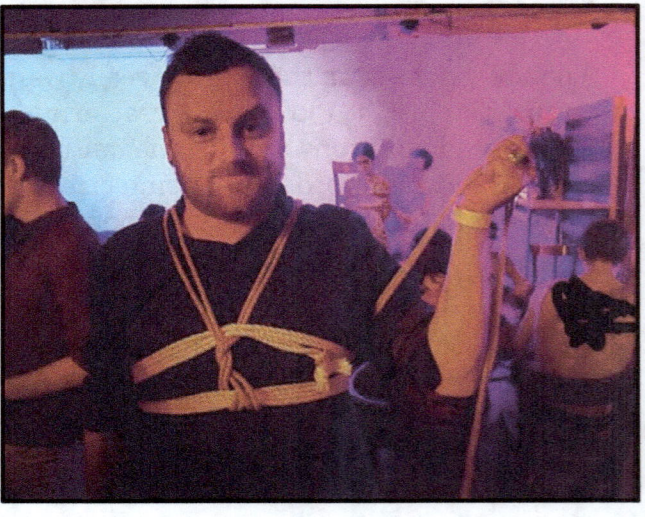

"Hmmm ... I guess you can tie me up," I told Tim. He was a nice-looking fellow and seemed amiable enough, but it's not a conversation two dudes, who had only met three minutes before, often have with each other, at least not in my world. Since we were the only two people without partners, someone had to be the one getting tied up, and I volunteered...

Earlier in the night, Quincy, Sasha, and I were hanging out with Joe and Jon at their place. "You guys wanna go to Shibari and Tea?" Quincy asked as we were sitting around trying to figure out what to do that evening.

"What's that?"

"Shibari is a form of Japanese rope bondage. There's an event at the Red Victorian, where people will be doing Shibari and drinking tea."

Of course, we were all curious. "So, is it a demonstration, a workshop, a sex party, or what?" I asked.

"I'm not really sure," Quincy responded, "but let's go find out." We hopped in the car and headed to Haight Street.

While the Red Victorian was a hippy bed-and-breakfast for several decades, it's now an intentional community, kind of like a co-op with specific intentions. Walking into the lobby the other night, we were greeted by a young, shirtless man and a woman wearing semi-revealing clothing. "The cover is sliding scale," he told us. "It starts at $10 and goes up $2 for every $10K you make a year." Nobody felt like doing math, so we each gave him 10 bucks and went in.

Spread throughout the large common area, people were either drinking tea while lounging on couches and chairs, or they were practicing tying each other up. It was definitely not a sex party, and it seemed like the demonstration was over. The couple came over from the front door.

"Since there are several newcomers, we'll do a little demonstration for whoever is interested. Who needs a partner?" (This is when I was matched up with Tim.)

If you read last week's column about me visiting a clown burlesque show, you're probably thinking, "Stuart is one kinky bastard." But really, I'm just interested in finding all the weird sub-cultural things San Francisco still has to offer — and I'm a big fan of saying "yes."

That said, despite my claims of being vanilla, my friend Amiee has now dubbed me "Vanilla with Sprinkles."

Even though there were tons of people being tied up in rope harnesses, it really wasn't too kinky an affair. It seemed most people were there out of curiosity, happy to find a safe and open space where they could figure out if Shibari and other forms of BDSM might be for them. Other than a few shirtless dudes, everyone was clothed, and the vibe was like 99 percent Burning Man camp and only 1 percent sex dungeon.

As Tim finished up tying the harness around me, a woman walked over and said, "Hey, you're Broke-Ass Stuart!" Because, of course. It was as purely a San Francisco moment as you could get, and so indicative of the weird life I lead. Only in San Francisco could I be recognized while randomly getting tied up by a perfect stranger in an old hotel lobby.

It's moments like this that make our city great. The interconnectedness of our lives, no matter how weird or placid they may be, is one of the truly unique things about San Francisco. And so is saying yes to new experiences.

FAINT LIGHTS FLICKERING IN THE FOG
San Francisco Examiner; 2019

"Every once in a blue moon, and by that, I mean ten years, we actually get to see the fireworks on the Fourth of July," Shanell said as we ascended the BART escalator at 19th Street in Oakland. "I have a good feeling that this is the year."

The weather was fairly warm, and there wasn't a cloud in the sky, so it felt auspicious. Anyone who's spent Independence Day in the Bay Area knows that it's almost a given that you won't get to see much in the way of bombs bursting in the air. There's usually a thick layer of fog hovering above the bay, turning the dazzling explosions into faint pops of muted color. About 15 years ago, a group of us thought we were slick and decided to spend the holiday on Treasure Island, reasoning that we'd be able to see all the fireworks in the whole Bay Area. We literally saw nothing.

But maybe Shanell was right. It was beautiful out, almost feeling like a real summer. This could be the year.

Shanell, Kayla, and I popped by Ben and Monika's place in Uptown Oakland for their get-together. People lingered around the chips and dip, drinking cider, champagne, and gin while talking disgustedly about the Trump Regime's concentration camps. I looked at Ben and Monika's sweet little one-and-a-half-year-old boy Jameson, and couldn't imagine the cruelty it would take to put people his age into such horrific conditions. There was a consensus amongst us all: we didn't have much to feel patriotic about. Somebody changed the mood, saying, "At least, we might get to see some actual fireworks this year."

We said our goodbyes and headed up to the Oakland Hills. Nick had left The City over a year ago and moved in with some friends who lived on a lush 2-acre lot. For months, he'd been trying to get Kayla and me to visit, rhapsodizing about how lovely it was. Being typical San Franciscans, we'd said, "Oh yeah, for sure. We'll get out there soon," knowing full well it wasn't likely. But this was the day! Everyone in the world seemed to be in Tahoe, and we wanted to do something outside of SF too, so we finally made it to Nick's place and brought Shanell too.

Nick had not been selling wolf tickets; the place he lived was beautiful. As we walked across a little bridge over a stream and entered the property, we saw redwoods, oak trees, and a massive backyard with dogs frolicking. We passed a crowd smoking and drinking, and went inside to find Nick. "Holy shit," I said, "You didn't tell me you lived in Terabithia!" He laughed and said, "See! I've been telling you to get out of here forever!"

We spent a couple of hours eating barbecue and chatting while I imagined what life would be like with all that space. Oakland somehow impresses me more every time I visit.

The people at the party were split half and half on whether we'd be able to see fireworks that night. But we knew if we stayed in the seclusion of Nick's place, we wouldn't be able to see anything, so when John and Anika offered us a ride back to The City, we hopped in.

Earlier in the evening, Shanell had left to go to another event. As John and Anika drove off towards the Haight, Kayla and I decided the best place to see the fireworks would be North Beach, where our friends had a rooftop to watch from.

It had been a long adventure of friends and exploration, and we were excited to finally see the thing we'd been talking about all day. Climbing the stairs, a glass of wine in hand, we made it to the rooftop just in time for the start of the fireworks.

And of course, the fog had rolled in. We couldn't see shit. Karl had won again.

As we went home that night, Kayla said to me, "San Francisco should just give up on the fireworks already. The City should consider hosting a laser light show each year, accompanied by loudspeakers playing booming sounds. Think about how much money they'd save."

I think she might be on to something.

I TRIED TO DRINK ALL THE WINE IN WINE LANDS. THIS IS WHAT HAPPENED INSTEAD
Fest 300; 2014

My assignment was to drink all 110 wines at Wine Lands. I mean, not all in one day because that would assuredly kill me, but the idea was to see how many I could get down my throat over three days at the Outside Lands Festival in San Francisco's Golden Gate Park. It was a genius concept, and one that Peter Eastlake, founder of Wine Lands, thought would be an excellent way for me to educate people about

Let's Get Weird

wine while simultaneously making a damn fool out of myself. I told lots of friends about it beforehand, so people stopped me all during the festival to see how many I'd made it through so far.

I drank exactly five glasses of wine throughout the entire festival. Yeah, that's it. Sorry to let everybody down, but the logistics and cost of it just didn't make it feasible. That said, not being a complete and total barf monster, covered in my own tears and urine while drooling from a purple wine-stained mouth, allowed me to fully take in the festival and make some pretty interesting observations. Here they are:

Photo by Jennye Garibaldi

— The main reason I go to Outside Lands every year is to see the young women in very skimpy clothing shiver to near death in the frigid San Francisco summer. Listen, girls, you have lovely bodies that look incredible in your *de rigueur* festival gear, but this isn't Coachella. I'm seriously considering visiting every Goodwill and Salvation Army in the Bay Area next year, buying up all their warm clothing, and selling it from a booth. I will make eleven million dollars.

— Kanye West and MDMA don't go well together. I found this out the hard way. Or maybe me and Molly and big crowds don't go well together. Regardless, even being on drugs didn't make Kanye's set good, which is a shame, really.

— Speaking of Kanye, he is, without a doubt, an absolute genius. He is also, without a doubt, an absolutely crazy person. It's just unfortunate for him (and us, really) that he lives in an era where media can convey a message to billions of people. Mozart was probably also balls crazy, but that motherfucker didn't have Twitter to let the whole world know that "Classical music is tight yo."

— I saw a goofy-looking white guy wearing a really poorly done Native American headdress. I guess he didn't get the memo that cultural appropriation as fashion is pretty shitty. Either that or he was just reclaiming headdresses for festival goers.

—If you wanna get a girl to love you, take her to see Big Freedia. Seeing you lose your shit in a moment of pure ecstasy, while trying to shake every bit of your body, to the music of a 6'3 transgender bounce artist from New Orleans, should be the moment she realizes you're the one. If not, she's dead inside. Dump her immediately.

— I drank a really great Gewürztraminer at Wine Lands. If I had drunk all the wines I was supposed to, I was gonna make a joke like "Gewürztraminer? That sounds like how I feel the morning after I drink 30 wines." In fact, I don't think there is a wine varietal whose name describes how I felt the morning after I spent all day consuming whiskey, beer, weed, and MDMA.

— If you live in San Francisco, Outside Lands is where you run into all your friends' ex-girlfriends. It's also kinda like homecoming for all of SF's creative folk. Everyone somehow gets in for free, and then we just party really hard for a few days.

— You know the saying "Necessity is the mother of invention"? That pretty much describes the amazingly creative ways people can smuggle booze into Outside Lands. These people even buried booze in the park way ahead of time and led people on a social media booze hunt.

—I'm getting too old for this shit.

—No one will ever watch that video you took of Tom Petty, dude. Honestly, you're never gonna watch it either. Standing at a show, *in real life*, and watching it through a little screen in front of your face, just so you can hopefully make your Facebook friends jealous, is well...ridiculous at best. At worst, you're just kinda a dick.

— Who are the people who spend the entire festival carrying around a stuffed animal or a Bill Murray head on a stick? I commend them for being the flag bearer for their group, but how is that decision made? Does someone actually volunteer to be that guy, or do you draw straws for it? Regardless, that person is a hero to somebody.

Let's Get Weird

— I saw a girl walking completely normally, on flat ground, but for some reason her beer just kept popping out of her cup as if she were going 60 mph over speed bumps. I still have no idea what the hell was going on there.

— Lykke Li dresses like a character from *The Matrix*. She puts on a hell of a performance, but I'd still like her better if she could do so while bending backwards and dodging stuff. She also has one of those faces that makes me feel like I've totally been wasted with her in the Mission at some point. That's a good thing, I'm pretty sure.

— After three days and nights of Outside Lands, I was in bed by 9:30 last night. Thanks for another great year, Outside Lands.

LYFT MIGHT CHANGE THE WORLD
The Bold Italic; 2012

I'm pretty sure I was the first non-tech writer to ever do a piece on Lyft. I was at their big unveiling press conference and then used them a bunch when writing this article for the Bold Italic. Nearly 15 years later, I was proven right. Lyft really did change the world... for better or worse.

Jen Friel and I are waiting outside of Dear Mom for a woman driving a car with a pink mustache to pick us up. Jen lives in LA and is crashing with me for a few days while she's in town for the TechCrunch something or other conference. She and I have such similar demeanors that I'm both excited and slightly worried about how tonight will play out. Fucking mayhem is guaranteed. She's wearing something called a Spirit Hood, which is a furry hood with dangling arm thingies to put your hands in and reminds me of *Where the Wild Things Are*. I'm wearing a clown nose and fluorescent orange sunglasses. The mantra we've been repeating all night is "let's get weird". It certainly feels like we're going to.

Eventually, the ride we've been waiting for arrives. Celeste is probably in her 50s and emanates a warmth that makes you immediately want to hug her. As we get in the car, she instead gives us each a fist bump and says, "Sorry, it was hard to recognize me. People try to steal my mustache when I leave the car, so I take it off when I park somewhere. I forgot to put it back on before coming to pick you guys up." The furry pink mustache in question is Lyft's signature. Every car in its "fleet" wears one on the grill. It's a clever and kitschy branding ploy as well as a way for those using the service to recognize their ride. Despite this and the mandatory fist bump that each driver is supposed to give you when you enter their car, what Lyft does is rather genius.

I had first heard about Lyft a week or so before when I was invited to a press conference at their SOMA headquarters. Like most of these kinds of things, I just went for free booze and food, but what I found was a service that has the potential to absolutely transform the way that people in San Francisco get around. What Lyft does is empower the citizenry of the Bay Area to use their own vehicles and effectively act as taxi drivers.

Each driver must be vetted, pass a series of tests, own a vehicle from 2006 or earlier, and pass a friendliness test. From the consumer's side, all you have to do is download the app, fine-tune the GPS cursor to your location, and then press "Request pickup here". Assuming all the drivers aren't occupied (as they have been the past few times I've tried), Lyft matches you with the nearest driver. A picture of them and their car appears on your screen, along with an estimated arrival time. You can practice your fist bump with passersby as you wait.

Unlike most SF cab drivers, Celeste plugged our destination into a GPS, and away we went to a free food and booze party being hosted by Zynga. This wasn't my first Lyft, and I'd been asking a handful of questions to all my drivers. I was curious as to what brought them to Lyft, how long they'd been doing it for, if it was their full-time gig, and a bunch of other shit. Celeste told us that she'd been driving for Lyft for a month and that she absolutely loved it. Her regular line of work was as a preschool teacher, and she was driving for Lyft to make some extra money so she could take her husband to Italy. God damn, she was sweet. She also dug it because she felt she was helping people out, it was fostering community, and it was fun. She smiled deeply when she mentioned all the great people she gets to meet. When she dropped us off at the Zynga party, Celeste got out to grab the pink mustache from her trunk, and we both opted to give her a hug instead of a fist bump. It felt like the thing to do.

As Celeste pulled away, the Lyft app popped up on my phone and suggested I donate $6 for the ride (the tip is included). Since you have to connect the app to your debit or credit card, you pay by tapping a button on your smartphone. You're then asked to rate your driver on a scale of one to five stars, and they do the same to you. If you don't have a good star rating, you're less likely to get picked up. It's this idea of a donation that's important, though, since it's what allows Lyft drivers to skirt around having to deal with actually being licensed taxis. They aren't technically cabbies or limo drivers since they aren't *technically* charging anything. While talking to the founders, the word "disruptive" was repeatedly used, and while it certainly felt like a hot business term from an MBA program, they had a great point; Lyft is going to shake things up.

I was curious to see what the taxi industry thought of this, so I asked a couple of my cabbie friends, MC Mars and Dirty, to give me their thoughts. Dirty has been driving a cab in SF for over a decade, and Mars has been doing it in NYC and SF for over 31 years. They're both intelligent and insightful cats, and Mars even authored the excellent cabbie memoir *Don't Take Me the Long Way*. When I asked Mars to weigh in, the point he kept coming back to is that there's a vast difference in oversight between cabs and Lyft. He said, "Cab drivers have to record each ride on a waybill; they have to renew an A-card annually (a super pain-in-the-ass), which can arbitrarily double in price from year to year. They must also conform to a whole book of strict rules and regulations, and, of course, they have to pay the gate. This last item puts tremendous pressure on the cab driver because on a slow night, he can spend a good part of the shift paying off his rental on the cab."

Dirty also had some valid points to make. He noted that, given the existing cab shortage, services like Lyft and Uber won't significantly affect his income during peak hours and days with bad weather. But it's when there's not a glut of customers that it will hurt his pocketbook. He followed this by saying, "One problem with the taxi business is that the drivers forget that they're not in the transportation business, they're in the service business. People who've been burned by cabbies before might be quick to turn to Lyft. Maybe this will help cause cab drivers to reevaluate their customer service." He certainly had a point.

As the night wore on, I thought about some of the other Lyft drivers that I'd had while experimenting with the service. Angel was an ex-Navy man in his 20s who was studying to be a paramedic and who'd gotten his first finger from a cabbie the day I rode with him. He liked Lyft because he got to meet cool people, and he especially liked the fact that he didn't have to carry cash. Boris, also in his 20s, uses the service himself to get to and from his Richmond District home when going out at night. He told me that he'd had a cabbie as a customer and that the guy was considering driving for Lyft. Rich had a bowl of mints for his customers as well as a full-time job. He dug that Lyft allowed him to choose his own hours and schedule. He was the only one I saw keeping notes on all the pickups and drop-offs, just like cabs do. And Henri told me he stopped using the mustache because he kept getting yelled at by cab drivers.

Everyone I rode with was interesting and had something to say. They were also proud to be part of something so new and unique that it had the potential to change the way San Franciscans get around their city.

As for that mantra Jen and I were chanting at the start of the night about getting weird, it absolutely proved true. Amongst the many things that happened that evening, we picked up a spokes model girl at Zynga who ended up sobbing into her drink for a bit while wearing a Peter Pan hat and then disappeared, we snuck into a Google Ventures party that culminated with me unfortunately puking into someone's drink, and the night ended in a PG rated threesome with another girl we met during the evening.

I'm not giving Lyft all the credit, but it certainly made getting around and getting weird a lot easier.

SAN FRANCISCO PRIDE NEVER CEASES TO AMAZE
San Francisco Examiner; 2016

This was the first year in over a decade that someone from my family didn't visit for Pride. So, for a couple of weeks leading up to it, I wasn't sure I was going to participate. I even considered leaving town. I told myself things like, "Oh, The City just gets so hectic," and "You've

Let's Get Weird

done Pride a million times before." But finally, as the Pride fervor began to be palpable sometime mid-last week, I got excited. I mean, it was PRIDE, one of the happiest and most loving times of the year.

On Saturday, I found myself at a rooftop party in the Mission with just enough of a view to see the upper part of Dolores Park. Thousands upon thousands of people covered nearly every inch of it so that instead of green grass, there was a multi-hued meshwork of bodies enjoying the sun. It was the pre-party for the Dyke March, and eventually, we heard the mechanical booms of Dykes on Bikes and watched from above while they led the procession through the Mission.

The day progressed into night, and we eventually found ourselves singing way too much karaoke while plotting and discussing our plans for the Pride Parade the following day.

None of those plans came to fruition, of course; few things ever do when plotted during late-night karaoke. But I woke up and got in touch with Ashkon to see about exploring the Civic Center festivities.

Though Ashkon had lived in the Bay for most of his life, he'd never been to the big Pride celebration in The City, so we walked through Civic Center, admiring all the beaming smiles that arched on people's faces like upside-down rainbows. "Happy Pride!" we'd say to anyone we made eye contact with, and hugs were given to plenty of strangers.

When you've been to Pride a dozen times, and you live in San Francisco, it's easy to forget how important the celebration is for people who live in places where they're not able to be so openly, boastfully, and fabulously themselves. For so many people each year, SF Pride is proof that there is a better future and that they are not alone. This radiated from everyone we saw.

It was impossible, though, to ignore the incredible amount of very drunk and most likely straight teenagers. Wobbling woozily through the crowd, doing drunk teenager things, it made me wonder how many people showed up in support of LGBTQ Pride and how many just came to party with their butt cheeks hanging out.

"What happens at Pride stays at Pride" or something like that.

Ashkon and I parted ways, and I went home for a disco nap, unsure if I would make it back out. But a little while later, Danielle convinced me to meet her and some friends at El Rio.

Hopping out of the cab, the line stretched halfway down the block. Every imaginable variation of queer was there, waiting to get into the party that each knew would be fantastic. And it was better than I could've imagined. I hugged and kissed people I'd known for years and sweaty danced with people I'd just met that day. The vibe was ebullient and effervescent. I ran into a woman I'd met on an airplane a decade ago, whom I see around town now and then. We talked about the strange corporateness and teenage drunkenness that we'd all witnessed downtown, and then she turned, looking into a crowd that was dancing and grinding and celebrating love, and she said, "But this, this feels like home."

For everybody there that day, it was.

THERE'S STILL MAGIC IN SAN FRANCISCO, IT'S JUST HARDER TO FIND
San Francisco Examiner; 2017

We were already a few Peronis in when the New Orleans-style brass band came sauntering down Green Street, humphing, booping, ba-ba-ba-ing, and making other beautiful noises that no onomatopoeia will ever get right.

Morgan's pocket-sized pup, Penny, searched for a pocket-sized place to hide her button-sized ears. Katie's marginally larger dog, Bear, was similarly nonplussed about the trombones, trumpets, drums, and sousaphone, giving his mom a look that said, "What kind of fuckery is this?"

"Yes! This is exactly why I love this city!" Morgan cried as we all pulled out our phones to catch the excitement. There simply aren't enough second lines this side of New Orleans, and few things light up a crowd better than one ambling toward you.

It was a lovely, warm-for-San-Francisco Monday night, and before the band arrived, we'd been sitting outside Bella Cora in North Beach, drinking beer and wine, and eating Bavarian pretzels covered in raclette cheese. Some days, heaven is almost attainable.

At one point, artist Winston Smith came by with some friends, and we talked about his collage art and the fact that he designed the Dead Kennedys' logo. "Can I get your info?" Alex asked, "We'd love to do a feature on you for BrokeAssStuart.com." I picked the last of the cheese off the pretzel when no one was looking.

Winston left, more drinks arrived, and artist Jeremy Fish came by and joined the group. I'd missed the release party for the new cannabis vape pen that Jeremy had designed the art for, so he brought me one. "Be careful," he told me. "It's 90 percent THC, the strongest stuff on the market." I put it in my bag, giving it a "not today, Satan" look, and had some more wine.

For a couple of years now, Jeremy and I have been talking about starting a sort of League of Extraordinary People club, where San Francisco's best and most interesting creatives can congregate to make more magic happen. One of the major obstacles has been that we don't have a space to do so. (If you have a space for us, please give me a shout!) The other obstacle is that so many of the artists, musicians, and writers who would've been in this club have been pushed out of The City. So, we all spent some time trying to figure out how to make our club happen anyway.

We didn't come up with any answers, but Nils and Danielle did come by our table with more drinks, which often is a good enough answer in itself. Then, the brass band rounded the corner, the dogs became excited, and the humans got riled up, too. Even though we'd just talked about San Francisco losing its soul, it suddenly felt magical again. Maybe I was high from all that cheese.

Since last September, I've been in Shanghai, Helsinki, Oslo, El Paso,

New York, San Diego, and Washington, D.C., to name a few. And even though I lament the changes The City has endured recently, I always love coming back to it because of nights like these. There's still magic in San Francisco, it's just harder to find these days.

WHEN IN DOUBT, JUST SAY YES
San Francisco Examiner; 2016

Just say yes.

It's a hell of a motto and, in a way, almost revolutionary. We spend so much of our lives being responsible and talking ourselves out of doing things we want to do. "I can't because I've gotta clean the house." Or "I've got work to do." Or "I gotta go to the gym." But nearly all of the best moments in my life have been when I just said "yes."

Granted, it's easier for me since I don't have kids or a mortgage to worry about ... I can already hear you grumbling and fumbling around, searching for your torches and pitchforks. But all of us could say a little more yes in our lives and a little bit less, "Well, you see ..." Last Saturday, all I did was say "yes," and it turned into a magical San Francisco day.

It started when I got a morning text from Amy, inviting me to brunch with her and Dan. I had planned on working on a few articles all day, because that was the responsible thing to do. But it was beautiful out, and I wanted to be with good people, so I said "yes" and headed out to meet them.

After tater tots done up like nachos and a few margaritas, they asked if I wanted to go to Dolores Park. That was the moment the day hinged on. I could go home and work all day, or I could say "yes" and see what adventures my "yes" had in store for me. Obviously, you know what I chose.

Dolores Park was a kaleidoscope of flesh, blankets, and booze, and we tucked in with Molly for her birthday picnic. Sitting on the grass, slathered in sunscreen, telling dirty jokes, and drinking wine is one of the best things you can do in life — and that's what we did. After a couple of hours, I remembered it was Morgan's birthday pub crawl in North Beach, so I headed that way.

Arriving at Tupelo, I was greeted by people decked out in wigs, sparkly leotards, and other weird costumes. A drink was shoved in my

Let's Get Weird

hand, and a blonde wig was plopped on my head. We floated amongst North Beach drinkeries 'til the birthday girl went home. I wandered down to Specs' to see what other things I could say "yes" to.

Two women at the other end of the bar yelled down at me, "Hey! You're Broke-Ass Stuart!" to which I replied, "Yeah! Wanna see my boobs?" When they agreed, I lifted my shirt and obliged. Then, I walked over to them, and they bought me a

drink. Shortly afterward, Christine sent me a text: "I'm at the largest private estate in San Francisco. You should come, like now."

Of course, I said "yes" and hopped in a cab. The Chenery Mansion is the largest private property in San Francisco. Bob Pritikin made a buttload of money in advertising back in the day and built the place in the Outer Mission in 1981. Weird and wonderful statuary, part of his purported $40 million art collection, sprang up all over the property. We weren't actually allowed in the mansion, though; a couple of Christine's friends live in the apartment attached to it, and they had thrown a little party. Drunk 20-somethings weaved amongst the tree house and metal sculptures. One of the girls had a 13th-century tapestry hanging in the room she rented. As the oldest and most responsible person there, I decided to take off my clothes and wear nothing but a little yellow apron, my underwear, and my socks. Eventually, I put my clothes back on and drifted home to go to sleep.

We're all busy, I get it. But sometimes you just have to say "yes." Every adventure starts with just that one word.

Jet Lagged, Hungover, & Homesick

(Travel)

Jet Lagged, Hungover, & Homesick

I started my professional writing career as a travel writer, so I would be remiss if I didn't include some of my travel stuff. The first pieces are some blogs I did for an incredibly popular travel guidebook company when I was in Ireland.

I included the introduction to my NYC book, and some excerpts from it, in this chapter because that's where they seemed to make the most sense.

Back when I used to travel a lot more, I would joke that "Jet lagged, Hungover, and Homesick" should be the title of my memoir, so I made it the title of this chapter instead.

IRELAND
A well known travel guidebook company; 2006

My first professional writing gig was the aforementioned travel guidebook company. In 2006, I was paid to go to Ireland to research and write the Ireland chapter for their budget travel and Western Europe books.

Customs Agents, Rock Stars, and Peyote.

Ugggh. I know I should have started this blog earlier. I'm sitting in Dublin's Easy Internet Cafe, breathing in the sickening yet delicious smell of the adjoining Subway sandwich shop and trying to make sense of a week's worth of: Guinness, irate customs officials, jet lag, sub-human bar bouncers, Irish rock stars and a revolving international cast mainly consisting of, you guessed it, Aussies and Kiwis. Oh dear reader, where does one begin? I guess the most logical place would be with the customs official.

I would like to take this moment to officially say, F*** that guy! I mean, I know he had to do his job, but after 14 hours of sleepless and uneventful travel, the last thing I needed was a disgruntled Irish customs agent giving me the third degree about how much money I had in my wallet. There was a point where I seriously didn't think he was going to let me into Ireland, and I'd be stuck in the airport forever like Tom Hanks in the movie, Terminal.

Stuart Schuffman

My first night in town was pretty cool; I stayed with my friend Victoria and her boyfriend Padraic. Victoria is a photographer who gets to hang out with rock stars and take their photos, and Padraic is a genuine Irish rock star. His band, The Thrills, isn't big yet in the US, so I'd never really heard of them. It wasn't until I saw the platinum record on the wall that I realized how big these guys were. On my second day in Dublin, Padraic and I were in the market when they played his band's song on the radio. Needless to say, I was impressed.

The next few days were spent drinking Guinness, not sleeping due to jet lag, and wandering around Temple Bar. During this time, I concluded that, much like the French Quarter in New Orleans, Temple Bar has become a parody of itself. It's almost as if it's so invested in being "Temple Bar" that it loses the very essence that makes it Temple Bar. The only actual Dubliners you'll find are the people working in the pubs and the lecherous guys looking to score.

I also realized, while wandering Temple Bar, that Magic Mushrooms and Peyote are legal in Ireland!! HUH?? There's a head shop in Temple Bar that sells these psychedelics as well as a crazy cross-breed of Peyote and San Pedro. I was so astounded by this that I've told just about every other traveler I've come across, and then shown them the photos to prove it.

One quick story before I go: I was going into this bar to get a pint when I stopped to ask a couple of ladies outside about the cover

charge. When they asked me where I was from, I answered, "California," and the wannabe Vinnie Jones bouncer immediately replied, half jokingly, but mostly seriously, "Well you can't come in here." He then asked me for ID, and as I pulled it out of my day planner, he said, "What is that a purse you're carrying? And ye've got two earrings? Ye must be some kind of fag." Yeah, he was super cool. Come to think of it, I think he might have a day job in customs.

Wexford, Indian Food, and Little Red Cars.

Wexford is a tiny town. I say this not because you can walk from one end to the other in less than 15 minutes, or because the population is roughly 9500 people. I say Wexford is a very small town because this morning, a girl in a little red car waved and honked at me as she drove by. This is by no means intended to imply that a certain small-town friendliness compelled her to do it. No, I say this is a small town because she was the exact same girl who drove by me last night and shouted out the window, "Nice arse!" as she sped away.

Truthfully, I arrived in Wexford a day or so later than planned. I had spent close to a week and a half in Dublin and was preparing to leave when my friends Victoria and Padraic made me an offer I couldn't refuse: "Wanna come with us tomorrow to Newgrange?" asked Victoria. "It's an ancient burial structure an hour north of here that predates the building of the Pyramids."

Padraic followed this by saying, "And then we're going to Belfast for the night to meet up with my mate Riggsy. You have to meet him, Stuart, he's a BBC radio host and simply one of the best people to know in Belfast." Before I could answer, though, I managed to miss pour our friend Traci's glass, and spill cabernet all over Padraic's flatmate's pool table.

Given the possibility for adventure, and the fact that I'd almost ruined a man's billiards room, I had no choice but to agree to go along. And I'm certainly glad I did. Newgrange was incredible, and I got some of the best photos I've taken yet on this trip. And Belfast, well, Belfast was a blast. We ate at what, in my minimal experience, is one of Ireland's most delicious restaurants, Archana. If you like Indian food and find yourself in Belfast, you must eat here!

After dinner and a well-deserved nap, we partied it up with Riggsy and the locals and then retired for an even more well-deserved night of sleep. I hadn't realized that I'd not slept more than 5 hours in a night since I'd arrived in Ireland. A week and a half in Dublin will do that to a person.

The next morning we took quite possibly the world's worst guided tour of Belfast, (Stephen Hawking would have been a more engaging tour guide) and then we zipped back down to Dublin where I picked up my gear, hopped on a bus, and managed to make it down to Wexford just in time to get cat-called by the girl driving by in the little red car.

Hitchin' for a Shave.

Every person has a mental list of specific goals they'd like to achieve before they die: visiting Machu Picchu, climbing Mount Everest, and witnessing the Northern Lights. Regardless of what your goals are, there are few things more satisfying than checking one off your list. Today I had something very special happen to me; I was able to both realize I had a goal and then check it off my list, within moments of each other. Today, I had my first Turkish Hot Towel Shave.

There is nothing in the world quite like having an unenthusiastic man from Istanbul take a straight razor to your face and neck after attempting to smother you with a hot towel. It makes you feel ALIVE, goddamn it! Although parts of my face are probably the smoothest they have ever been, the man's lack of pride in his work resulted in me being left with a few rough patches along my jaw and one of my sideburns half an inch longer than the other.

Truly, though, on Thursday, I did have one of the most amazing experiences thus far on my trip. I was staying in the beautiful medieval town of Kilkenny when I heard about Kells Priory, the romantic ruins of a 12th-century monastic castle. Kells is about 13km out of Kilkenny, and since no buses really go there and I'm terrified of driving on the opposite side of the road, I had to hitchhike out to the site. My first ride was from an old man who told me that the only time he'd been to the US was for one day in New Mexico. Since he didn't elaborate and let me out shortly afterwards, I'm still completely puzzled as to why someone would travel all the way from Ireland just to spend a single day in New Mexico. The next car that picked me up was driven by a Romanian man whose job it is to travel all over County Kilkenny teaching children to play chess. He was able to drive me to the elementary school in Kells.

The Priory was absolutely awe-inspiring, and the best part about it was that I had the site entirely to myself. Well, completely to myself and the sheep. There were loads of sheep just hanging out, doing their thing, being sheep. I hung out there just taking photos and walking around and thinking how cool it would be to have a giant broken-down castle, next to a stream, right across from your town?

I hitched back into town with a sociology professor whose work focuses on the changing nature of Irish society concerning the Celtic Tiger. She was terrific and dropped me off right at my hostel, where I grabbed my gear, got on a bus, and headed for Cork, where I've been ever since. Cork is a lovely town which I'll tell you about later. Wish you were here.

> Goin' to leave this Broke-down palace
> On my hands and my knees I will roll roll roll.
> Make myself a bed by the waterside.
> In my time - in my time - I will roll roll roll.
>   – Robert Hunter

The People's Republic of Cork.

Come to Cork. Seriously, stop reading this blog, open up your browser, and buy a plane ticket. Come on, do it! What was that? You've got work tomorrow? Alright, I understand (sigh). No, I'm not hurt; it's just that I was really looking forward to sitting with you in this great little pub I found, listening to some traditional music and drinking some Murphy's (that's the big stout down here, not Guinness). I also really wanted to take you to this Nigerian restaurant I went to the other night. There were three of us: a German guy named Kevin, a

Stuart Schuffman

British guy named Stuart (good name), and me. We were hungry and walking down MacCurtain St. when we found the little unmarked restaurant. Oh, it was SO good, and seeing that we were the only non-Nigerians there, it'd be pretty safe to say that the food was authentic and not some kind of new-age fusion. But then again, I've never been to Nigeria.

Anyway, just a couple of days ago, I went to visit the town of Cobh (pronounced Cove), where the Titanic made its final departure. The day before, I went with Evalina and Maria, two Greek girls I had met, to visit Blarney Castle. Yes, I did kiss the Blarney Stone, and yes, I do know that the locals supposedly pee on it at night so the dumb tourists can kiss their urine the next day, but how could I make it all the way up there and not kiss it? Especially when there is this crazy 65-year-old guy up there whose job is to support you while you hang upside down to it.

I'm telling you, you would love this place. Did you know that Cork was the 2005 European Capital of Culture? I'm not exactly sure what that means, but I do know there were all sorts of fireworks, festivals, concerts, and *craic*. *Craic* (pronounced Crack) is what the folks over here call having fun, or a good time. You'd say, "Let's go over to An Brog, it's good *craic* over there." In fact, An Brog really was a good time. On Sunday, a Canadian named Eli took a group of us — a Hungarian, a Swede, a Croatian, an Aussie, and me — to An Brog. It was easily my favorite night here so far. The DJ played Stevie

Jet Lagged, Hungover, & Homesick

Wonder, James Brown, and Curtis Mayfield; the whole bar was dancing, jumping, sweating, and screaming, and it was incredible!

So are you coming or what? Seriously, if you come to Cork, you won't regret it. It was the 2005 European Capital of Culture for Christ's sake!

Well, anyway, this is your boy Stuart signing off from the People's Republic of Cork. Wait, what was that? Oh yes, I really look forward to hearing from you again, too. Peace.

Dublin...Again.

All roads lead to Dublin, and I think it's because of this that I find myself here again. I'm on the better end of three and a half weeks in Ireland, and, just as the water on the banks of the river Liffey seems to rise every day slightly, so does my affection for this city. This has been a city considered in the up-and-coming category of European capitals for the past 15 years or so, but anyone who visits today can clearly see that Dublin is far more "up" on the spectrum than "coming". Having emerged from the fog and rain of history, it is now Ireland's day in the sun, and nowhere is this more evident than here in its capital. Just today, I read that Dublin is the 16th most expensive city in the world (just as a point of reference, New York is 27th). Every single day of the week, the streets are packed with people shopping, just spending money for the sake of it, and never in my life have I seen so many "Help Wanted" signs. Luckily, with the advent of the EU, every week Dublin sees new immigrants coming from different parts of Europe, who are more than happy to fill these vacant positions.

There are certain by-products of this Celtic Tiger economy, though that were completely unforeseeable, things that the famous capitalist theorist, Milton Friedman, could never have imagined. One thing in particular is that Dublin is a city full of men with very dirty hands. I mean this literally. Somewhere along the line, the bar owners of Dublin decided that, since people have more money to spend, they should make their establishment appear upscale by having a bathroom attendant in every men's room in the city. Big mistake. Given the choice of using the sink and having to tip the attendant, or just walking out of the bathroom, hands unwashed, no drunk man in his right mind is going to choose option one. That is, at least no one that I know (present company excluded, of course). And so it is that the nasty underbelly of capitalism is shown to us again, making one wonder, is there not a better form of commerce? One where men can feel free to relieve themselves without the guilt of not tipping after washing one's hands? I leave you with this to contemplate, dear reader.

Viva la Revolution!

Cape Clear.

I've found that trying to leave cities like Dublin and Cork is a lot like trying to leave the mafia. Every time I attempt it, they GRAB me and pull me back in. I've somehow ended up in Cork three times in less than two weeks, and each time, I run into this guy named Andy (I think), and he laughs at me for not making it out yet. The most recent time was two days ago when I was just supposed to transfer in Cork, but I missed my bus. This time I've made it out though; I've cut the damn umbilical cord, and I'm not going back to Cork...I think.

Yesterday, I took the bus from Cork to Skibereen and then from Skibereen to Baltimore, which is a small town of roughly 250 people. To give it credit, though, it is supposed to get packed in the summer, and is apparently famous for its scuba diving. It was here in Baltimore that I caught the ferry over to Cape Clear Island. For some reason, during the ferry ride, two high school girls adopted me and basically told me their (short) life stories, after which they also told me about the small island and informed me that at the dock, I'd be able to catch the bus up the hill to my bed & breakfast. Upon disembarking, I found the "bus" to be a woman named Mary who drives a silver van around the island, and will take you where you need to go, for â,¬2. I spent most of the 10-minute ride talking to a guy from El Salvador who was elated to find someone else who spoke Spanish.

The family who ran the B&B were fantastically warm and, after I dropped off my bags, my landlady put a flashlight in my hand and sent me out the door to find the pub. You see, Cape Clear only has 120 people, so during the winter, there is only one pub/restaurant open, which serves as the social center for the entire island. Another woman named Mary runs the pub and can tell you about EVERYONE'S business on the entire island. She was amazingly sweet, but given her vantage point, I'd imagine that this is not a woman you'd want to cross if you plan on staying in Cape Clear for any extended period.

Cape Clear is magnificent; I don't think I could spend more than a day there. Cape Clear is absolutely beautiful; I think I could spend the rest of my life there. I'm not really sure how I feel about the place, but I know it's unlike anything I've experienced before. The smallest place I've ever lived in had a population of 50,000 people. At 120 people, Cape Clear is just slightly smaller.

The Importance of Being Loved.

What a weird day. I arrived back in Baltimore after my night on Cape Clear, just in time to miss my bus. Instead of waiting four hours for the next one, I took the initiative to thumb it to Skibbereen. It was about half an hour before a guy finally stopped and picked me up. Apparently, he thought I was one of the two Lithuanian guys he was supposed to pick up to work at his son's mussel farm. Still, due to his incredibly thick West Cork accent, I didn't realize this until ten minutes later when we were still sitting idly in the car waiting. Once it was cleared up that I was neither Lithuanian nor had any plans to work on his son's mussel farm, we proceeded to spend the next hour waiting for the men and then ultimately going door to door so I could inquire about the missing Eastern Europeans. Thankfully, no one answered their doors; I really didn't want to have to explain to unsuspecting Irish folk why a Californian was canvassing their neighborhood in search of a couple of lost Lithuanians.

Later that day, back in good old Skibbereen, I was waiting at the bus stop when I spied the cutest little old-time store in the world. Of course, I had to go inside. Instantly, I was in a different era. A very old couple sat behind the counter, chatting with a local woman who had probably popped into the store every single day of her life. We got talking and inevitably the question of whether or not I had any Irish ancestry arose. When I answered, "No, I'm all Eastern European Jew," the local woman squealed, "Ooh! We LOVE Jewish people!" The three lovely people then earnestly told me that they loved Jewish people because, in their view, they were essentially doing God's work by being in Israel and fighting the good fight that would help bring about the End Days and the return of the Messiah. "We're basically Zionists," the local woman told me.

With a new odd sense of being, I guess, appreciated, I caught the bus to the town of Schull, where I intended to stay the night. Almost immediately, I managed to get myself adopted by a group of 15 or so university students from Dublin who were in town for some type of sailing competition. Evidently more intent on partying than sailing, they very easily persuaded me to go back to their place and start drinking at 5:30 pm. Jesus, I forgot what college binge drinking was all about. Let's just say that at one point, an entire room full of Irish people began chanting, "U-S-A! U-S-A!" out of nowhere, which they then followed by changing the name of the guidebook company I was writing for. Of course, after each time cheering happened, we were all meant to down whatever beer we had in our hands. The funny part about the whole thing was that they weren't even doing it to take the piss out of me; they were actually being sincere. Ah, it's nice to feel loved.

Driving with Tom.

The Irish countryside rips past me as I push The Beast harder. The kilometers per hour are clocking up: 90, 100, 120. I have no clue what this means in miles, but right now, I am King of the Road, I mean, I am F-L-Y-I-N-G, man. The Beast is really moving now; I am at one with my machine. Then there's the sign - "Improved Road Now Ending." DAMMIT! I knew it was too good to last.

Now it's back to the little, bitty, curvy, two-way roads where, each time a truck passes you, you grip the steering wheel for fear that it might be the only thing in this entire world that you have a grip on. Just minutes ago, I was King of the Road — now I'm back to being me, Stuart, a guidebook writer who's tired from driving all day and just wants to make it to Dingle before nightfall. And The Beast? Well, The Beast is still The Beast; a determined, tiny, silver Hyundai Accent that I rented at the Kerry Airport for an exorbitant amount of euros.

But it's all worth it. The Kerry countryside is gorgeous out here; there's no room for complaints. Smoke scrapes the sky as farmers set fire to their fields in an almost yearly ritual of renewal. The greens of the fields, the browns of the mountains, the blues of the ocean; this is the Ring of Kerry, baby. The most common sound heard here must be the smack of someone's jaw hitting the ground at the sheer beauty of the place. Descriptive words don't quite do it, but that's all I've got; that and maybe a few pictures. Definitely not enough. The downside to all this beauty is the constant fear that I'm about to die in an inferno of silver car parts, green fields, and brown mountains.

Driving these roads is a beautiful yet harrowing adventure, one where I've realized that the roadway infrastructure in Ireland was planned out by either a madman or a junkie. I'm driving on pure

adrenaline; I feel like I'm constantly on the brink of crashing the car. Combine this with the fact that I'm listening to Tom Waits' The Heart of Saturday Night and driving on, what is for me, the wrong side of the road, then the sum of all parts equals a truly vivid, unforgettable day.

In the summertime, the road around the Ring of Kerry is bottled up like the arteries of a doughnut factory worker, but today? Today, the road is all mine.

On to Dingle, baby, follow the road, here we go.

Stuart's Euro Saver Secret of the Day: The rental car companies in Ireland are carnivorous heathens who hold you by your ankles and shake until the last cent falls out of your pocket. If you must hire a car, approach the situation as one who approaches a battle for one's life.

Glowing in Galway.

I am glowing in Galway. I am in tip-top shape, baby, hip, happening - something is going on here. You don't just walk down Shop Street, you glide. Galway has an energy that you can feel and you know, you know, that there is no place like it in all the rest of Ireland. Slide baby, glide baby, crawl honey, it doesn't matter - just do your thing.

You can creep through the medieval streets at night, drunk on stout, high on hash, energized from espresso, or sober as hell. You can bounce from Trad session to Indie rock, swanky lounges to old man pubs. "What do you want, lads?" Galway seems to whisper. "Whatever it is, we got it."

Ah Galway. It was on the wire from the second I landed in Ireland. I was tired of walking into tiny pubs in tiny towns and getting the hairy eyeball from all the locals; not so here. You can let it all hang out in Galway.

Dingle was cool, a tiny little place with eccentric shop owners and charismatic bars. It's suitable for a night and a day, two if you plan on seeing the friendly dolphin in the bay. Then there was Limerick, good old "Stab City." Not nearly as dangerous as the moniker suggests (especially when you've been living across the Bay from Oakland, CA, for the past four years of your life). And now, Galway. Did I mention that I like this place?

It was from here that I caught a ferry to the Aran Islands, three tiny islands surrounded by water, where the locals speak mostly Gaelic and the ruin-filled landscape looks like the deities got too lazy to give the place proper vegetation. It was wet, cold, beautiful, and old. I hiked up to Dun Aengus, which is a roughly 2000-year-old stone fort whose back end is perched upon a sheer cliff. Up there, I imagined myself as an ancient warlord looking out across my domain, satisfied that I had protected my people correctly. I also got rained on a lot.

I've got plenty of photos of the Aran Islands, but unfortunately, Galway cast quite a spell on me and I didn't get around to taking many photos. You'll understand what I mean when you get there.

Stuart's Euro Saving Secret of the Day: Make friends with bartenders and bar owners; when you do, shots of Jägermeister flow like the River Euphrates.

Rugged Shamrocks.

Letterkenny, County Donegal; last stop on a blitzkrieg three-day tour of the Republic of Ireland's wild and untamed northwest. Three days prior, I pulled out of Galway in a brand new rent-a-car, pristine, like a newborn baby in swaddling cloths. "Extra insurance?" the devil behind the car hire desk asked. "You bet your ass," I answered; I knew what those god damn roads were like.

The upside to this road trip, though, was that at least I had a traveling buddy. My friend Elodie's friend Camille was headed in the same direction as me. For Camille, it meant not having to take the bus, and an excuse to practice her English (she's French). For me, it meant one less car ride spent talking aimlessly into a digital voice

Jet Lagged, Hungover, & Homesick

recorder.

We lit out of Galway and headed for the Connemara, the northwest region of County Galway. The thing about Ireland is that each time you think you've seen all the beauty this island has to offer, you enter a new region and are awestruck once again. Between the placid mirror-like lakes, pale mountains, deep valleys, and more than occasional rainbows, the Connemara is so gorgeous it hurts.

We hit Westport by nightfall, and this was where the wear and tear of a week in Galway finally caught up to me. I was worn out, tired, and sick. But I'd heard that Westport had a must-see traditional music scene, so of course we went to the pub that night, where I managed to thoroughly insult a local man when I wouldn't let him buy me a beer because I felt too lousy.

The next day rivaled its predecessor in sheer physical beauty but completely outdid it in bodily sickness. We flew through West County Mayo, a region even more unruly and wild than the Connemara, hitting remote places as the stunning and almost haunting Achill Island (only accessible by a little bitty bridge). By nightfall, we were in Sligo, the famous muse of WB Yeats.

Hugging the lazy river Garavogue, Yeats' Sligo is a charming town with brightly colored buildings and absolutely nothing to do on a Sunday afternoon. So we headed out of town to find Queen Maeve's grave - roughly 40,000 tons of stone sitting atop a hill, with a 360-degree view of County Sligo. Apparently, if you take a stone from the bottom of the hill and carry it with you for the duration of the 35-minute hike to the top, you can place it on the enormous pile of rocks and make a wish. Unfortunately, we didn't know this until we got back to town.

It was getting dark by the time we left Queen Maeve, so I dropped Camille at the station so she could catch her bus, and I headed to Letterkenny, where I now sit, exhausted and coughing up phlegm.

Stuart's Euro Saving Secret of the Day: Learn how to drive a stick shift - it'll save you LOADS of money.

Stuart Schuffman

Hello Belfast, Goodbye Ireland.

I tore into Northern Ireland's capital like a madman recently released from military service. My stretch of recuperation was done, and I planned on letting this city do what it wished to me. The days are long here, and I continuously wander among the marvelous architecture, just trying to absorb as much of Belfast's energy as I can. Queen Victoria would be proud of the way her pet city looks today. It's a fine mixture of 19th, 20th, and 21st-century buildings, all blending together in a way that's not exactly harmony, but more like a coexistence. I guess buildings can reflect the people who live within them.

Take Great Victoria Street, for example. On one side, you have the newly refurbished Europa Hotel, a modern-looking 20th-century building which at one point had the lovely distinction of being 'the world's most bombed hotel'. Directly across the street is the Crown Liquor Saloon, built in 1885 with enough beautiful Victorian decadence inside to bring a drunk of any era to tears. These buildings don't look odd standing across from each other; on the contrary, they almost look natural.

Despite the coexistence of the buildings and, for the most part, the people, there is still an air of tension in some parts of the city. One day, I took a Black Taxi Tour, which brought me through both the Falls Road area (the hard-line Catholic neighborhood) and the Shankill Road area (the hard-line Protestant neighborhood). I saw the amazing murals and heard the rugged stories of Belfast life from the mid 60's until the 1994 ceasefire between the IRA and the various Ulster armies. The "Peace Wall" is still up, separating the two sides. Those whose houses border this wall still worry about the occasional Molotov Cocktail that manages to find its way over.

Jet Lagged, Hungover, & Homesick

But this is a new era in Belfast. Cafe culture is taking root, and the nightlife is insane! The people here, especially the young people, don't want anything to do with the Troubles of the past. Good things are happening here; it's impossible not to feel it.

As for me, I'm tired of the road, and it's starting to snow here in Belfast. In three days, I'll be back in San Francisco. I'm going to miss the stout beer, the lovely lasses, the random pub conversations with old men, and most of all, the *craic*. I'm definitely gonna miss the *craic*.

Goodbye Ireland.

Stuart's Euro Saving Tip of the Day: Throughout Northern Ireland, you'll find a restaurant chain called Lloyd's No. 1, which offers 2 for 1 meals all day long. So if you go in for lunch and order 2 meals, you can box up the second one and bring it home for dinner. Genius, I know.

Stuart Schuffman

Photo by Nicki Ishmael. Cover design by Kenny Liu

NEW YORK

For those who don't know, I got my start making a zine called *Broke-Ass Stuart's Guide to Living Cheaply in San Francisco*. That eventually became a series of books, including one for New York, and one that could apply to broke-asses anywhere in the country. What follows are some funny excerpts *Broke-Ass Stuart's Guide to Living Cheaply in New York City*. They were all written between 2007 and 2008.

Jet Lagged, Hungover, & Homesick

NYC BOOK INTRODUCTION
Broke-Ass Stuart's Guide to Living Cheaply in New York City; 2008

I'm sitting now in my Bushwick apartment, coming to terms with the realization that my time here in this strange and brutal city is quickly coming to an end. I maintain that, no matter how much you love New York, this city fucking hates you. Don't take it personally; this bitch is just badder than you are. Her game is tighter, her mind is quicker, her swagger is more believable. She's not the one who got away; she's the one you never had a chance of getting, and this is what makes just being near her so exhilarating. There's a quote from Thomas Wolfe that goes something like, "One belongs to New York instantly, one belongs to it as much in five minutes as in five years." And I think old Mr. Wolfe was on to something; New York will never be yours; you will always be hers. She's got you pussy-whipped, and you fucking know it.

But, I'm leaving. In two and a half weeks, I'll be gone. I'm filling my days (and notebooks) wandering through these streets, getting to know them as well as one gets to know a friend with benefits who lives in another town. I'm learning and admiring the creases, cracks, and character of these thoroughfares, but I'll never know what it's like to be with them forever. This has just been an affair, and I'm heading home to my wife in California, San Francisco, the one who takes the love I give to her and repays it in spades.

But I'm gonna miss New York. It's quite possibly the best city in the world. I'm gonna miss the electric fervor of summertime rooftops and the girls who wear next to nothing on the humid and fetid subway. I'm gonna miss the snow that sneaks in while I'm dreaming and piles itself up on the cars while they sleep in the street. I'll miss the little badge of pride that comes with saying I live in Brooklyn, not Manhattan. I'll miss all the beautiful people who have nothing to say, and all the ugly ones who say too much. Anything you could ever want is here, as long as you're willing to work for it and know where to look. Magic happens daily; the hard part is finding time to take it all in.

Thank you, New York, you've been a sweet and charming mistress who deals out pleasure and pain equally, the way a blackjack dealer can just as easily give you 21, or make you bust. I'll be back, probably sooner than you'd like, but this is it for us, kiddo. This affair is over. I want to ask you never to change, to stay just the way you are, so that when I do come back, you'll be just as you are now. But you and I both know that can't happen. At least I'll have my book, which will let me pin you down to exactly who you were, to me, for the past 10 months. Just do me one favor after I leave: tell all the developers they can suck my dick.

The Strand: 828 Broadway btw E 12th & 13th Sts.

You know how in commercials the Keebler Elves always seem like they're having a great time because their job rocks and they're making people happy by baking delicious cookies? Next time one of those commercials comes on, look into the Elves' eyes and you will catch fleeting glimpses of pure terror. It's like they know that if they don't convince you of how great their jobs are, there's gonna be hell to pay when the cameras turn off.

Those Elves are shuckin' and jivin' for their lives. Whoever employs those little guys must be kicking the shit out of them on a nightly basis, and I'm pretty sure that the same person runs The Strand. The only difference is that the people who work at The Strand are in open rebellion; they want you to know how much they hate their jobs. It's the only plausible conclusion that I could come up with, considering how extraordinary The Strand is.

How could you hate working at one of the best used bookstores in the world, a place famous for having 18 miles of books, unless they were chaining you to the wall and attaching a car battery to your genitals every night? The only other explanation is that The Strand exclusively hires total fucking assholes. I wonder which of these explanations is true.

P.S. I heard the Elves tried to go on a hunger strike, but that they just couldn't resist eating those delectable baked goods.

McSorley's Old Ale House: 15 E 7th St. @ Cooper Square

Founded in 1854, McSorley's is New York's oldest bar, and because of this, its slogan is, "We've been here since before you were born." Are you kidding me, McSorley's? You've been here since when my ancestors were getting raped and pillaged by fucking Cossacks. No shit, you've been here before I was born.

And you know what McSorley's? I love you for it. I love that your walls are crammed with photos and memorabilia from over 150 years of dedicated drinking. I love that your chandelier probably hasn't been dusted since the time they used to call WWI "The Great War". I love how your urinals are weird and old and bigger than some of the apartments in this strange city that you and I both inhabit. And you know what else I love about you, McSorley's? I love that you only serve two drinks, light beer and dark beer, and that they're both delicious and only cost $2.25 each. Who cares if it wasn't until 1970 when you begrudgingly let women through your hallowed doors because of some namby-pamby Supreme Court case? You've had Abe Lincoln, John Lennon, and Woody Guthrie hang out at your tables! Who needs chicks, right? I guess what I'm trying to say, McSorley's is that you might be the best bar in the world, except for Friday and Saturday nights when your sublime atmosphere gets screwed up by too many guys whose favorite band is Sublime.

Palace Fried Chicken: Manhattan Ave @ Nassau

Every time Paul walks into Palace Fried Chicken, Abdul, the guy behind the counter, shouts in his Afghan accent, "MEEESTER CHEEEESE-FRIES!" It happens to be an almost daily ritual since Paul eats here almost daily. This is quite understandable because a) it's incredibly cheap, b) it's pretty damn good, and c) Paul lives virtually next door. But it might be more than that, too; Paul and Abdul seem to have a special relationship.

For example, when Abdul told Paul that it had been "seex months since I have push-push in de bush-bush", the two of them agreed that if Paul got Abdul laid, he'd get free Palace Fried Chicken for the rest of his life. So, Paul spent the next month trying to pimp out his female roommate. He began slyly by asking questions like, "So, what do you think about Abdul over at Palace Fried Chicken? You know the guy with the mustache who always stares at you? He's pretty dreamy right?" and when that didn't work, he tried the direct approach of, "Come on! Just fuck him once. We're talking about free Palace Fried Chicken for the rest of our lives!!" Needless to say, she moved out shortly afterwards.

Another time, Abdul asked Paul to look at a website for him to help him figure out why he wasn't allowed to go back to Afghanistan to visit his family. So Paul took the information, went home, checked out the website, and entered the ID number Abdul had given him. Apparently, Abdul wasn't allowed to leave the country because our government was concerned about his reasons for wanting to visit Afghanistan. Luckily, though, Paul was able to help Abdul get his trip home okayed by the state department because everybody knows it's pretty hard to get some "push-push in the bush-bush" if the US government thinks you're a "threat." Girls just don't really dig that sort of thing.

Kenka: 25 St. Mark's Pl. btw 2nd & 3rd Aves.

Oh Kenka...Kenka...Kenka...Kenka. You are one of the weirdest fucking places I've ever eaten in my entire life, and for that, I salute you. I'm literally sitting here in front of my computer trying to find the proper words with which to describe you, and the only thing that keeps popping into my head is "bull penis". Yes, bull penis. You sell bull penis. To be eaten. By people. For $5.50 a pop. And yet there is more to your menu than just penises, squid beaks, and cow tongues; there's also the drawing of a guy sticking a revolver up the ass of a bound, half-naked chick. While I'll admit that I am just pointing out some of your more...er, colorful qualities, it must be noted that *everything* on your menu is amazingly cheap. Most of your food (including your more standard dishes) rings in at around the $5-$7 range, and you sell beers for $1.50 each or $8 a pitcher. That my friend is beautiful; almost as beautiful as the scores of vintage bondage porn posters that line your sacred walls or the rules written on the bottom of your menu saying "No fighting, masturbating, having sex or drugs. You will be ejected." Kenka, you're my kind of place and I just wanted to say thanks for the cotton candy that you give out at the end of the meal; it helps to get rid of the lingering bull cock taste.

P.S. For those interested, I think Kenka is only written in Japanese on the outside sign, which can make it harder to find when searching for it.

Yaffa Café: 97 St. Mark's Pl. between 1st Ave. & Ave. A

No write-up about the East Village would be complete without the inclusion of Yaffa Café. I love the fuck out of this place, but not for the usual reasons. The food isn't really that amazing, and the prices are just a tad bit more expensive than what I'd consider cheap. So what makes this place so great? It's got mad soul. And I don't mean "soul" in the way kinda racist white people use the word when describing hip things created by black people. I mean soul in the sense that there's something ineffably cool about Yaffa Café.

It's a 24-hour joint that has excellent wallpaper (zebra, floral, and even that faux Victorian one with the velvet designs), cow print tables, leopard print seats, random hanging beads, and off-colored X-mas lights. It's kinda like what I imagine the inside of Cindy Lauper's vagina to look like. And since the restaurant is on St. Mark's and is "Open all night", you get an incredible variety of people who dine here.

Jet Lagged, Hungover, & Homesick

So here's my advice: next time you're having a late night in the East Village, stop in for a bite at Yaffa, you might just see me there.

Shakespeare & Co.: 939 Lexington Ave., btw E 68th & 69th Sts.

When I asked the girl working at this independent bookstore if it was related to the famous Shakespeare & Co. in Paris, she replied, "No. They just stole the name." And you know what? I can appreciate that. This was initially supposed to be *Broke-Ass Spencer's Guide to Living Cheaply in New York*, but I stole the manuscript and buried Spencer somewhere in the desert 45 minutes outside of Marfa, Texas. The shitty part is that my partner in crime was a guy named Dan Brown, and though we both got to take one of Spencer's two unpublished books, Dan got something called The Da Vinci Code, while I got stuck with this piece of crap. See what happens when you try to determine all your important life decisions by playing Rock, Paper, Scissors? Apparently, there are a few bookstores like this throughout the city. Due to its location, this particular one focuses primarily on books for old, rich women and students, with a particular emphasis on the former. Fabio sells tons of his romance novels here.

Radegast Hall and Biergarten: 113 N 3rd St. @ Berry St.

Ten years ago, if you had told a local that there would be a Bavarian-style beer garden in Williamsburg, they would have responded, "*Vhut, are you meshuggenah? Vee moved to Brooklyn to escape ze farkakteh Bavarians!*" But lo and behold, today there's one sitting right on the corner of Berry and N. 3rd and it's fucking great!* Look, I know that I constantly rail against kitsch, irony, and faking the funk, but considering that this place was opened by guys who used to run the 100-year-old Bohemian Hall and Beer Garden in Astoria, I'd have to say it's about as authentic as possible without being the real thing. As for the price, I'm not gonna lie and say it's uber cheap, but every once in a while, a person wants to eat sausages and drink delicious beer out of a giant glass brought to them by cute girls dressed like beer wenches. You feel me? They even have a retractable roof for fuck's sake! These guys thought of everything.

Publisher's note: Stuart is an insensitive prick who obviously can't tell the difference between a Bavarian beer garden and an Austro-Hungarian one. When confronted with this mix-up, he responded, "All white people look the same to me."

The Eagle: 554 W 28th St., btw 10th & 11th Aves.

I consider myself to be a fairly knowledgeable and well-traveled person. I'd like to think that I'm hip to a lot of different subcultures and that I know enough about them that I can pick up on most of the slang. But when I came to The Eagle, I was totally surprised by the entire subculture within the Bear/leather community, which is in itself already a gay subculture. I learned that, not only are there Bears (big, hairy lumberjack-looking guys), there are also Otters (skinny, playful, hairy guys), Wolves (aggressive, muscular, hairy guys), and Cubs (younger guys who are growing into Bears). Since when is being gay like being in the Cub Scouts? Do Wolves eventually become Webelos? Are there merit badges for safe sex and reach-arounds? If you identify as one of these woodland creatures, or just wanna see them at play, stop in at The Eagle on a lovely Sunday for their rooftop beer blast. You might just get to pitch a tent.

Ninth Avenue Bistro: 693 9th Ave., btw W 47th & 48th Sts.

Occasionally, you stumble into a bar on what happens to be the right night; completely irrational events unfold in front of you, and you wonder if this type of magic happens regularly. When I first staggered into Ninth Avenue Bistro, I lurched into a barstool just as an older-looking version of John Waters screamed out "Bingo!" In my condition, I wasn't quite sure what had transpired; I thought he was so excited to see some fresh, young meat in the joint that he jumped up and screamed with glee. I started to mumble something about being flattered and that I'd take a vodka tonic if he were buying, when a loud voice said, "Alright, it's Jim again, folks! He's on fire tonight! Come on up for your copy of the new *Ass Crusin'* DVD!" It was then that I noticed everyone in the bar had a Bingo card in front of them. Although I was the youngest person by 40 years, nobody had noticed me stumble in, let alone jump for joy. Nobody, that is, except for the hiccupping drag queen with the 4-day beard and disheveled wig, who sat on the next stool over.

She managed to squeeze out a "Welcome to Porno Bingo, sweetie" between hiccups before pinching my ass so hard I bruised. Truthfully, I didn't stay around much longer, but I did manage to ask Miss Pinchie Fingers how often this type of thing happened. Apparently, it's every Wednesday night.

Jet Lagged, Hungover, & Homesick

The Cottage: 360 Amsterdam Ave. @ W 77th St.

As Americans, we aren't used to getting shit for free, so when we do, we often misbehave. It's not our fault, really. The Capitalist system we grew up in has reared us towards an "I'm gonna get mine motherfucker!" mentality, and living in New York only exacerbates this. Just go to Costco on a hectic day and watch as grown ass men slyly try to cut in front of each other for their third sample of Annie's White Cheddar Macaroni & Cheese.

So, it's with this shirking of culpability in mind that I relate to you The Cottage's policy of giving out unlimited complimentary wine with dinner. Just as inviting me to an open bar event is the surest way of getting me in trouble, offering me all the wine I can drink with dinner only assures my inevitable response, "None of this is my fault." Yes, I know that it was my choice to drink carafe after carafe of the Dionysian drink, and that this decision led to me eventually being cut off, arguing for more wine, getting kicked out, and ultimately puking dumplings and sweet & sour chicken all over 77th St., but it's not my fault. It's capitalism's fault; I was never taught to say "no" ...ok, maybe it was a little bit my fault.

Fried Dumpling: 106 Mosco St. btw Mulberry & Mott Sts., also at 99 Allen St. btw Broome & Delancey Sts.

The only English words the ladies at Fried Dumpling know are "How Many?" And that's enough because the answer is usually five. Yes, friends, you get five of the best dumplings you've ever had for $1. And apparently, instead of change, they give you dumplings. I bought a 75-cent Coke, and instead of giving me back a quarter, she just gave me another dumpling. Sweet right?

The funny thing, though, is that if you come and say you want $20 worth of dumplings. The ladies kind of bug out, curse at you in Chinese, and then go into hyperdrive. My fantasy is to bring in that Japanese eating champion kid (Kobayashi or something like that) and challenge him to a $50 showdown against the dumpling ladies. It would probably be the best fifty bucks ever spent.

Stuart Schuffman

HARAJUKU HEARTBREAK: NOTES AND OBSERVATIONS ON TRAVELING THROUGH JAPAN
BrokeAssStuart.com; 2013

This was written in 2013. My observation about face masks was unfortunately proven very true during the pandemic

My good friend Sato is a Japanese-American who now lives in Japan. A few years ago, I had a dream that he was getting married. Although he wasn't there at the time, I decided to attend his wedding when he got married, which I did. Between October 15th and November 2nd, I traveled in Tokyo, Osaka, and Kyoto. As you probably know by now, I'm a strange person who looks at the world through a very particular set of eyes. Below are the notes and observations I made while traveling. Most of them are both weird and funny, and they were written drunk. I think you'll enjoy reading them and may learn a little about what it's like to travel as a foreigner through Japan:

— I showed up during what the news was calling a "death typhoon." I didn't die, but I got very wet and realized I didn't pack the right kind of shoes. I also got incredibly drunk those first few nights in Tokyo. It made up for having soggy shoes.

— The Tokyo Park Hyatt (hotel from Lost in Translation) put me up for free for two nights. It was one of the nicest places I've ever stayed in my life. Perfect for nursing hangovers in.

— Maybe it's because everyone says Japan is incredibly safe that, despite not knowing anything and looking like a total mark, there wasn't the slightest bit of menace in the air.

— On my first night, I got misled into a whorehouse. A guy from Ghana told me it was a place where I could drink unlimited for 90 minutes for US$40. He didn't tell me it was a whorehouse. I was sorely disappointing to a Filipina prostitute since I wasn't gonna pay her for sex. I'm not opposed to prostitution, as long as it doesn't involve sex slavery, but I'm just too young and good-looking to pay for sex, maybe in 30 years or so.

Jet Lagged, Hungover, & Homesick

— Making a *thizz* face, while waving your hand in front of your face to demonstrate that you're very excited about something, is apparently not a universal thing. I think they thought I was having a seizure.

— America, while you may be #1 at some things (like being a big fan of saying that you're #1), the toilets in Japan make your toilets seem like well...simple receptacles for going #2. I never knew having a butthole was so awesome until I used those Japanese toilets!

— Whenever I saw another white dude, we made eye contact and nodded at each other as to say, "Hey whitey. I see you too!" Actually, the nod happened with pretty much anyone who wasn't Asian.

— My sense of "otherness" was immense. I stood out so much, but I was often treated as invisible while walking down the street. I'm not hideous by any means, but the only time I was ever checked out was out of curiosity more than lustfulness.

— Not only do a good portion of the men spend a ton of time on the way they look, but many of them also carry giant purses. They basically broke my gaydar.

— Tokyo is not a sexy city. Whereas in New York, you can feel sex appeal virtually seeping from the buildings, Tokyo feels completely asexual. Kyoto and Osaka did as well.

— The social contract in Japan is far different than ours. They are so much more community-minded. For example, when you see people wearing doctors' masks in public, it's not because they don't want to get sick, it's because they don't want to get YOU sick. Just think about that for a second. In the US, we're like, "Ya, I'm sick. Fuck you if you get sick too." We could learn a lot from the Japanese when it comes to looking out for each other and our community.

— Japan is incredibly clean, and it's impossible to find a trash can! People actually save their trash and dispose of it when they get to the train station or home.

— Nobody steals in Japan. People will be in a crowded bar and, to save their seat, they'll put their wallet on the bar while they go to the bathroom. YES REALLY!

— My second night in town, I randomly ended up back at a bar I had been to the night before. I had vague recollections of it and said to the barkeep, "Hey! I think I was here last night!" He responded, "Yes, you were too drunk", to which I said, "Was I an asshole?" He responded, "Yes." I then gave him a Broke-Ass Stuart sticker, to which he responded, "I already have one of those." He was very funny about it all, though.

— Tokyo is vast. It is so much bigger than you can even imagine. From a certain viewpoint, the city seems to go on forever.

— Most foreign things are taken entirely out of context. You'll see a guy dressed like a Crip from South Central Los Angeles, and it will absolutely have no meaning whatsoever. It's just the way he likes to dress. He has no concept of the socio-economic implications of dressing like that.

— Tokyo is hip without pretension. Everyone seems stylish without judging other people's style. And there are SO many styles. It seems like every style that has ever existed in the history of the world currently exists in Tokyo. If a dude dressed like Socrates, he wouldn't look that out of place.

— Cute local bars are only so when you speak the language.

— I'm pretty sure I was the only male traveler in Japan who didn't have an Asian girl fetish. I still don't.

— One strange thing, compared to every other place in the world where I've been very obviously "the other", is that the street barkers ignore me entirely. Anywhere else, travelers and tourists are the targets of the "I have a deal for you! Come this way, my friend." However, Japanese people often feel embarrassed about not pronouncing English words correctly, so they tend to ignore me. The only exception to this is that clubs in places like Roppongi will hire dudes from Africa to do the street hustling and barking.

— In Osaka, there is a red-light district that's way off the beaten path called Tobita Shinchi. When I asked the lady who ran the hostel I was staying at for a suggestion of something to see that most people don't, she sent me there but said I should be back before it got dark since it was dangerous. She had never been there herself. It's essentially a network of small alleyways lined with prewar buildings, where young girls sit and smile at passersby. Meanwhile, older women sitting next to them call out, trying to sell the girls' services. The yakuza run the whole neighborhood, and there were signs everywhere showing a camera with an X through it, so I didn't take any pics. I didn't want to get my phone taken away. Tobita Shinchi was the only place where I got looks that read like "Whoa...what's this white dude doing here?" Most of the time I was in Japan, I felt invisible even though I was incredibly the opposite.

— I saw very few children in Japan. It's actually a problem there. People aren't having kids. It's a combination of various social pressures, including tradition, the economy, and possibly technology. Most of the time when I saw kids, their parents were incredibly hip, looking like Japanese versions of the Beckhams.

— The most important notes you take are the ones you take when you're drunk. If you're not taking any, it means you're drinking too much.

— The "train arriving" chimes in Osaka sound just like the first few notes of "Dancing in the Moonlight". It's actually quite lovely. Of course, the song was stuck in my head the entire time I was in Osaka, but I still love the song.

— I never score at weddings. The wedding in Kyoto was no different. Maybe it's because people at weddings are looking for love, and I look like more trouble than I'm worth. I probably am.

— Hostel friends are people you have quick, tight bonds with who just as quickly become just someone whose stuff you "like" on Facebook.

— Some kind of mad MC Escher on LSD designed the central train station in Osaka. I got so lost in there, while incredibly hungover, that

I came very close to tears.

— People in Japan are SO good at lining up. I mean, they are so orderly that it makes Americans look like drunk kittens.

— No one gets cut off at the bar. People are allowed to drink until they pass out. In fact, you see people passed out everywhere. Since they know no one is gonna rob them, they just kinda go "whelp, this looks like a place to zzzz..." and literally, NOBODY ROBS THEM. Where I live, they'd wake up wearing nothing but a homeless man's poop.

— There are bathrooms in every train station, and they are both very safe and immaculate. Plus, no homeless people are living in them. In fact, there are very few homeless people visible in Japan. I've been told it's because they are far too ashamed to be seen in public.

— While there are like no thugs, there are also no hugs. There's minimal intentional physical contact in Japan. I went through a sort of hug withdrawal. I really like giving and receiving hugs.

— Cat cafes smell like cat piss.

— Maid cafes are terrifyingly creepy in the sense that the women are so utterly infantilized. But the dudes that hang out in maid cafes? Those, my friends, are the really creepy ones.

— I want to make a song or poem called "Killing Me Softly in Kyoto". It's about being forced to eat and drink way too much at a wedding.

— There's a song by Australian singer/songwriter Paul Kelly called "Every Fucking City Looks the Same". There should be one for Tokyo called "This Whole Fucking City Looks the Same" because it mostly does. Once you've been here for a while, everything in Tokyo looks vaguely familiar and completely foreign.

— Tokyo is not particularly good-looking, but she is bright.

— When the trains are resting, the systems (hydraulics, maybe?) sound like the faint and distant sounds of sea lions.

Jet Lagged, Hungover, & Homesick

ISRAELI-PALESTINIAN CONFLICT THROUGH AMERICAN EYES
San Francisco Examiner; 2018

This was written in 2018, far before the tragedy of October 7th 2023, and the subsequent annihilation of the people of Gaza that we have all watched unfold at the hands of the fascist Israeli government.

I hope with every ounce of my soul that by the time this book is in your hands, the people of Gaza are no longer being killed, there is a permanent ceasefire, the hostages are brought home, and Netanyahu is arrested for war crimes.

"It's complicated." That's what nearly everyone said.

Traveling through Israel and Palestine just two weeks ago, we met with professors, journalists, activists, industrialists, and generals. We broke bread with Ethiopian Jews, Palestinians, Israelis, Ultra-Orthodox Jews, and secular Muslims. We tried to learn as much as possible about the intricacies of the Israeli-Palestinian conflict during an 11-day trip, during which 10 hours of each day were devoted to listening to lecturers and asking questions.

We were a diverse group of Bay Area civic leaders, representing various ethnicities and backgrounds, who were brought to Israel by the Jewish Community Relations Council to gain a deeper understanding of the complexities of the situation there. And it is complicated — incredibly so — but I learned a Hebrew word that sums it up even better: *balagan*.

Balagan means "chaos" or "fiasco" or "mess" or, as we say in colloquial American English, "shit show."

That's precisely what the Israeli-Palestinian conflict is, a complete and utter, century-old *balagan* that doesn't seem to be getting any better.

This week has been horrific. On Monday, more than 50 Palestinian protesters were killed by Israeli Defense Forces. Any death at a protest is terrible, but really, think about it. Think about the times you've been at a demonstration or seen one on TV, and consider what it would be like if the authorities opened fire on the crowd with live ammunition. Of course, we've seen it before: The death toll at Kent State was four; Bloody Sunday in Northern Ireland was 14. But Israeli forces killed dozens of people this week, armed with little more than rocks, bottles, Molotov cocktails, and apparently some kind of incendiary kites.

The protesters' use of incendiaries is wrong. But what are Molotov cocktails compared to well-protected snipers with high-powered assault rifles? This underscores one of the significant issues with the current iteration of the conflict: Both sides have lots of blood on their hands after a century of violence, but Israel has significantly more power, both politically and in terms of weaponry. Gaza is a veritable open-air prison, where Israel gets to decide who leaves and when, and the economic blockade keeps the people of Palestine impoverished. The fact that Israel enforces these things with state-of-the-art weaponry and deadly force leaves the Palestinians in Gaza in a desperate situation.

Israel is not the only one to blame. Hamas, a terrorist organization funded by Iran, has been in control of Gaza for a decade with the stated purpose of wiping out Israel completely. Much of the international aid that goes to Gaza to help build things like hospitals and infrastructure gets taken by Hamas and is used for bunkers, tunnels, and weaponry. And Egypt, which borders the other side of Gaza, refuses to let the Palestinians live on their lands.

The situation is only slightly better on the West Bank. While the Palestinian Authority has control of 18 percent of the land and joint control with Israel of another 22 percent of the territory, they are wildly corrupt and don't really have much power. For example, all the buildings in the West Bank have big water tanks on their roofs. That's because Israel controls their access to water and sometimes turns it off. All this is occurring while Israel financially encourages religious Jewish zealots who settle in designated Palestinian lands because they think they were promised it in the bible. And just like Egypt, Jordan, which borders the other side of the West Bank, won't allow Palestinians to move onto their land.

So why does Israel insist on exerting such tight and anti-humanitarian control over the Palestinians? From their view, it's to protect Israeli citizens from the kind of terrorism that rocked Israel during the Second Intifada, which took place from September 2000 to February 2005 and resulted in 1,000 Israelis being killed. Since the day it declared its independence, Israel has had some very legitimate security concerns.

Total *bala-freakin'-gan*, right?

A Palestinian journalist from Ramallah suggested that even though Hamas and the Palestinian Authority hate each other and have been to war with each other, they need to sit down and decide what's best for the Palestinian people. As it's evident that Israel isn't going anywhere, the leaders in Gaza and the West Bank need to acknowledge Israel's right to existence and move forward with plans on how to live peacefully next to Israel. Once they have that, they can start negotiations with Israel.

Israel has a ton of work to do. First, they need to get all the Jewish settlers out of the West Bank. Not only are their settlements wrong, but they are also illegal. Israel should also pull back to its 1967 borders and give sovereignty over to whatever unified Palestinian leadership comes out of Hamas and the PA, making peace. If peace is ever to happen, Israel will need to completely reconsider the wall in the West Bank, if not tear it down altogether. While the wall has significantly reduced terror attacks inside Israel, it has done so at the cost of jobs lost, families divided, land divided, and the freedom and dignity of innocent Palestinians. Besides the humanitarian issues, it's not even all that effective: Twenty percent of Arabs already live on the Israeli side, and people sneak across the wall all the time for work opportunities.

Since Jerusalem is viewed as such a holy place for both the Jews and the Muslims, it's a huge sticking point in the Israeli-Palestinian conflict. The best possible outcome would be if Israel or Palestine did not own it, but instead it was an international city where Jews, Muslims, and Christians could still live, pray, and make pilgrimages to.

This is just one way peace can come to the region, but there's a long way to go before any of this happens. So, what can we do as Americans?

At home, we start by electing a government that is not in bed with the right-wing extremists who are currently running Israel. Even then, Israel needs to get rid of its right-wing government, Gaza needs to oust Hamas, and the Palestinian Authority needs to have leadership that doesn't believe Jews brought the Holocaust on themselves, as Mahmoud Abbas recently suggested.

Our most significant task is dealing with our relationships with Israel.

Many will suggest the movement to boycott, divest from, and sanction (BDS) Israel. Given its booming economy, that movement has been largely ineffective. Beyond that, it does nothing to help the Palestinians with what they need: jobs, security, education, and health. Journalist Peter Beinart suggested a targeted BDS of anything manufactured in the Jewish West Bank settlements might be more effective. Supporting Israeli and Palestinian organizations that work for a peaceful two-state solution and human rights for all is another way you can help.

We also need to deal with our own personal relationships.

Fellow Jews: Stop blindly siding with Israel. Their government is committing atrocities, things that, if it weren't Israel, you'd be condemning. You can support the State of Israel while also denouncing its government. It's what we do every day here with our own country. The things the Israeli government is doing to the Palestinian people are things that were done to us in other countries for centuries. The only way the Jewish state can have legitimacy is if it ends the occupation of the Palestinian territories and stops persecuting the people in them.

Non-Jews: Please stop equating all Jewish people with things the Israeli government is doing. There are millions of Jews around the world who can see Prime Minister Benjamin Netanyahu for the criminal he is and who are dissenting against what the Israeli government is doing. In fact, many of them are Israeli citizens living in Israel and working for peace. Israelis in Tel-Aviv took to the streets to protest Monday's massacre of Palestinians. Just because Israel is a Jewish state doesn't mean its government represents every Jew. Anti-Semitism is on the rise worldwide, and this kind of thinking is helping fuel the flames.

Jet Lagged, Hungover, & Homesick

MEXICO CITY IS MOVING ON UP
San Francisco Examiner; 2015

I'm currently sitting on the 23rd floor of the Hilton Mexico City Reforma. The city stretches out in front of me as far as the eye can see, its sloping buildings and sputtering sidewalks slowly sinking into the marshy earth. The *Torre Latinoamericana* pinpricks the low-hanging clouds, looking like a Mexican Empire State Building. I call it the Mexpire State Building, but my girlfriend Ashley replies, "I think you've still got some work to do on that one."

She's probably right.

After planning and running a mayoral campaign from February to November, I desperately needed a vacation. So, Ashley and I booked a trip to The City of Palaces, hoping to find ... well, we weren't exactly sure. We were both physically, mentally, and emotionally exhausted from the campaign grind, and the idea of having a vast city — that might be heading towards its summit instead of barreling downhill — to explore sounded incredibly appealing.

You read that right: Mexico City is moving on up. Long associated with horrible traffic, abysmal smog, and violent kidnappings, Mexico City is actually moving towards becoming a world-class city, achieving the kind of renown it hasn't enjoyed since the days of Frida Kahlo and Diego Rivera. Creative young expats are moving here because it's supremely affordable. Artists, writers, performers, and designers are trickling in from all over the Americas because rent is cheap, and the scene is burgeoning. Plus, the food is off the hook. From street tacos to high-end French bistros, the ingredients are fresh, and the flavors are brilliant. Ideas like farm-to-table and organic produce are percolating, and fantastic culinary mashups are opening next to little mom-and-pop tacos spots.

That's not to say everything in this city of more than 20 million people is perfect — far from it. There are a lot of really fucked up things about Mexico City. The sidewalks often look like they've been bombarded with cannonballs, the police seek any reason to extort you, muggings are not uncommon, drinking tap water could hospitalize you, there's immense poverty, the entire government is utterly corrupt... the list goes on.

But it's an excellent time to be here, especially as an American. The dollar-to-peso ratio is 1:16 at the moment. "This is what it must feel like to be rich," Ashley mentioned as we spent the equivalent of $36 on six glasses of very fine mescal. And then the little girl selling flowers at midnight came up to us, and our conversation quickly switched to being about privilege and how nothing we ever did caused us to be born in the United States.

Mexico City opens your mind and breaks your heart at the same time.

It's almost hard to imagine that all of this is happening only a three-and-a-half-hour flight from SFO. At $350 for a round-trip, nonstop flight, it's easier and cheaper to get to Mexico City than it is to get to New York. And so we're here, on the 23rd floor of the lovely Hilton Mexico City Reforma, gazing out at the beautiful *Palacio de Bellas Artes* and the *Hemiciclo a Juarez* as the sunset lights the clouds on fire. It's nice to be away from San Francisco for a little bit to be reminded how good we really have it, while at the same time realizing how much better we can be.

REVISITING AMSTERDAM
San Francisco Examiner; 2019

It's been 18 years since I last visited Amsterdam. In 2001, I was 20 years old, backpacking through Europe with my buddy Nick, overjoyed to be in a city where weed was legal, and ecstatic to be on a continent where I was old enough to drink. To me, Amsterdam was heavenly: I smoked my way through the coffee shops, drank lots of fine beers I'd never heard of, and had hot sex in a hostel with a 25-year-old woman (five years older seemed so sophisticated to me at the time).

It. Was. Glorious.

Nearly two decades later, it's exciting to be back, albeit on a very different trip. This time, instead of being on what amounted to an international pub crawl with my buddy, I'm traveling more leisurely with my fiancé (we just got engaged in Belgium!!). The focus is less on

Jet Lagged, Hungover, & Homesick

booze and drugs, and more on culture and exploration. Rather than sleeping in a hostel dorm with 16 other snoring dudes, we're staying with friends and in hotels. While I was obviously a very different person from the one who visited in 2001, I was curious to see how much of this old city has remained the same.

Walking through the center of Amsterdam today feels like little has changed in the past few decades. Beautiful 400-year-old buildings still line the canals as cute boats float by. Bleary-eyed international cannabis pilgrims shuffle between the coffee shops and the gazillion vendors selling a cornucopia of stoner foods. Sex tourists from around the world crawl the Red-Light District, patronizing the attractive women standing behind the glass doors. If I were to stay only in the city center, then it would seem like nothing had changed at all. But that's not remotely true.

To be fair, there was a whole lot of Amsterdam I didn't see last time around, but the evidence that this city has changed, and is continuing to do so rapidly, is incontrovertible.

Sitting in my hotel room at the Double Tree Amsterdam NDSM Wharf, I've got a panoramic view of a city that is quite literally on the rise. I can count at least 12 building cranes from my window, and while there has always been stuff to see, do, and consume outside the city center, it feels like things are really popping off right now.

Just take the neighborhood I'm staying in. The NDSM, located northwest of the Ij River from the Central Station, is an abandoned shipyard that's exploding with underground arts and culture. The actual old Nederlandsche Dok en Scheepsbouw Maatschappij (NDSM) building is filled with over 200 different artists and artisans, and considers itself a breeding ground for creativity. Around this have sprung up hip restaurants, performance spaces, and outdoor bars and cafés.

Other neighborhoods are going through similar transformations. Noord, located just north of the Central Station across the river, has until recently been a more neighborhoody area, but it is now experiencing a surge of eateries and performance spaces. It's also got the major tourist attraction of the A'dam Toren, which has a swing at the very top, allowing you to swing over the side of one of Amsterdam's tallest buildings. I nearly pooped my pants!

As we know in the Bay Area, though, all this exciting change comes at a cost. Amsterdam is experiencing a housing affordability problem, too. Due to factors such as Airbnb, a booming economy, and foreign investors purchasing property, it was recently ranked the least affordable city in Europe to buy a home. A bartender I met at Café Hegeraad, an incredible bar that is more than 100 years old, told me that if her 25-year-old daughter moves out, the daughter will most likely have to leave Amsterdam completely.

Photo by Kayla Brittingham

Similarly, some artists I spoke with at the NDSM building expressed concerns that the area's cool art spaces might eventually be converted into condos and offices. As one guy put it, "First the artists move in, then they make things cool. Then businesses start popping up, and soon the artists can no longer be there." Doesn't that sound familiar?

By the time you read this, I'll no longer be in Amsterdam. We're off to Berlin for a few days before heading home, but I'm so glad I got to revisit this city and see it through grown-up eyes. Amsterdam is beautiful and charming, and it has so much figured out that we can't seem to nail yet (hello bike friendliness and mass transit ease). Obviously, it's going through the same struggle as most major cities right now, but I can't wait to come back here again.

Jet Lagged, Hungover, & Homesick

LIYUAN PARK BLUES
(OR HOME IS WHERE THE HEARTBREAK IS)
Previously Unpublished

Sitting in Liyuan Park in Shanghai
Beautiful old men are dancing with each other
Couples are foxtrotting to Chinese pop
The air is crisp and perfect a few days after a typhoon

I spent the morning and afternoon
Hungover and irritable
Overwhelmed by my otherness
Lusting for something familiar
And I got it

The news from home is not good

Another black body lying on
Black pavement
Bleeding out red blood
While the white police who shot him
Do nothing to help

The world's cutest babies toddle and tipple
around the park while
adults look at me queerly
as I sit and write

My whiteness not exactly rare
But my interest in them is

Trying so damn hard to hold back the tears of
Everything so beautiful in front of me
And everything so ugly back home.

Bombs in New York and New Jersey
Donald Trump is on the move
A second black man murdered in just a few hours

The news from home is not good
The news from home is not good

Stuart Schuffman

Gil said "Home is Where the Hatred is"
But home is also where the heartbreak is

I saw a man with a pet monkey the other night
The monkey was on a leash and
held tightly to the man's leg

Sometimes I wish I had someone's leg to hold on to

I want to cry a lot these days
It all sits there, deep like a well
And then a divining rod comes along and
strikes home setting the water free

I wept on a bus to Zhujiajiao
A town famous for its canals
where the water doesn't hide underground
but acts as avenues through which things move

As I read the news about Rose Pak
I never knew her but she was the divining rod
I wept for my city
and for my country
and for all the people who never get to go home
like Terence Crutcher and Keith Lamont Scott
as I was doing in a few days

A sweet wonderful Chinese baby
laid his head on me while he slept
I don't know if his mother saw me weeping

The news at home is not good
But I'm heading there anyways
San Francisco your boy is coming home
Even if the news is not good

Jet Lagged, Hungover, & Homesick

4TH OF JULY AT THE MARIJUANA MANSION
San Francisco Examiner; 2016

Jen Friel had reached out to me the week before. "You should come to L.A. for the Fourth of July. We're invited to a party at the Marijuana Mansion."

I don't really smoke weed very often, but it was such a curious invitation that I couldn't say no. I hadn't seen Jen in a few years, but every time we hang out, shenanigans happen — like the time we got smuggled into a Google Ventures party dressed like absolute freaks.

Twenty minutes after the invite, I had a plane ticket to Los Angeles.

"Bring a costume" was the last thing she messaged me. I obliged.

The afternoon before Independence Day, I found out what the costumes were for. "Today, we're gonna dress up and go down to Hollywood and Highland so people can take photos with us. We'll donate the tips they give us to charity."

There's a whole scene of people dressed as famous characters and actors near Grauman's Chinese Theatre, and we were going to join them for shits 'n' giggles and see what a day in their lives was like. Jen dressed up as Katy Perry and looked remarkably like her. I put on a Day-Glo psychedelic muumuu and a captain's hat. Those, coupled with my beard, made me look like a combination of Mama Cass and Zach Galifianakis. For obvious reasons, no one wanted to be photographed with me.

We quickly grew bored with the picture-taking and instead went on a weird, costumed bar crawl throughout Hollywood, making friends and drawing strange looks everywhere we went.

The following day was July 4, the day of The Marijuana Don's big party at the Marijuana Mansion. Michael Straumietis made millions selling fertilizer for legal weed grows and has since become an Instagram celebrity, with an account consisting of photos of hot girls in bikinis, weed, private planes, mansions, and more weed.

When we arrived, there was a girl in a bikini sitting on an armored tank in the front yard. There were a couple of young kids sitting on the tank with her. I'm not quite sure where they came from. Walking into the waterfront mansion in Malibu, the crowd was exactly as I expected. Beautiful women, in patriotic bikinis barely covering their fake boobs, splashed around in the hot tub and pool while 20-something stoners moved glassy-eyed toward the back. There were a few bars on each floor, including a marijuana bar where girls in bikinis rolled you joints and packed you bong loads. Seemingly endless

supplies of king crab legs, oysters, and sushi were on an ice castle of sorts, and the rest of the buffet had pretty much anything you could desire. People were set up in the middle of the kitchen, making fresh ice cream for everyone to enjoy.

Nearly every conversation Jen and I had with people started the same way: "This is absolutely insane."

An industry town is an industry town, and depending on the industry, that's what most of the conversations end up being about. Since this was L.A., nobody was talking about their new app or their startup. Almost everyone worked in entertainment. Some were film producers, some were models, some were ... well, I'm not really sure. Everyone else there worked in the cannabis industry and was somehow connected to The Marijuana Don.

It's always interesting to see how other people live, whether they dress as Spiderman for a living or have a waterfront mansion paid for by weed fertilizer. San Francisco has a lot of different ways to live a life — 800,000 or so — but none of them were quite like what I experienced in L.A. Despite all the freakiness, though, it's always nice to come home.

MAKE AMERICA FINLAND
<small>SF Sounds; 2017</small>

In Finland, women on Tinder list all the languages they speak, which are at least Finnish, Swedish, and English — and often more. I imagine the men do as well, but I don't date men. That said, in the US, we're lucky if people don't spell "your" as "ur" on their profiles.

These are the things I think about and notice when I travel. And I travel a lot. Sometimes it's just for the sake of going somewhere new, but other times, it's for work. At that time, in late November/early December, I found myself in Helsinki, covering a tech conference called "Slush," of all things. What kind of idiot leaves California and goes to the Nordic region *during the winter*? Apparently, me, but it's hard to say no to a free trip.

Helsinki is a fantastic city. With excellent transit, beautiful old churches, and charming cobblestones, it's a treat for all your senses. It's also incredibly cold and dark during the winter. Throughout the entire week I was there, the temperature remained below freezing. The trickle from water drains becomes solid, and so does the puke on the sidewalk outside bars, which I surprisingly didn't see too much of — considering how big a drinking culture Finland has. You'd drink a lot too if you lived that far north. It's so cold and dark there in winter that there's even a word for drinking alone at home in your underwear. It's called *Kalsarikännit*. A very lovely Finnish woman taught me this before she came back to my hotel room, and we drank without wearing any underwear. God bless Tinder.

If you're attracted to white people, Finland is a magnificent place to be. There are a lot of them. And goddamn, they're good-looking. Plus, considering the dearth of sunlight, they don't really seem to age. Finland is quickly becoming more diverse, though. Recent waves of immigrants and refugees have added a bit more color to the traditional Nordic palette. This has led to some interesting results.

Finland is an incredibly progressive country, offering excellent, free education and healthcare, but an influx of people seeking work and/or asylum puts a strain on the social safety net due to the increased demand on resources. While there are the expected racist right-wingers who want to kick out all non-Finns, a fantastic organization called Startup Refugees is instead helping asylum seekers start their own businesses with the skills they came to

Finland with. In the one year they've been in existence, they've helped more than 40 refugee-owned and-operated businesses get off the ground. I literally raised a fist in the air in solidarity with them when I heard their representative, Camilla Nurm, give her presentation during Slush.

One thing I've learned is that most Americans who travel internationally are progressive, and most of us have such a huge wound inside of us right now that's painful to talk about. On two separate occasions, I became emotional when discussing the political situation in the United States. One instance was when talking to a group of journalists from around the world about Donald Trump's election as president. Explaining the sorrow, hurt, and fear on the left got me more emotional than I expected. The second time was when I was explaining the horrors of the Prison-Industrial Complex to a couple of Finnish friends. In Finland, prison is actually set up to rehabilitate people, unlike the United States, where private companies make billions of dollars from incarcerating a populace that is mostly poor and/or people of color. When I asked my friend Tuomas if cops in Finland carry guns, he said yes, but they seldom use them; the *police only fired six bullets in the entirety of 2013*. SIX!! (I actually researched this, and the Guardian UK substantiated the statistic). America really is #1... just mostly in the wrong things.

In the States, I'm considered a radical leftist (well outside of the Bay Area, anyway), but my beliefs are pretty standard in Northern Europe. If nothing else, my trip to Helsinki was proof that my ideals are achievable and are being implemented in other countries. Although the population of Finland is relatively small compared to the US, we have sufficient capital and resources to compensate for this. Finland is positioning itself to be a world leader in digital healthcare, and a significant number of startups receive seed funding from the government, rather than venture capitalists. Plus, healthcare is free. Their world-renowned free public education system, which already produces people fluent in three or more languages, will soon make learning to code compulsory for all students. And they support the arts! There are museums and galleries everywhere you look in Helsinki.

Of course, there are negatives to the Finnish system. Still, I'd rather pay more taxes and get more for them, and watch all

Jet Lagged, Hungover, & Homesick

Americans become better off, than watch as my country horrifically tears itself apart in late-stage capitalism.

Can we make a hat that says, "Make America More Finnish?" I'd rock the hell out of that thing.

ITALIAN GIRL IN DUBLIN
Love Notes & Other Disasters Zine; 2014

I love your tiny breasts
and the way they come to rest
on me when were naked and trying to catch our breath
and lying here beside you
makes me feel like I am special
cause we are both so lonely from following our devils
but lets not talk of things we've done
or lives we could've changed
let's just stay here whispering
and listening to the nighttime Irish rain

I traced your giant scar
from your belly to your sternum
but didn't ask you questions cause I was sure you always heard 'em
and you explained it anyway
a car wreck in the rain
said doctors took an organ but you don't know its English name
then you pointed to my beer belly
said none of us are perfect
i laughed out loud and kissed your neck
and we began another circuit
i watched you from the bed

While you smoked out of the window
and thought you looked like someone from a 1920's photo
all you wore were black socks
black thong and black turtleneck
the curtain partially covering you as you finished your last cigarette
then you came back to the bed
pulled down the covers and got in
i'll always remember that night and you
my Italian girl in Dublin

ACTIVISM IS NOT A CONTEST

Design by Lil' Tuffy. Photo by Chad Riley

(ACTIVISM)

Activism Is Not A Contest

While I've been involved in activism in some form or another since protesting the Iraq War in 2003, it wasn't until I ran for Mayor of San Francisco that I realized how important it was to be engaged on a local level. My mayoral campaign kicked off just after I began my Broke-Ass City column in the *San Francisco Examiner*, and so suddenly I was able to speak up about broken things in the world and The Bay and have a whole lot of people hear me.

I made a lot of enemies and haters, but I also gained many fellow travelers and co-conspirators. Considering that the process of putting together this book started before Trump's second term, all these pieces were written before the horrors that have taken place since he regained power. The only exception is the piece titled "I Didn't Cry in the Bar When Trump Won This Time."

The title of the chapter comes from a piece with the same name.

HOW TO LOSE AND ELECTION BUT WIN A CITY
Slouching Towards Neverland Zine; 2022

This was originally written for Vice and was twice as long. Considering how much I learned while running for Mayor, even that felt short. Vice ended up not taking the piece after a few months of going back + forth, making the piece managable. I feel like Vice and I have been flirting with each other my entire career.

Let me begin by saying I have absolutely no business being mayor of San Francisco. The only "public office" I've ever held was in high school, and I mainly used that as an excuse to get off campus so I could smoke pot. Beyond that, I recreationally use drugs like LSD, I drink more than I should, I'm a 35-year-old who lives with three roommates, and I can't balance a budget to save my life. And to top it off, I'm publicly known by the name Broke-Ass Stuart.

That's not to say I'm a lazy slacker; I've done some pretty cool things in my life. I've written three Broke-Ass Stuart travel books, created and hosted my own TV show (Young Broke & Beautiful on IFC), founded an influential arts & culture site (BrokeAssStuart.com), been a columnist at three publications, had my work translated into four languages, and been paid to travel the world and write about it. Still, none of that even remotely qualifies me to run a city with a $9 billion budget.

So what does that say that I still managed to get nearly 20,000 votes in the 2015 mayoral race? It says that San Francisco is a deeply fucked up place.

* * * *

Almost since its inception, San Francisco has been the place you went if you didn't fit in anywhere else. It's always been a haven for artists, queers, immigrants, refugees, writers, drag queens, communists, and anyone else who was "other." But over the last five years or so, the explosion of the tech industry and the resulting housing crisis have created a city that's tearing itself apart.

There have been record numbers of evictions, record numbers of homelessness, record numbers of local business closures, and all in the shadow of companies making record numbers of dollars.

When I read that a greedy pigfucker of a landlord was trying to evict a 98-year-old lady, I was finally like, "Alright, this shit has gone too far! Can't the dude wait two years? I mean, she's 98 for fuck's sake!" I assumed one of the established progressives would throw their hat into the ring to take on Ed Lee, San Francisco's "Tech Mayor", the man who has literally been selling SF to the highest bidder. When none of them did, I figured I might as well do it. What better way to stir shit up?

When I first considered running for mayor, it was 100% a publicity stunt. San Francisco has a great tradition of strange characters running for office, people like Jello Biafra, lead singer of the seminal punk band Dead Kennedys; Sister Boom Boom, member of drag nun activists the Sisters of Perpetual Indulgence; and Chicken John, an underground showman involved in marginal circuses and Burning Man.

Plus, there's a tradition of outsider writers, like Norman Mailer and Hunter S. Thompson, who've run for public office as well. It seemed like a no-brainer: I'd be taking part in a beautiful and ridiculous tradition. I'd also get to stick up for the city that I love while pushing important issues that people weren't talking about, and of course, pick up some new fans for all things Broke-Ass Stuart along the way.

Activism Is Not A Contest

* * * *

I was sitting in Nate Allbee's living room when the plan came together. As the campaign consultant, he and I had spent weeks trying to figure out the best way to go about it. Then, late one spring afternoon, while his dog was trying to hump my leg, it clicked: my entire run would be one giant gonzo media campaign. The goal was to use humor to make important points about shit that wasn't being paid attention to, and use my network of small business owners, media outlets, and local influencers to spread the information. We'd make funny videos and articles and pull pranks to keep people interested. On top of it all, I'd be writing about the whole thing as a journalistic experiment in my weekly Broke-Ass City column in the San Francisco Examiner.

When the May 21, 2015, issue of the SF Examiner came out with me on the cover announcing my mayoral run, all the madness started. After a couple of my columns came out, the Ethics Commission decided I could no longer write about my campaign in the Examiner, but the few that did get published helped immensely. People came out of the woodwork to get involved, and folks I'd only known peripherally before became an all-volunteer staff that used Mission Comics & Art as our campaign headquarters. We actually had one paid employee, Amiee Kushner, a former CFO, who became my campaign manager and treasurer. She was the only person we could afford to pay.

Yeah, money is a motherfucker, especially in a political campaign. Or rather, not having much of it is a motherfucker. Imagine spending a few hours each week calling everyone you know to ask for money. It's a hell of a thing to do, but unfortunately, it's the primary way campaigns are funded. I mean, sure, we threw lots of rad parties, but a huge chunk of the roughly $30,000 we raised came from sitting down with my phonebook while my campaign fundraiser, Marina Javor, plied me with whiskey and goaded me into calling people. And while $30k might seem like a lot of money, it's nothing considering Ed Lee raised something like $1.5 million before even officially announcing his run.

We focused on several key areas in the campaign, including corruption, affordable housing, and saving local businesses. Still, San Francisco is facing a homelessness epidemic, and because of this, there is literally human shit all over the streets and sidewalks in neighborhoods like SoMa and the Mission. While solving homelessness was obviously a more complicated issue, fixing the poop problem wasn't. All we needed to do was open more bathrooms, many of which already existed at BART and Muni stations and public parks but had been closed over the years. So, we used this as our launching point. For each plank of the platform, we wanted to put out an article, a video, and take some kind of action. Although I was no longer allowed to mention my campaign in the Examiner, I could still write about issues. I laid out a plan to fix SF's poop problem, which included going into City Hall and putting Out of Order signs on all the bathrooms that the Mayor and the Supervisors use. That way, they could feel the cramps of what it would be like to be homeless and not have anywhere to shit. Then we released a video to go along with the article and the prank. It went viral.

As it turned out, I wasn't the only one running against Ed Lee. There were five challengers in total, and three of us — Amy Farah Weiss, Francisco Herrera, and I — banded together to try and use ranked choice voting to get a larger percentage of the vote collectively. I won't go into explaining the labyrinthine process of ranked choice voting, but we created a movement called Vote 1-2-3 to Replace Ed Lee that garnered over 11,000 Facebook members! Have you ever heard about three people in the same race running a campaign together? Neither had we, nor had anyone else in San Francisco, for that matter, and because of this, the Vote 1-2-3 movement caught fire.

While the grassroots activism inspired by Vote 1-2-3 energized people into getting involved, my gonzo media campaign seemed to be inviting the attention we hoped for. Hundreds of businesses all over town had my posters in their windows, our videos were getting hundreds of thousands of views, and the pranks were keeping social media channels buzzing. Plus, many local media outlets and even some national ones started paying attention: There were stories about my campaign in the SF Chronicle and the LA Times, it was covered in tons of local blogs like SF Station and SFist, I was interviewed on the KPIX (CBS affiliate) Sunday morning news, I appeared on Live 105, four or five times, and AJ+ (Al Jazeera's main digital property) made a video about the campaign that was viewed over a million times on Facebook. That said, we had no idea how well we were doing, considering we couldn't afford any polls.

Activism Is Not A Contest

* * * *

In early October, the word came in: Ed Lee was going to debate me and the rest of the candidates. I'd been fucking with him for weeks on Twitter and my website, and I'd even gone to his office and taped a note to his door challenging him to a debate. When we finally got the word, he'd participate in the 2015 Mayoral Candidates Forum put on by the League of Women Voters, I honestly didn't believe he would show up. But he did, and while it was a forum and not a debate, the other candidates and I lit him up! While I got in a few solid zingers, it was really Amy Weiss who stole the show that night. She was ON FIRE! So much so that the Vote 1-2-3 Facebook group nearly doubled that week, and there was so much momentum that some people felt like maybe, just maybe, this ragtag grassroots opposition could actually dethrone the big tech money bankrolled machine.

There's an old tradition that on Election Day, a big lunch is thrown at the historic John's Grill for everyone involved in politics. Former mayor Willie Brown puts it on, and everyone from Lieutenant Governor Gavin Newsom to political junkie journalists like Tim Redmond shows up. This year, I was one of them. My girlfriend, Ashley, and I arrived early, having come straight from some early morning campaigning. As a result, we got to meet some other movers and shakers.

I was introduced to Lee Houskeeper, an old-school press agent, and he told me that Ron Conway was going to be there and that he'd introduce me to him. Conway is the evil tech billionaire who is using his money to buy SF and turn it into a playground only for the rich. He's also Mayor Ed Lee's major financial backer. I'd spent the past few months fucking with Conway on Twitter and even dressed up like him for Halloween (with an Ed Lee puppet, of course). It was election day, so I was wearing one of the "Beat Ed Lee" shirts that I'd been selling to raise money for the campaign, but since my jacket was buttoned, Conway couldn't see it when we were introduced. "Let me get a photo of you two," Houskeeper said, and as soon as I was on Conway's side, I unbuttoned my coat to reveal the shirt for the photo. It might be my favorite moment from the entire campaign.

We were at El Rio for the Election Night party when the results started rolling in. Hundreds and hundreds of people showed up to support, so many that I turned to Amiee and my Ashley, "Where were all these people when we needed them to show up for our fundraising events?"

"Come this way," Nate led a few of us down a hallway to check out the results on his phone. The drunk and rambunctious sounds of the crowd careened towards us as he revealed the preliminary results. "It's not looking good," he told Tom Temprano, his other client, who was running for the City College board. "And Stu looks like you're not gonna be mayor of San Francisco." A wave of relief washed over me as I headed to the stage to make my conciliatory speech.

When all the votes were finally tallied, I got 4th place with 18,211 votes, which is nearly 10% of the vote! Collectively, "Vote 1-2-3 to Replace Ed Lee" garnered almost 37% of the vote. In comparison, Mayor Ed Lee secured only 55%, a notably low number given the major media outlets' assertions that he was running uncontested and would win by a landslide.

While Ed Lee is still the mayor of San Francisco, we helped galvanize a ton of people who are now far more active in the community. Many of the members of the Vote 1-2-3 group are now involved in organizing efforts to tackle homelessness and hold City Hall accountable for things like corruption and the murder of Mario Woods. And since 2016 is a huge year for district races, the momentum of the group will be funneled into getting even more progressives on the Board of Supervisors. Everything said and done, running for mayor was the smartest dumb thing I've ever done in my life.

PUSSY HATS AND TRUMP HATS, IT'S TIME TO TALK
San Francisco Examiner; 2017

When this article came out someone called me a Nazi sympathizer on twitter because of it. I responded that being a Nazi sympathizer sure made things awkward for me every year at Passover with my family.

Activism Is Not A Contest

There is no shortage of heart-warming stories, sad anecdotes, and think-pieces about what went on last week in Washington, D.C. Some say this is the American Experiment finally taking an unrecoverable nosedive. Others say this is the start of the next grand social movement.

Having been roughly 30 rows back from where President Donald Trump was inaugurated and also having been in the thick of the Women's March, I'm still trying to piece together my final thoughts about what it all means. I can say I'm grateful to legendary press agent Lee Houskeeper for putting me up and getting me tickets to the inauguration. I'm thankful to my buddy Chef Ryan Scott for giving me airline miles to get out there. The rest of it I'm still digesting.

Of all the many people I met and the fascinating interactions I had, the most important one was at the airport right before I left to fly home. The airport that day was surreal. There seemed to be just as many Trump hats as there were Pink Pussy Power hats. Yet despite the intensity of the previous few days, everyone was behaving as if things were normal.

Sitting down next to a middle-aged white woman, I noticed her pink coat and asked if she'd been at the Women's March.

"No," she told me. "I know I look like it because of my coat, but I was bumped from a flight and just happened to be here. I'm on my way home to Minneapolis from Costa Rica."

We got to talking about the previous few days. I had told her how I'd gone out to D.C. specifically to protest the inauguration and to partake in the Women's March.

"Wow, that's neat," she said. "Are there women in your life that make you want to do that?"

"I was marching for all the women in my life and all the women in the world," I told her.

Things progressed from there. I told her I was an agnostic Jew; she told me she was a Christian who did missionary work and that she had a lot of respect and admiration for the Jewish religion.

"I don't have a problem with any kind of people other than Muslim terrorists," she said.

"All religions have extremists," I replied. "Even Christianity has terrorists. Just look at the KKK or the Westboro Baptist Church."

This blew her mind. "Wow, I never really thought about that."

We talked some more, and she told me how, in her previous job as a teacher, being white had excluded her from getting work because of hiring quotas. She followed that with, "But being a woman helped me get my current job in advertising because they were hiring for diversity."

On the other side of the woman I was talking to was another middle-aged white woman, with whom I began chatting when the first woman got up to use the restroom. She was a federal prosecutor, also from Minneapolis (that's where my connecting flight was), and had come to D.C. to participate in the Women's March with her daughter, who lived there.

Once the first woman returned, the three of us continued to talk about the Women's March. The second woman had been doing pro bono legal work for the Minneapolis Planned Parenthood for more than a decade. This led to her and me explaining to the first woman how little of what Planned Parenthood does is actually abortions. The first woman didn't know that most of what PP does is give free health care to men and women who can't afford it otherwise.

"That's so interesting," she said. "Nobody ever told me about that."

Shortly after that, we all boarded the flight, and I never saw either of them again. But it got me thinking ...

The only way we can start to make things better is by finding venues for us to have respectful and engaging conversations with people who might disagree with us. I don't know how or where, but I just know that being in an airport full of both people in Trump hats and people in Pussy hats is a very rare thing.

If one of you reading this wants to help facilitate these conversations, I will do everything I can to support them.

Activism Is Not A Contest

WHAT HAVING A BROTHER WITH SPECIAL NEEDS TAUGHT ME ABOUT SOCIALISM
San Francisco Examiner; 2020

I've got a special needs brother. He's high-functioning, and if you met him, all you would think is "Well, he's a strange and funny fellow," which he is. But he's also never going to be intellectually or emotionally older than a 12-year-old, even though he's currently in his late 30s.

From doctors to therapists to special schools, raising a kid like my brother nearly bankrupted my parents. I have distinct memories of my mom crying as she and my dad tried to figure out how they were going to pay for all his bills.

It took many years until my folks found an advocate who could navigate the labyrinthine healthcare system to get my brother on disability and SSI, meaning that now Medicare covers his medical bills. He receives a small stipend from the government to cover essential expenses like rent and food, as he is unable to work. And it took my folks even more years to finally be able to pay off the advocate because she was expensive, too.

I mean this in all seriousness: If my brother didn't have the family and the support system that he has, if he didn't have parents who were willing and, in a position, to fight tooth and nail for him, he would be one more disabled, unmedicated, desperate, heartbreaking and heartbroken homeless person that you pass every day on your way to work. He wouldn't have the opportunity to be a "strange and funny fellow."

This is not the American Dream. This is the American Nightmare. And it's far too common. Every person reading this knows someone who has been ruined by medical debt. Or has contributed to a GoFundMe to help someone whose medical bills are obscene. Or they have been afraid to go to the doctor because they simply couldn't afford it. And if you don't know someone who has, they just haven't told you because they've been ashamed.

Why is it that we keep voting for politicians who believe a corporation's right to make money is more important than our right to live and be healthy? Why is it that our government has no problem spending $2 trillion on a war in Afghanistan (which, according to the Afghanistan Papers, we knew we couldn't win), yet thinks funding

Universal Healthcare is impossible? Why have we allowed our government to practice socialism for corporations but tell us that wanting it for ourselves is un-American? It's time to stop being scared of the word socialism and start

realizing that our country already practices it. The fact that we have a postal system, roads to drive on, and firefighters to save us is because our tax dollars pay for them. That's a form of socialism.

And when our government gives tax breaks to corporations so that billion-dollar companies like Amazon and Netflix don't have to pay federal taxes, that's a form of socialism too. Our government gives subsidies to oil companies, factory farms, and retail megastores like Walmart, making it so our taxes cover their financial losses. Yet, they get to keep their financial gains. As the saying goes, "Socialism for the rich and capitalism for the poor." It sure doesn't sound fair to me.

The socialism Bernie Sanders is offering is democratic socialism. It's not Stalin, it's Sweden. It's a chance to live in a country where people don't die or go bankrupt because they can't afford health care, where 23-year-olds aren't saddled with $100K in debt just because they wanted to go to college. Where the federal government partners with cities to alleviate the housing and homelessness crises by helping to build more government-owned affordable housing.

Last week, news broke that 22 separate studies concluded that Medicare for All would be the cheapest and most effective way to fix our broken healthcare system. According to a study by Yale University, the University of Florida, and the University of Maryland, Medicare for All would "save $450 billion per year — about $2,400 in annual savings per family — and would prevent more than 68,000 unnecessary deaths each year." While you should check out Bernie Sanders' website for a further breakdown of how all these things are paid for, the short answer is by making the billionaires and corporations finally pay their fair share.

Our tax dollars shouldn't be used to make billionaires and corporations richer; they should be used to take care of us, even if that is called socialism.

After all, the whole point of socialism is to make sure people like my brother don't fall through the cracks.

Activism Is Not A Contest

WHY WOULD ANY JEW BE A REPUBLICAN?
San Francisco Examiner; 2019

IN CASE You don't Know, I'm Ethnically + Culturally Jewish

I completely get why so many rich, white, straight, Christian men are Republicans. The party's ethos is devoted to serving that segment of the population. What I don't understand is why anybody else would be one.

Why would working-class people support the GOP when it creates laws that give tax cuts to the rich, while taking services away from the poor? Why would people of color be Republicans when the party has done everything in its power to undermine the socioeconomic advancement of black and brown people? Why would queer people join the GOP when they continually try to deny the LGBTQ+ community their civil rights? Why would women vote for men who don't want them to have autonomy over their own bodies?

As a Jew, a loud, obnoxious one at that, I'm also repeatedly flabbergasted that other Jews are Republicans. I'm not talking about the people who believe in small government and lower taxes – while I disagree with them, we can have a dialogue about our ideological differences. It's the entire rest of the party that is so vile.

If you're a Jew, your ancestors were kicked from country to country for 2000 years. If you're an American Jew, there's a 75 percent chance that your ancestors fled Europe to get away from pogroms, Nazis, and other murderous things. The people who are coming to America now as refugees are fleeing the same types of evils our ancestors did. To know that some of my fellow Jews support the camps at the border, and support raids that take parents away from their children, and don't see the similarities between what happened in Nazi Germany and what's happening now...well, it sickens my soul. But the fact that there are Jews who still support Donald Trump after he refuses to condemn white men marching in Charlottesville, chanting "Jews will not replace us!" ...well, that wrecks my head. Anti-Semitism doesn't get any more blatant than that.

Just this week, Donald Trump promoted himself as "King of Israel" on Twitter – yes, really. And he also pulled out a tired antisemitic trope when he said that Jews who vote for Democrats are disloyal. The dog whistle here is that Jews are never loyal to any country they are in and that they are constantly working to overthrow it. Yet, somehow, there are Jewish people who still back this insane bigot.

Luckily, for my peace of mind, most Jews do not support the white supremacy pushed by the GOP. Nor do they back the Golem of hate that sits in the Oval Office. A total of 71 percent of Jews voted for Hillary Clinton in 2016, which is a substantial number, and I imagine that if that election happened today, it would be even higher.

Despite the vast majority of Jews despising the Trump Administration – and their fascist actions — the lying, sniveling, hate-filled GOP keep hiding behind their "Jewish friends" when they do or say something racist.

When Donald Trump got backlash for finger-mashing out tweets calling for four congresswomen of color to "go back" where they came from, he then raised up the specter of anti-Semitism to defend himself. In further tweets, he called the congresswomen "Anti-Semitic," "Anti-America," "Anti-Israel," and "Pro Al-Qaeda."

Just last week, Ilhan Omar and Rashida Tlaib (two of the congresswomen told to "go back") were denied the ability to visit Israel and Palestine because Trump encouraged the country's Prime Minister, Benjamin Netanyahu, to bar them. Both congresswomen have been highly critical of the Trump and Netanyahu administrations, and they've endorsed the Boycott, Divestment, and Sanctions (BDS) Movement as a way to curb Israeli aggression towards the Palestinian people. Senator Lindsey Graham used this as an opportunity to try to score points by hiding behind anti-Semitism, saying, "If you openly joined an international movement to destroy the state of Israel, then you'll suffer the consequences." As these congresswomen have been vocal about the horrific things the US government is doing, Graham is trying to punish them by saying they are anti-Israel and, therefore, antisemitic.

This is problematic in so many ways.

First off, you can be critical of Israel and be critical of the United States without being antisemitic. I do it every day. Trust me, there is plenty to be critical about both places (that's for an entirely different article, though).

Secondly, American Jews don't represent Israel, and Israel doesn't represent us.

Thirdly, and probably most importantly, these racists don't actually care about Jews or Israel. The Republican Party only started caring about Jews and Israel (which they equate as the same thing) around the time George W. Bush got elected. A large portion of Evangelical Christians believe an interpretation of Revelations that says the Jews need to be in Israel for the Second Coming of Christ to occur. Since it was with Bush's election that Evangelicals became a serious power in the Republican Party, Israel suddenly became important to the GOP.

It was 9/11 that made the rest of the GOP care about Israel because suddenly they were the United States' ally (or pawn) in the never-ending War on Terror.

So to my fellow Jews who still somehow support this ugliness, I'm asking you to wise up and realize when you're being manipulated by people who honestly don't care about your well-being.

IF YOU SUPPORT THE DETENTION CAMPS, YOU'RE A BAD PERSON
San Francisco Examiner; 2019

Driving down Interstate 10 toward the hotel, I could see the border wall running alongside the Rio Grande. It seemed to trail off into the distance further than last time I'd been in town, but that could just be because I wasn't paying as much attention.

This was not my first time in El Paso, Texas. My grandma, mom, and brother were all born there, and I lived there from ages 2 to 7. Since moving to California in the 80s, I'd been back at least once a year, but this time might very well be my last. I'd flown to El Paso to bury my grandma, our matriarch, and with most of the family now living in California, there won't be much of a reason to go back.

El Paso is the ultimate border town. Until recently, people talked about the El Paso/Juarez region as a singular place, but after the cartel wars in the 2000s, things changed. The fluidity of the border tightened, and many Americans stopped crossing. Now, El Paso is making headlines for a different reason: thousands of immigrants fleeing horrific circumstances are ending up in internment camps there. The conditions are inhumane. Children are being taken from their parents and held in savage conditions, while Fox News and Trump convince the Right that this is a just punishment for parents fleeing massacres and war.

Sitting on my grandma's living room floor with my family, sifting through boxes of old photos, postcards, letters, and ephemera dating back over 100 years, I began thinking about my own family's immigrant story and how we came to be Jewish from El Paso.

My great-grandfather, Lazar Kopilowitz, was born in Pokroi, Lithuania, a small Jewish *shtetl* that was part of the Tsarist Russian Empire. Tired of the terror of Cossacks and pogroms and fearing conscription into the Russian army to fight in WWI, he took what money he had and began walking East. He ended up walking all the way East, eventually taking a boat to Japan, and from there to Hawaii, ultimately landing in San Francisco on November 1, 1915. One of his first jobs in America was helping to dismantle the Panama–Pacific International Exposition. His other job was working as a busboy for $15 a month plus room and board.

Great Granddad Lazar Kopilowitz

Lazar eventually saved enough money to head to New Jersey, where he worked in a relative's candy store and learned English. Once the U.S. joined the war, he found himself in the Army, which was somewhat ironic considering he had left Europe to stay out of the Russian one. In the Army, he contracted tuberculosis, and since this was 1919, the best treatment they had for it was "go live someplace warm and dry and work outside." Leaving the East Coast, Lazar headed to Fort Bayard, New Mexico. Still, before he did so, he was brought before the Supreme Court and naturalized as a US citizen, along with other foreign nationals who'd served in the Army. That's how simple it was to become a citizen back then.

I'm telling you all this to make a point, but before I do so, let me give you a very truncated version of the rest of the story. Lazar ended up staying in the Southwest. In 1921, he brought over his childhood sweetheart, Lillian, who was my great-grandmother, and shortly after, they established a goat farm in Deming, New Mexico. Realizing they wanted to raise their family among other Jews, they relocated the goat farm to El Paso, where there was a Rabbi and a congregation. They had three daughters — one of whom was my grandma Blanche — and of the three girls, two married men who came to work at what had become a dairy cow farm. By the time they sold the family business in the 1970s, The Wholesome Dairy was one of the largest dairies in the Southwest. Lazar Kopilowitz truly achieved the American dream.

My great-grandfather's story is a remarkable one, but not unique. This is a country founded by immigrants, and those of us who've had the privilege of being born here grew up hearing stories about the sacrifices and journeys our ancestors made to create a better life.

And this is the part that I can't seem to wrap my head around. During the few days I was in El Paso, I talked to other people whose family immigration stories were similar — they began with fleeing persecution and violence. Yet some of these people still somehow supported the camps.

As we were grieving, I was on my best behavior, following the golden rule of "Don't start no shit, won't be no shit," but I wanted to take a moment to address this now.

Let me be unequivocal: there is no argument you can make that justifies separating children from their parents. There is also no argument you can make that justifies depriving people of fundamental human rights and dignity.

Those of you saying "They are criminals because they came here illegally" are misinformed. The vast majority of the people coming across the border are seeking asylum because they're fleeing violence in Central America. This is not illegal. The United Nations Universal Declaration of Human Rights states that "Everyone has the right to seek and to enjoy in other countries asylum from persecution." Just like my great-grandfather, Lazar Kopilowitz, these people are leaving untenable situations because they have no choice. Think about it like this: how bad would things have to get for you to leave everything you know behind, and show up in another country without a penny to your name?

Those of you saying, "Well, it was worse under Obama," are also misinformed. While it is true that there were more deportations under the Obama administration, it was Trump's senior policy advisor, Stephen Miller, who came up with the "Zero Tolerance" policy that separates families at the border. Regardless, that's a stupid argument anyway: "It's ok to do it because the other guy did it" is a weak-ass excuse for putting children in subhuman conditions.

Those of you saying, "They should do it the right way like my family did," are not only misinformed, but you're also arguing in bad faith. I know for a fact that my great-grandfather became a legal citizen because we found his naturalization papers while cleaning out my grandmother's belongings. How many of you who argue "They should do it the right way like my family did" can say the same? How many of you have the paperwork proving that your ancestors came here and became legal citizens? Do you have the name of the boat they came in on? How about the port? The thing is, none of that actually matters because there's a very good chance that when your ancestors showed up, we didn't really have a "right way."*

Congress didn't pass the National Origins Act until 1924. Before that, you could just show up, and if you weren't diseased, you were let in. The idea of "illegal immigrants" is actually a relatively new concept in our country. Still, even that shouldn't matter, considering that the United States committed genocide against the Native Americans just to get our "sweet land of liberty."

What I'm getting at is this: the camps at the border are not only unjust, they are evil. There is not a single good argument that can prove otherwise. If you support them, you're a bad person.

My great-grandfather came to the United States because otherwise he would've been killed. There's a good chance your ancestors came here for the same reason. How can you deny that opportunity to someone fleeing something equally horrific and still be considered a good person? The answer is: you can't.

Activism Is Not A Contest

*That is, of course, unless you were Chinese and it was between 1882 and 1943, when the US government adhered to the Chinese Exclusion Act, which forbade Chinese immigration. Or unless you were one of the thousands of Jews turned away in the 1930s because FDR was afraid they could be Nazi spies or Bolsheviks. Those Jews went back to Europe and died in the Holocaust.

MAYBE WE NEED TO RE-BRAND SOCIALISM
San Francisco Examiner; 2018

I'm a Democratic socialist. I know some of you just sneered reading that sentence, which is totally justifiable because I'm sure you're a billionaire and Democratic socialists want to raise your taxes.

Oh, you're not? Well, surely, you must at least be a multimillionaire.

No, not even a millionaire, and you're seriously bandying around the idea that socialism is evil and wrong?

Not to sound patronizing, and this honestly comes from a place of compassion, but you've been duped. Hoodwinked. Hornswoggled. Taken for a ride. Swindled. Bamboozled.

My friends, you've been lied to. The idea that capitalism and the free market will fix everything is a myth made up by those who stand to gain the most from us believing it. The truth is that capitalism is what has gotten us to this awful place in history — and things are only getting worse.

Why do I refer to this era as awful? Just look around: The environment is falling apart, jobs are being replaced by automation, people can't afford health care, and income inequality has reached staggering heights. Oxfam just published a study that found 82 percent of the wealth created in 2017 went to the top 1 percent. And these are the individuals who somehow manage to continue receiving tax breaks. Someone who makes $1 million a year is making $83,333 a month; why on Earth should their taxes be lowered?

Now, I know the word socialism sounds scary. Growing up in the United States, we've had it beaten into us that socialism is evil and leads to things like the USSR and Cuba. And to be honest, socialism could stand a little rebranding. Maybe, instead of calling it socialism, we should call it "health-care-and-education-for-you-and-your-kids-ism." Because that's what it is.

Democratic socialism is Sweden, not Stalin. It's the idea that, by making the ultra-wealthy pay a lot more taxes and the rest of us pay a little more in taxes, we can have things like great free health care, excellent free education, fair payment for the work we do, and security for when those jobs disappear.

Unless your job covers your health care — which is less than 50 percent of Americans, according to the Kaiser Family Foundation — you're probably already paying far more for your health insurance than you'd be paying in total taxes if this country had universal health care. And if you want bright, well-educated kids who can compete globally, a good, well-funded free education is a must.

Just look at Finland: By heavily investing in public schools, students not only end up speaking at least three languages fluently by the time they graduate, but they're also now learning how to code, starting in kindergarten. And they don't have any student debt after college. In fact, people in most developed countries leave university without debt.

Our current predatory system, allowed to flourish because "capitalism and the free market will save us," has gotten us to a place where regular Americans end up assuming crushing school and health care debt. And, of course, those who already have money are getting even richer by investing in the health care and educational institutions to which the rest of us are indebted.

Now, how is that fair?

The U.S. government is currently giving welfare to multibillion-dollar corporations in the form of subsidies and tax cuts. Don't you think that would be better spent on citizens instead of some of the most profitable companies in the history of the world?

I'm not alone in my beliefs.

Socialism is having one of its most significant rises in popularity since the labor movements of the early 20th century. And look what that got us: weekends, eight-hour work days, workers' compensation, and oodles of other laws that protect us from rapacious bosses — even if some people have spent the past 40 years undermining these laws and trying to give more power and profits to those at the top.

So, don't let the bogeyman scare you. Don't be afraid of a word

Activism Is Not A Contest

that's been given a bad rap by the greed monsters who don't want to pay their taxes. Join the Democratic Socialists of America today and get involved; there are local chapters all over. Together we can make this country work for all of us, not just the 1 percent.

That's what socialism is about after all.

I'M DISGUSTED BY THE CORPORATIZATION OF PRIDE
San Francisco Examiner; 2017

> *This piece is especially poignant after watching most of these corporations back down from supporting Pride in order to appease Trump. Fucking cowards!*

"Pride reminds me of the America I want to live in," I said to whomever was next to me. I was standing near Fourth and Market, a few vodka Red Bulls in, and watching as the beautiful, multi-hued, heartfelt people of Glide accompanied their float. Rainbow flags stretched down San Francisco's main artery as far as anyone could see, and the crowd was so full of love and, well, Pride that it was hard not to fall head over heels for this messy and complicated city all over again.

This year, as nefarious Republicans tried to dismantle health care, give tax breaks to the wealthy, and pass anti-LGBTQ laws, Pride felt especially significant. It was a beacon, screaming, "We will not go backward. Everyone deserves equality, justice, and love."

Then the Walmart float went by.

"Fuck this shit," I said to my friends Matt and Alyssa. And all the screaming and cheering that had echoed down the thoroughfare for grassroots organizations, like the Berkeley Free Clinic and Swords to Plowshares, noticeably diminished. How am I supposed to cheer for a company that pays its employees so little that some stores hold food drives for them during the holidays? The irony wasn't lost on us that the International Brotherhood of Electrical Workers passed by shortly afterward with only a fraction of the marchers that Walmart had.

The corporatization of Pride is a strange thing. On one hand, the money that big corporations like Chipotle, Facebook, and Apple pay each year helps fund the day of festivities that so joyously heartens our city. It's also crucial that these corporations demonstrate their support for their LGBTQ employees. The visibility of Fortune 500 companies supporting their queer workers is integral to the movement toward equity and equality.

But also, this is San Francisco. Being pro-gay is, at the very minimum, a great PR move. If these companies really wanted to show that they believed in LGBTQ equality and women's rights and that no human is illegal and that Trans and Black lives matter, they'd put their money where their mouth is.

Burger King's rainbow crowns and burger wrappers are cute. Budweiser's rainbow beer bottle advertising is just darling. But honestly, fuck them. Fuck all of them.

Don't use the struggle for human dignity and the fight for access to equal treatment and safety as some marketing ploy. If these companies really gave a shit, they'd instead be spending that money on giant billboards in Mississippi that say: "Budweiser supports marriage equality and thinks the new law you're trying to pass is really mean." Burger King should identify the districts of everyone voting for TrumpCare and take out ads saying: "Our customers deserve health care to cover the maladies they get from eating our food." And Walmart should just start paying its employees living wages.

The morning of San Francisco Pride 2017, I read about the bravery of the people in Istanbul who gathered despite the ban on their Pride parade. At risk to themselves and their loved ones, they showed up to say, "We won't be silenced and we won't go back into the closets." It was the same sentiment that launched the gay pride parades in San Francisco and New York all those decades ago. And even though it seems like we've come a long way, we still have politicians trying to pass laws that are horribly anti-LGBTQ.

The message of Pride is just as important now as it was then.

So, I've got an idea for the Pride organizers in major cities like San Francisco, New York, Chicago, Los Angeles, and anywhere else where major corporate money is used to advertise: Insist that these companies spend an equal amount of money promoting equality in regions where the message needs to be heard. In San Francisco, we already know that love is love. I'd like to see Walmart promote that same message in Arkansas, where they're from.

WHY WE'RE MARCHING IN THE STREETS
San Francisco Examiner; 2016

"I'm just so tired of having to do this," I told Kaeli. We were marching up Market Street, toward the Castro, with a crowd of 4,000 other people. "How many times have we done this? I mean, even this year, we've been out in the streets a dozen times."

It was the evening after Donald Trump was elected the next president of the United States, and both Kaeli and I were exhausted. Mentally, physically, emotionally, we were suspended in a state of weary disbelief.

"But this time ..." Kaeli responded, "I can't believe what we are protesting. It's still hard for me to wrap my mind around the fact that he won."

Walking up Market that night, amongst the chanting and the yelling and the crying and the singing, it felt like all the things we'd been fighting for over the past years had suddenly fallen apart. We'd marched against police violence, against homelessness, against oil pipelines, against evictions. We'd shouted that Black lives did, in fact, matter. As did Trans ones. And that no humans were illegal. We'd held candles on our slow stride to City Hall when our queer brothers and sisters were murdered in a nightclub in Orlando. And that night, as we tried to find the energy to keep shouting "Fuck Trump," it was like we were marching for all of those things at once. The weight of it was almost unbearable.

But it still didn't stop us. Even though we were tired and grieving and heartbroken, the people on the receiving end of Trump's hate speech — and on the receiving end of hate crimes perpetrated by his emboldened supporters — don't have the luxury of stopping. People of color, queer people, immigrants, and Muslims don't get to check out from being marginalized when they are tired. So, there we were, people of all ethnicities, religions, genders, ages, abilities, and income levels, marching up Market Street as allies and co-conspirators.

That was why so many of us were in the streets and why we

continue to be. We do so not just to protest what has already happened, but also to stand against what has yet to occur. We march as a statement that says, "This man who espouses homophobia, racism, sexism, and xenophobia does not represent me." We march because of the rising occurrence of hate crimes, and because we must defend one another, and because we can't allow this ugliness to become normalized.

That night, we marched because we didn't know what else to do.

For so many people, Trump winning was more than demoralizing; it was the absolute unraveling of reality. Suddenly, our neighbors, friends, and family members were not the people we thought they were. The ideals that we knew our country stood for proved to be empty, valueless lies. Hate had unfathomably triumphed over love and destroyed our notions of who we were. For more than sixty million people, the definition of what it meant to be an American changed in the blink of an eye.

Or at least it did for many "good" white folks, including myself. People who are used to being kicked know what a boot looks like, so those who've been treated as second-class citizens by this country for years, decades, centuries ... well, those people knew the score. While they might have been feeling grief and heartbreak, what they weren't feeling was surprise. They woke up Wednesday morning to the same America they'd gone to sleep in every single night they'd lain their head down in this country.

For many white people, though, it was the first time they realized they were complicit in all this oppression, simply because they benefited from it. Just being one of the "good" white people wasn't enough. The entire goddamn system, from schooling to lawmaking to policing to city planning, was set up to keep them benefiting from their whiteness. It was rotten and decaying from the inside, and, suddenly, for the first time in their lives, they could smell it, too.

As we neared the Castro that Wednesday night, I looked around and took in the crowd. I saw many of the same allies I'd protested with for years. But there were also new ones, younger ones, many of whom were in high school. Seeing the sheer number of them and witnessing their burning indignation gave me hope.

This is precisely why we march in the streets: Times are dark right now, but if the future is anything like those young people who are protesting all over the nation, a change might really, finally, actually come.

Activism Is Not A Contest

LET'S TAKE A KNEE ON THE NFL
San Francisco Examiner; 2017

Since writing this piece there has been a number of allegations that Shaun King misappropriated a lot of the money he raised over the years. Just thought I'd let you know I'm aware of it before you send me angry emails about it.

I must preface this column by letting you know that I'm basically sports agnostic. I'll watch a game if it's on in front of me, but I don't really care who wins or loses.

I think it's exciting when the Warriors win the NBA championship, and I think it isn't very comforting when people burn Muni buses when the Giants win the World Series. As a bartender, I love it when our teams are in the playoffs because my fellow barkeeps and I make stupid money for a few weeks. But if all professional sports ended tomorrow, I'd just shrug and go on with my life.

I nearly boycott the NFL every year, simply by accident, so that this year won't change much for me. But since I'm about to ask you to boycott the NFL, too, I want to acknowledge how much it means to many of you: I'm sorry something that brings you so much joy (or pain, depending on how your team fares) is such a rotten, manipulative, and racist organization.

Let's be honest, from suppressing research surrounding the brain damage many players leave the league with, to not paying taxes on its billions of dollars of profit because it passed itself off as "nonprofit" until 2015, the NFL has always been a shady-ass organization. The league's treatment of Colin Kaepernick, though, takes it from being underhanded and conniving to outright racist.

There's a long list of rapists, wife beaters, and dog fighters who the NFL has treated with a "boys will be boys" attitude. Still, Kaepernick's silent protest against police violence was somehow enough to get him blackballed from the league entirely.

Let that sink in: There's video of Ray Rice knocking his girlfriend out, and the NFL's initial reaction was a two-game suspension. Michael Vick went to jail for running a dog-fighting ring — in fact, he spent more time in jail than the police officer convicted of killing Oscar Grant, but that's another story — and he came back to the league as a starting quarterback. But Kaepernick's decision not to stand for the national anthem effectively got him kicked out of the NFL.

Even if you disagree with his actions, you can't say it's fair. And don't give me that shit about it being based on his performance or skill as a player. As the Guardian UK points out, "there are still 11 current starting QBs in the league who are objectively worse than Kaepernick," and that, judging by statistics, he is "currently better than a third of the starting QBs in the league."

As Shaun King, the activist and journalist who initially called for the NFL boycott, notes, all of the NFL team owners are white, and at least seven of them gave $1 million or more to Donald Trump's campaign. King goes on to say, "These white men hate Colin, like Donald Trump hates Colin, and like Trump hates Obama, because they cannot believe a black man stepped into power without their permission."

I love you, Bay Area. I love you like you love your sports teams. And one of the main reasons I love you is that one of our core values is sticking up for people who can't always stick up for themselves. That is precisely what Kaepernick was doing when he took a knee, and that is exactly why we should have his back. Because police violence against black and brown people is real, and it's heartbreaking and terrifying. Just ask Michael Bennett.

Here is my ask: Will you join me and thousands of others in boycotting the NFL? You can't call Muhammad Ali a hero for boycotting the Vietnam War and not support Kaepernick. You can't look with admiration at the image of Tommie Smith and John Carlos raising their black-gloved fists at the 1968 Olympics and not see the importance of Kaepernick's silent and peaceful protest.

What we do with our money matters, and nothing angers billionaires more than when you stop giving them yours. So stop doing it. Avoid going to games or watching them on TV. Don't buy any NFL merchandise. Cancel any subscriptions that give the NFL money.

I know this sucks and that it might fundamentally change what you do with your Sundays, but think about all the things you will suddenly have time to do instead. Plus, think about how much this will piss off Trump.

THE DEMOCRATIC PARTY IS DEAD TO ME
San Francisco Examiner; 2016

I wrote this the morning after Trump won in 2016. I still feel the Democratic Party is a piece of shit. Unfortunately the only thing worse than it is the Republican Party.

As I write this, it is a beautiful day in San Francisco. It's in the mid-60s and will probably reach the 70s. This is gorgeous weather — possibly perfect — but it doesn't matter. There is a dark and inconsolable cloud hovering over this city like a funeral veil.

On election night, I was at El Rio. We watched the TVs and drank and soft-laughed, trying to push away the gnawing feeling that tragedy was waiting for us just around the corner. And it was, with a bludgeon the size of nearly 60 million scared and angry white voters. I was about to order a drink when I looked up and saw nothing on the screen.

"Hey, why's the TV off?" I asked Astrid Kane.

"It's over," they responded. "They turned it off."

"Wait, what do you mean?" I couldn't quite process it. "Are you fucking with me?"

"I wouldn't joke about this."

I felt my face fall from confusion to desolation, and I crumpled, weeping into Astrid's chest as they hugged me. I don't cry very often, especially not in public, but there I was, gushing a river in the middle of El Rio while the low hum of heartbreak passed through the crowd.

This whole time, we thought the 2016 Election was the end of the Republican Party when, in actuality, it's the end of the Democratic one. Those of us who fought hard and banged and yelled, mean as hell for Bernie Sanders ... well, we got took. When finally there was a candidate who was sick of the corporate shill job that is the Democratic Party, the DNC did all it could to bury him. They obfuscated his message because it was Hillary's turn, goddammit, and they didn't build this system to work for them just so that a socialist Jew from Vermont could actually deliver on the promises they'd been breaking for all these years.

Looking back now, it's like it was pulled straight from Dostoevsky's "Grand Inquisitor."

They sabotaged Bernie and then made us feel bad about it, selling us on apocalyptic damnation, to scare us into line. They got us like the suckers we are, but apparently just didn't do a good enough job.

This was not a case of the "Silent Majority." No, this was the unsilent one. The loud, obnoxious one. The onerous one. The terrifying one. The one that represents the dark side of all these truths that we hold to be self-evident. Because it is devastatingly clear that we are not all created equal, not in the eyes of this country, not in the eyes of nearly 60 million people who voted to elect a man who grabs women by the pussy while calling Mexicans rapists. This is who the fuck we are as a country, and it is harrowing.

I can barely look at myself in the mirror.

I didn't stand there in El Rio, weeping into Astrid Kane's shirt, because I gave a shit about Hillary Clinton. I cried for us. I cried for those of us who knew better but went along with it anyway. I cried for those of us who towed the party line out of fear instead of principle. I cried for all my brothers and sisters who are queer, or black, or Latino, or Muslim, or Jewish, or anything but chickenshit, scared white people. I cried because I realized that this election wasn't about democracy or making the world a better place; it was about who could do a better job of scaring citizens into voting.

And the Democratic machine couldn't even do that right.

So, I'm done. I'm out. You lost us, many, many of us. I don't mean I'm done fighting for justice, equality, and equity — hell no. I'm done with the Democratic Party, if there still is one. And now that I'm done crying, it's time to pick up the pieces and keep pushing. There's a whole lot of ugliness on the horizon, and we've got work to do.

And one last thing: Fuck you, Donald Trump.

Activism Is Not A Contest

I DIDN'T CRY IN THE BAR WHEN TRUMP WON THIS TIME
Previously Unpublished

I was actually afraid to go to El Rio last night, which is a terrible feeling considering it's one of my favorite bars in the world. My wife and I had our first kiss there and even had our wedding reception under the twinkling string lights of its spacious backyard. I love that bar.

But I really didn't want to be there for Election Night. I didn't want to jinx things. I've spent far too many Election Nights at El Rio, watching as candidates and propositions I believed in lost at the ballot box, and it's broken my heart. I was there in 2016 when Trump won the first time, and found myself weeping, snotty, sniveling into Astrid Kane's shirt.

I didn't cry in a bar last night, though. In 2016, most of us were blindsided by Trump's win and the seething anger and resentment that his campaign had unleashed. Not this time. We've spent the past eight years watching it grow while right-wing media and influencers fed the petty hate machine. Horrible things that would've tanked any campaign ten years ago were uttered every week to a crowd who either cheered along or simply shrugged. We knew what was at stake this time; we'd already survived one Trump presidency and been subjected to three of his harrowingly vile campaigns. And while the constant debasement was no longer shocking, we were still able to think, maybe, finally, this will wake people up.

Nothing did. Not the convictions, not the rape, not the easily debunked lies, not the insane yammering about immigrants eating pets, not the simulating of a blow job on a microphone, nothing. Not a fucking thing could change the mind of his followers. Somehow, they actually seemed to grow. As we see today, Trump at least didn't lie about one thing: he really could shoot someone on a crowded street and not lose any voters. In fact, they'd probably justify it by saying the person was transgender or an immigrant or a journalist or a Democrat.

* * * *

Yesterday, while walking to the Election Day Luncheon at John's Grill, I watched a construction worker apply a Trump sticker to his hard hat on Market Street in the middle of San Francisco during Election Day.

He did it slowly and precisely, reveling in the act as people passed by on the way to vote, or get lunch, or get high.

It struck me that right here, in the center of San Francisco, someone who was very likely a union member was proud to be voting for Trump, a person who has been vocally anti-union for his entire life. That's when I knew we were fucked.

For anyone who's been paying attention, it's evident that working-class people have been moving to the right for a long time. Decades really. But it's really been during Trump's reign of error that the shift has become so complete.

I blame the Democratic Party. (I also blame the social media platforms for allowing themselves to be manipulated just to make shareholders wealthier, but that's for a different essay.) To be honest, I despise both parties. The Democratic party has a terrible history of racism, sexism, homophobia, Islamophobia, antisemitism, xenophobia, etc., and the only thing worse than it is the Republican party. The difference is that the GOP is willing to exploit anything to win. They realized a long time ago that if you win, you get to call the rules of the next game. And if you push the bullshit a little further each time, and you keep winning, you can fool the other team into playing by rules that you no longer even pretend to follow. Just ask Al Franken.

Since the Democrats have decided to play as the good guys, there's no way they could've won. You can't win a game where the other team doesn't follow the rules. And the thing is, none of us really gave a fuck if they were the good guys or not. We want affordable housing, healthcare that won't bankrupt us, education that won't give us crippling debt, food that won't poison us, and corporations that won't buy elections. Being the good guys, the respectable party, wasn't going to win this election, and right now there's gonna be a lot of finger-pointing – people blaming Jill Stein or blaming pro-Palestinian protesters. You know what would've won this election, though? Giving people the things I just listed above. That's because these are all the same things Trump's voters want too.

I don't hate his followers. To a large extent, I feel where they're coming from. We've all been so thoroughly screwed over by the wealthy and the corporations and both political parties that we should all be on the same side. We should be collectively pulling down the exploitative system that keeps us struggling while the 1% get richer and richer. The right calls them "elites," and the left calls them billionaires. But they are the same thing. And that's why Trump won. Because he knows that, or at least the people in charge of him do.

Divide and conquer. It's the oldest trick in the book. Convincing people that the person on the rung below them is the cause of their problems, while you're the one actually harming them, has been the key to success for tyrants for millennia. It's how fascists get their followers to do unspeakable things. And Trump, being the natural predator that he is, is the perfect candidate for fascism. It's just bewildering how successful he's been at it, considering he's an absolute buffoon.

As a Jewish person, I hate Hitler, but at least he and Mussolini had pizzazz. Trump is a sloppy, orange mess who still hasn't figured out how to do his makeup right despite wearing it every day for decades. But a fascist he most certainly is. He's been telling us he is one all along, even saying he will be a dictator on his first day in office.

The GOP has already taken the White House and the Senate. If they take the House of Representatives, this will have been our last real election. Sure, they'll let us pretend our votes still matter, but they will gerrymander, pass laws, stack the Supreme Court, and make it so that anyone who isn't like them can never win again. They've even told us they're going to do this. It's called Project 2025.

So where do we go from here?

To be honest, I don't fully have all the answers, but I just saw something posted by my friends at Indecline that said this:

• Fascism is deathly allergic to compassion and empathy. Fascism hates joy as an act of resistance. Never forget that.

• Take the time you need to reset. Get outside. Get your closest friends around a table of food. Let your emotions get the better of you, but don't let them turn you apathetic. Read, exercise, fuck, and remember, we are ungovernable.

After that, we have to organize, collectivize, and build up solidarity networks to look after each other. And then, most importantly, we have to figure out how to reach across the divide. We need to find ways to get all those people in MAGA hats to realize that a better world isn't made by demonizing other working people, no matter where they come from, who they love, or what gender they are. The only people we need to take our country back from are the corporations and billionaires who profit off our struggle and suffering.

* * * *

After spending a few hours at another Election Night party, we ended up going to El Rio after all. We knew the jig was up. We knew Trump was going to win, and the Senate was also lost. But we wanted to end the night with our allies from so many other political struggles.

This time, there was no weeping. Sure, there were forlorn looks and lots of sadness, but looking around the room, there was also the feeling that all we had was each other and that together we'd get through this. It's the only option we have.

ACTIVISM IS NOT A CONTEST
San Francisco Examiner; 2020

It's been over a month since protests, sparked by the police murder of George Floyd, began independently springing up around the country. Not only have they yet to cease, but they are also hardly diminishing. We've been keeping a running list, updated every day, on my website, and just this week, there are nearly 40 protests in the Bay Area alone.

This sustained civil disobedience appears to be having some effect. Cities throughout the U.S. are pledging to divert money from their police departments to badly needed social services, and some places, like Minneapolis (where George Floyd was murdered), have begun the process of abolishing their police departments altogether. Several officers involved in recent murders have even been arrested and will face trial. But that's all too rare, as evidenced by the fact that the police who killed Breonna Taylor still have not been arrested.

That said, there is still a whole lot more that needs to be done. We've barely scratched the surface. If we could dismantle centuries of systemic racism with just a month of protesting, it would've been done ages ago. The work we are involved in now is only possible because of the sacrifices, struggles, and yes, protests, of all the many righteous activists who came before us.

So, it's essential to understand a few things about the nature of activism if we intend to ultimately change the world, especially if you're just now getting involved.

Let me begin by saying that, despite being an activist to varying degrees since we first invaded Iraq in 2003, I am also still learning. Not only is that OK, it's vital. The only way we can win against something as powerful as systemic racism is by building community and working collectively. And one of the best ways to do that is to listen to and learn from each other. Below is what I've gleaned from the past few decades of giving a shit, being involved, and listening to my allies and co-conspirators:

Activism is Not a Contest.

This one is critical, especially for white people. The goal of this entire movement is equality, equity, and liberation for people of color. It's not a contest to prove you're the white person who cares the most. Nobody is getting a "Wokest White Person Award." So, stop tearing each other down when people don't get everything right.

One of our most important jobs as white allies and co-conspirators is to talk to other white people and try to educate them. But we have to remember that learning is a process and that not everyone is on the same timeline as we are. Not everyone reads the same publications or spends the same amount of time on social media. People get awoken at different times. Before publicly attacking someone online for a misstep, consider calling them in instead.

This means that you should reach out to them privately and try to educate them compassionately, rather than using it as an excuse to show how much better of an activist you are. You're far more likely to bring them over to your side and expand their thinking than if you publicly shame them.

That being said, if you're dealing with someone whose racism isn't a misstep, who repeatedly deals in racist tropes and language, who refuses to learn or accept that systemic oppression is real and a form of terrorism, and/or is endangering the lives of people of color by unnecessarily calling the police, they need to be held accountable. No call-in necessary. We need to make racists scared again.

Activism is Not a Sprint; it's a Marathon.

Protesting is exciting! There's an exhilaration that comes with being surrounded by like-minded people while fighting to make the world a better place. But not only is it impossible to be involved in every demonstration, it's a terrible idea. This is not a sprint, it's a marathon. Set yourself up for a sustained lifetime of activism by being part of the actions you think will have the most impact. You're no good to anyone if you're burned out. Which brings me to:

Self-Care is Very Important.

I'm pretty sure I first heard the term "self-care" in 2016 while deep in the Black Lives Matter protests surrounding the police murders of Philando Castile and Alton Sterling. We'd been in the streets for days, shutting down the freeway, marching up Market Street, and I was exhausted. But I felt it wouldn't be doing my duty if I wasn't at every single protest.

Then someone shared an article about self-care with me, and it changed my outlook. Just as activism can be thrilling, it can also be stressful, heartbreaking, and even demoralizing when the change you're fighting for doesn't seem to be coming. Taking a moment to unplug from the toxicity of the internet and spend time doing things you really love allows you to recharge your battery and give more to the struggle.

Wear a Mask and Social Distance from Others.

The world is ever-changing, and so is the nature of activism. Another form of self-care is literally not getting sick and dying. It's also not spreading a deadly sickness to others. Right now, COVID is spreading like wildfire throughout the nation. If you plan on protesting, take care of yourself and your allies. There is free testing in many places around the Bay Area and the country. Just Google it.

Educate Yourself and Have Uncomfortable Conversations.

There are numerous excellent lists available, featuring books on anti-racism. Consider buying some of those books and reading them. Then get involved with groups like Standing Up for Racial Justice (SURJ), where you can have tough conversations and also put that knowledge into action.

Follow Black Leadership.

While it's always important to learn from those with experience, in a social movement dedicated to Black liberation, you must follow Black leadership. If you're white, you'll never fully understand what it's like to live in America as a person of color. That's OK. Acknowledging this allows you to see that the movement isn't about you. Your activism doesn't need applause or congratulations, and the only prize

Activism Is Not A Contest

is winning a better world for people who don't currently have the same level of privilege as you. Stand up, show up, listen, and learn.

LOVE NOTES & OTHER DISASTERS

(LOVE & LUST)

Love Notes & Other Disasters

I've been very blessed to have been in love with and been loved by a few incredible women in my life. I've also been very blessed to be in lust with far more of them. The pieces in this chapter are about love and sex, some poetry, and some prose: some naughty, some sweet. A few of them are about my wife, whom I'm excited to write love notes to for the rest of my life.

The title comes from the zine I put out in 2014 with the same name. A few of the pieces here were in that zine, but I've also included lots of stuff that's been published since then.

WHY YOU SHOULD FUCK A WRITER
(OR THE PLEASURES AND PERILS OF LOVING A CREATIVE PERSON)

BrokeAssStuart.com; 2014

I worked on this piece on and off for a couple years. I eventually got help from fellow writers Jennifer Maerz and Anisse Gross to get me out of being stuck. It ended up going viral on Medium and random fans of the piece translated it into Russian, Spanish, and Polish.

Fuck a writer because he can make you hard or wet just by typing. Kiss him because he can turn a one-night stand into a life-defining poem. A weekend fling into a highly praised novella. A short love affair became a bestselling book. Grab his hips so he can turn that rainy night in a Dublin hostel into three stanzas that speak to the heart of lust and loneliness everywhere. He will use literature to undress you. He will use his words to turn you on. He will quote someone else's work, at just the right moment, to get you into bed. You won't realize he accidentally misquoted it until you go home and Google the piece just because you need to feel those words one more time.

Have sex with a writer because she chooses art over money, even if she's always complaining about being broke. Unclasp her bra because she's 31 and still living with three roommates, squeaking by on rent, sliding by on bills, bartending a few nights, working in a bookstore, doing odd jobs, hustling; all because she's convinced that she will

Stuart Schuffman

Why You Should fuck a Writer

Art by Jon Stich

create something masterful that may one day make all of this worth it. Pull off her jeans because you admire the sacrifices she makes to do what she loves, knowing you could never do the same. Fuck a writer because she shivers and starves for her chance to carve her name on the world.

Sleep with a writer because he'll begin a beautiful poem about the bottoms of your feet, black from wearing flip-flops on Brooklyn's streets, and the way they contrast against your light blue sheets. And know that he'll never finish the poem, but sit up late at night, five years later at a desk in San Francisco, drinking shitty red wine, lamenting not just the loss of your love, but the fact that the poem was never finished. He'll think that maybe if he had finished the poem, you'd still be in love with each other. And then he'll think that he's just reading too deeply into it. Unbutton his shirt because he'll give you copies of the books he writes, and inscribe them with cute, heartfelt love notes. Those same notes will make him weep while he separates his library from yours, after the breakup, during the moving out. He'll take all his books with him, giving you more room for the new furniture he always said the two of you couldn't afford.

Lay with a writer because she'll build you up in her mind to be way more than you ever could be in real life. Climb on top of her because she'll tell you elaborate things you both know aren't true, but wish were. Fuck her not for who she is, but for who she believes herself to be, and because you almost believe it too. Do it for her brain or because she's read more books than you or because at her core, she's a romantic, even when she's jaded, heartbroken, and full of self-doubt. Slip off her underwear because she's mastered the art of grand gestures. Can get away with earnestly sending you 16th-century love poetry. Can quote Pablo Neruda, hum Leonard Cohen, memorize Rumi, cry Sylvia Plath, and use E.E. Cummings to make you think about cumming. Fuck a writer because wordplay is one of the sexiest kinds of foreplay.

Make love to a writer because he needs muses even though he hates that word. Leave bite marks on him because he can compose you something so exquisite, you'll show your grandchildren. Do it because he trades in metaphors and similes and crafts sentences that make you pause, pull the book to your chest, and sigh. He spends his life trying to distill heartbreak and love into something tangible. Fuck a writer because this piece could so easily be turned into a Twitter account, or a Tumblr, or a Facebook page, but is so much more potent as a single, solitary piece.

Screw a writer because she's crazy. Do it because you're crazy too. Pull her hair because she can make moody and forlorn seem sexy...for a little while. Do it because she's intolerable when she has writer's block, and she's intolerable when she's in the groove and doesn't wanna be touched or talked to. Because she'll sit in a room, working for eight hours, sometimes only to produce eight lines. Because she'll sit in a room for eight hours and produce 18 pages. Fuck a writer because she'll sit in a room for eight hours and produce nothing at all.

Bang, bang, bang a writer because he'll send you electronic love letters from across the world, writing you daily with words that burst with the feelings he wasn't able to say in person. He'll wake up each morning with a flutter in his stomach, excited to see what bits of tenderness are sprinkled within your emails detailing all the little pieces of life he's missing by not being home. Curl up next to him because he'll understand the meaning of love-sickness and will pine for you and use what little money he has to help you buy a ticket to meet him. You will believe in him, move across the country with him, and sacrifice so much for him, all while knowing he will never fully appreciate any of it. Because he always puts his work first. Fuck a writer because you will love him so much more intensely than anyone who's come before, even though he will probably fuck it up.

Don't fuck a stockbroker. Don't fuck a real estate developer.

Don't fuck a politician. Don't fuck someone in finance. Don't fuck people who've never created something lovely simply for the sake of creating it. Fuck a writer because you'll probably marry someone more consistent, someone who makes a salary, someone who says stupid shit like "weekend warrior" and "work hard, play hard." Those people are assholes.

But more than anything, fuck a writer because I really need to get laid.

FALLING IN LOVE ON THE 71 BUS
Slouching Towards Neverland Zine; 2022

During the fateful summer of my internship at Bill Graham Presents in 2002 I met a girl on the 71 Haight/Noriega Bus. We ended up being together for 3½ years after that day. It was my first serious relationship and the first time I fell in love. It also helped me fall in love with S.F.

The following story was written about 13 years or so ago so I could read it at the Live Muni Diaries Show. And that was about 10 years after we met on the bus.

I met my first love on the 71 bus. I had recently moved to San Francisco for a summer internship at Bill Graham Presents, and I was sharing a room on Haight St. with Mani, a friend from UC Santa Cruz. I was abysmally broke because my sense of honesty, which I thought was a good thing, kept me from lying to potential employers about how long I planned to stay in the City.

It was the summer I lived off of two pieces of Fat Slice pizza a day; the summer where cheap beer and whiskey were consumed each night on a rooftop in the Upper Haight; the summer where I found my neighbor dead in the hallway (which is another story all together); the summer when I first fell in love with San Francisco and the summer where I first fell in love with a person other than myself. I was twenty-one years old.

Mani and I were underemployed and had lots of time on our hands, so we investigated and learned the city by riding the bus. Sometimes we would get on and travel until the end of the line, just to see what possibilities were held in this brand-new world. The different colored bus lines on the Muni map looked like the veins and arteries in those anatomically correct drawings of the human body in medical books. San Francisco was ours to explore.

One day, our adventures led us to Fisherman's Wharf because we were craving In-N-Out, and it was the only one in the city. Later that summer, Mani would make a pilgrimage by foot to the one in Daly City. Afterwards, we headed back to Market St. and caught the 71 bus back towards the Haight. We were young, single, in a vast new city, and not shy. We'd started chatting with this blonde girl who said her boyfriend was in a Swedish rock band called the Hellacopters. Apparently, they were big. I'd never heard of them. Mani was sitting next to her, and I was next to a middle-aged Latina lady.

At 7th and Market, a short, black girl got on the bus and we locked eyes for a good three seconds before looking away. She was the most enchanting thing I'd ever seen in my life. She had long, brown, wavy hair, light caramel skin, rounded facial features, a button nose, a Julia Roberts smile, and a healthy set of tits, almost too large for her slight frame. On my end, I was young, reasonably good-looking, cocksure, and daring. The mop hiding beneath my brown beanie was a color that only exists when hair that had once been brightly dyed, fire hydrant red with black tips, gets quite faded out.

In those days, I met women everywhere; hell, I probably could've taught classes on how to be successful with them, but I was suddenly, and very uncharacteristically, nervous. This angel of the 71 Haight/Noriega looked to be in her early 20s, at the most 23, and she was getting hollered at by an older black guy at least twice her age. I overheard him telling her something about being a rapper or a rap producer or something else along those lines. She was very politely disinterested, but had said something about wanting to be a music journalist. When he got off at Fillmore St., she sat down, and there was an empty seat next to her. This was my chance. I got up from my seat, scooted in next to her, and said, "Excuse me. I couldn't help overhearing that you wanted to be a music journalist. That's something I'm interested in too. My name's Stuart. What's yours?"

Her name was Tia. She was just in town for a few days, exploring the city and considering a move here. She was on her way to get a tattoo at Mom's in the Upper Haight. "What are you gonna get?" I asked.

"A treble clef right here," she rubbed her inner wrist with her thumb.

"That's amazing. I'm a music junkie. I even work at a rock and roll concert company right now, and I throw concerts where I go to school in Santa Cruz." Nervousness made my usually rapid speech pattern feel sped up to the point where my words came out like machine gun bullets.

It turned out that music was even more a part of her life than it was mine. Not only was she equally as obsessed with it as I was, but her dad was a famous songwriter and producer from Philadelphia in the 70's.

"Holy shit," I said. "That's so cool! I know so many of his songs!" We were locked in. Deep eye contact. Butterflies in my stomach, a sense of hyper awareness. A peak experience, maybe. We arrived at my stop, Haight and Central. I looked at Mani, and he understood. I'd meet him at home later.

"That was my stop," I told her after the bus pulled out from the curb, "but I'm really digging our conversation, so I'll ride with you to yours." It was true, I wasn't spitting game. I was absolutely hooked.

Two stops later, we got off in front of Mom's Tattoo. "So wait, how long are you in town for?" I asked. It was Thursday.

"I'm here until Sunday."

"Well, I know you said you didn't know anybody in San Francisco, but now you do. Here's my number. Give me a call and I'll show you around." I said it like I knew everything about the city. I didn't know a goddamn thing.

As she entered Mom's Tattoo, I walked up Haight St. in a daze, wandering the wrong way, away from my apartment. I was pretty sure I was in love. She was gorgeous and came across as down-to-earth and cool. I called the apartment in Santa Cruz where all my music junkie friends lived, and which I'd be going back to after the summer. I rapidly spittled out the information to my boy who answered the phone that: I had just met a girl on the bus and she was gorgeous and had great taste in music and was a famous music producer's daughter, and that I gave her my phone number and that she would probably never call and that I was probably in love. He thought I was being hyperbolic, as usual, but I wasn't so sure. We both agreed, though, that she definitely wouldn't call.

* * * *

A half a week or so before that fated In-N-Out trip, Mani and I had gone out, and I'd gotten the number of a pretty blonde girl named Shayna at The Gold Cane. Shayna also lived on Haight St., and after getting her digits, I had imagined a cute little summer romance involving smoking pot in the park and getting to use her internet connection. The year was 2002, after all, and the apartment we were staying in didn't have internet. It's funny to think of that now.

A few hours after I had swooned over Tia on the sidewalks of Haight Street, I made my first call to Shayna. We chatted for a couple of minutes on the phone before I got an incoming call from a number I didn't recognize. I put Shayna on hold while I answered the other call, "Hello?"

"Hi, is this Stuart?" I thought to myself, *"There's no fucking way."*

"It sure is," I said, probably smiling or grinning through the phone.

"It's Tia, we met earlier today on the bus."

"Hey! Good to hear from you. Hold on one sec, I've got another call." At that moment, I had to make a decision: either try to hang out with a girl who lived down the street and would be here as long as I was, or try to catch this fleeting beauty like a sunset while it lasted. The choice was obvious for me. I clicked over and told Shayna that I had to take the call and that I'd talk to her soon. Then I clicked back over to Tia, not realizing at the time what a fateful decision it would prove to be. We chatted for a bit before I invited her to come out for a drink.

"I would, but I'm uh, afraid to leave my hotel room," She answered.

"Really? Why, what's going on?"

"It's in a really shady neighborhood. It seemed ok during the day, but there are a lot of really weird people out and I don't wanna go out at night."

"No worries, I'll come to your hotel and then we can go out from there."

Tia agreed to it and then told me the room number where she was staying at the Flamingo Hotel near 7th and Mission St. Considering how seedy that part of San Francisco is, I wasn't surprised that she was hesitant to go out at night. After hanging up the phone, I looked over at Mani, who was on his mattress on the floor. "Dude! It was that girl from the bus! She wants me to go meet her at her hotel room."

"Oh shit! Really? Her hotel room? Bring a condom."

I grabbed my beanie and threw on my coat, two essentials for a San Francisco summer night, and bounded out of my apartment. I caught the 71 bus and headed downtown.

* * * *

At 7th and Market, I got off the bus. I'd only been in San Francisco for less than a month, and while I knew the Mid-Market area was shady, I hadn't spent any time there at night. Walking down 7th Street towards Mission, I saw an emaciated man crouching with his back against a car for support while he shit rivers of what was probably dope sickness out of his bare ass. I could certainly see why a pretty young girl unaccustomed to our special brand of depravity would be terrified to leave her hotel.

Opening the door to her hotel room, she gave me a big, toothy smile and invited me in. "I'm glad you came over," she said. "I'm only in town for a little bit, and I wanted to have fun, but there are so many fucking weirdos out there." As it turned out, she was also only 18 years old, and while she had a fake ID, she didn't want to risk getting it taken away. We decided instead to grab a bottle of Captain Morgan and drink it in the hotel instead. As we went to the liquor store, I chose a route that would allow us to avoid the shitting homeless man. I am a gentleman after all.

Getting back to the hotel room, I cracked open the bottle and took off my beanie. Tia gave me a look of surprise, and I realized it was the first time she had seen my odd-looking hair. I smiled, took a pull off the bottle, and handed it her way. Sitting in that hotel room on the second floor of the Best Western Flamingo Hotel, Tia and I passed that bottle back and forth, alternating between sips of rum and Coke, and talking about things like history, music, love, and heartbreak. At that moment, neither of us realized how much of the last two we would cause each other to feel over the next three and a half years.

"I was so surprised when you came and sat next to me. I mean, I thought you were cute, but it looked like you were with your girlfriend." She told me. By this time, our bodies were relaxed and we were lying next to each other on the bed. We'd been talking for hours.

"My girlfriend?!" I laughed, "I was sitting next to a 50-year-old lady! You thought that was my girlfriend?" We both cracked up at this, and I inched closer. We began comparing scars, both physical and otherwise, touching this and that of each other until I could no longer resist. I leaned in and kissed her. Her lips tasted of Carmex and cigarettes. Soon, we were taking off our clothes, and I was finally freeing her tits from the bondage her garments had subjected them to. They were even more beautiful than I imagined. Her body seemed to defy gravity. She was 18 and had the physique of a porn star without an ounce of silicone. I gave a silent thank you to the 71 bus.

After our initial run, she told me I was the first person to make her cum. She might've been just saying that, but I was drinking her potion by that point. I would've believed anything she said. She'd only slept with two people, so it was possible.

I didn't go home the entire next day. I called in sick to my internship and we spent the day wandering through Chinatown, lying in Washington Square Park, exploring the Exploratorium, and then making love at the Flamingo Hotel. We were definitely making love by this point because we were already falling deeply into it. We were together for three and a half years after that day on the 71 bus. When we finally broke up, it was devastating. Love is a powerful thing, and the first time you feel it, you don't act like a sane person. It took me nearly a year to fully get over her, and the thing that really helped the most was falling in love again.

I'm writing this story now because it was 10 years ago. These days, I'm mending from a recently ended relationship of five years, and that one is just far too raw for me to be able to put it on the page right now properly. Maybe in 10 years.

Despite the first awkward six months to a year after we broke up, Tia and I have remained good friends ever since. Recently, we hung out over Pride weekend like we always do, and we drunkenly ended up in bed together. It was the first time we'd had sex since shortly after we broke up, and it was almost ten years to the day from when we first met. We made love again this time, but it was a different kind of lovemaking. It was a lovemaking created from binding up old wounds and kisses that felt less like fireworks than like visiting the home you grew up in, but that your family moved out of years before. It felt warm and comfortable, but also filled with the knowledge that you were in a place that would never be yours again.

And yes, she still looks amazing naked.

LOVE IN THE TIME OF HOUSING CRISIS
San Francisco Examiner; 2018

I met my wife KAYLA on Bumble (yes really!) in 2017. Despite having to postpone our wedding a year and a half cuz of the pandemic, we got married in March 2022 on a hill in Fort Mason overlooking the Bay, the G.G. Bridge, and the Wave Organ. We had our wedding party at El Rio. When you read the following piece you'll understand why. San Francisco really is a wonderful city to fall in love in.

San Francisco is a wonderful place to fall in love. Sure, Paris might be the "City of Love," but anyone who calls it that has never walked up Columbus Avenue, arm in arm with their sweetheart, as Coit Tower winked at them from above.

In our city, multi-hued buildings sprout from undulating hills like ebullient spring flower stalks reaching toward heaven. Fog quietly creeps in like a lover softly padding into the bedroom from the kitchen to join you under the covers for just 15 more minutes of sleep. The Bay and the ocean embrace each other so deeply beneath the Golden Gate Bridge, it's as if they're trying to say, "Look, we still got that spark after all these years."

When you find someone whose inner jinn sings the same song as yours, The City rewards you and manages to shine just a little brighter than before. Yes, San Francisco is a city of romance and beauty. What a remarkable place to fall in love.

This week marks a year since Kayla and I had our first date. That night, we tumbled through Mission Street dive bars, high on booze and pheromones, flirting our way toward our first kiss right beneath a heat lamp in El Rio's backyard. A week or so later, we found ourselves at the Wave Organ, chaperoned by a bottle of Jameson, leaning into each other's stories, telling them laughingly, until we ended up singing loud songs beneath the dome at the Palace of Fine Arts.

Falling in love is always glorious, but doing so in San Francisco is breathtaking. It's like The City cheers you on. Even when times are tough and it feels like you keep hitting roadblocks, San Francisco encourages you by saying, "I may be mean and unforgiving, but don't I make you feel beautiful?"

It's not as easy as it sounds, though...

Ask anyone single in San Francisco, and they'll tell you finding that spark with someone feels impossible. From Tinder to Teslas and bitcoin to booty calls, it can feel like everyone is too busy working or playing to let love in. And while falling for someone has always been both brave and precarious, only in San Francisco must you worry that your new darling might get evicted at any time. But even then, it's still worth it.

Sure, it might just be limerence, that chemical explosion in the brain that causes young people to do foolish things and emboldens bards to sing passionate songs. And, yes, even Fresno probably seems buoyant when you've met someone who fills your chest cavity with Motown music. But Fresno doesn't have deep kisses with a luminous view outside the Legion of Honor. Paris doesn't have sandy September hand-holding at Ocean Beach. That T-shirt might say "Virginia is for Lovers," but the person wearing it never ambled down Haight Street with their fingers in the back pocket of their favorite human's jeans.

So, I'll take San Francisco's blessings and I'll thank her for them profusely. I'll walk down Mission Street on my way to Emmy's Spaghetti Shack, holding Kayla's hand as we laugh at inside jokes and feel The City's radiance. Falling in love in San Francisco is a marvelous thing, and celebrating a year of it is even better. I hope all of you find what you're looking for, whatever that might be.

ELECTRICITY IN TUPPERWARE
Slouching Towards Neverland Zine, Limited Edition; 2022

I wrote this poem for Kayla shortly after we started dating. I love reading it now and remembering what things were like when we first started.

Cooking dinner in my apartment
kissing between cutting cloves
of garlic, giggling at the beauty
exploding between us

Two people filled with lightning
trying our damnedest to put that electricity
in Tupperware, just like leftover dinner
hoping to save some for later
worried about filling up on each other
or running headfirst into a storm

LOVE OVER BRUNCH
Slouching Towards Neverland Zine, Limited Edition; 2022

We made eyes at each other over
fried green tomato Benedict
giggling at jokes that could
only be understood
by the tension between us.

THE BOTTOMS OF YOUR FEET
Previously Unpublished

The bottoms of your feet
black from wearing flip-flops
through these Brooklyn streets
stick out from the cover
of our light blue sheets
as you sleep through this July humidity.

in this city
where you can't kill them with kindness
they simply kill your kindness

sitting in this messy room
in this filthy house
at our one desk
that doubles as your vanity
and my place to write

I watch you dream
and watch you breathe
for what you do for me
for what you do to me

with your perpetual femininity
with which you made tolerable
this shitty room
in this shitty brownstone
we share with eight other people
and we're stuck calling home
at least until September

and I love you
for following me to this city
on your terms

and tonight I pulled off your boots
and helped you get undressed
because you were tired from working a double
while I continue to look for a job
continue to bring us stress

and it breaks my heart that I'm just finishing this poem now
over five years after I started it.
after just passing through our old neighborhood
after thinking about all we struggled through together
and I love you more each time I think about it

and it breaks my heart that I let you go

IT'S SO BEAUTIFUL SHARING YOUR LIFE WITH SOMEONE
Previously Unpublished

It's so beautiful sharing your life with someone
the little morning murmurs when they stir next
to you
still sleeping, but smiling
when you lightly kiss them
before padding off to begin your daily
routine.

You share a secret
language, often conversing with just looks and smirks or
nonsensical noises and strangely uttered
phrases that form
the patois of your
island of two.

Sometimes you look over while
they are captivated
by a project and their toes twinkle asynchronously
to Erykah Badu's "Danger" and
somehow, impossibly, your love grows deeper
as you witness them
so fully.

When you share your life with someone
the best holiday can be a
Sunday with nothing to do
interweaving your legs with
theirs while watching pirated movies
in bed
all day
arm tickles
making them tea.

That feeling of coming home to
your person whether you've been gone for a few
hours or weeks
is the finest kind of addiction since
it's the only one that makes you
feel complete.

Not that you're incomplete without
them but rather
the joy of being a We
is when two glittering beings conjoin
not to fill each other's missing pieces but
to create a grander whole.

THERE'S NO MISTAKES IN DANCING OR SEX
Love Notes & Other Disasters Zine; 2014

She said something like
There's no mistakes in dancing or sex.
It's something my grandmother once told me.

We were naked on a bed sheet
on the roof of the music center.

Meadow, redwood, eucalyptus, and oak stretched on all sides of us
the scents traveling up our noses.
Stars glistened through the big dark Santa Cruz sky
like pinpoints of light.
that trickle through blankets,
knit by grandmothers,
and used as ceilings for pillow forts.

She smoked cigarettes
and always wore the same perfume.
We often drank too much and sometimes
to this day
when I ride the bus
I smell the combination of
booze and smokes and that particular perfume
on somebody else,
and I think of her.

A star fell across the heavens and she said
Make a wish.
And I said
I wish I didn't always shoot my load
faster than that shooting star.
We both laughed.

I was 19 and she was the fourth person I'd ever slept with.
I was a lousy lay
but she kept fucking me anyways
because she thought I was cute and sweet and other things
even though I didn't want to be her boyfriend.
There goes another one.
Now it's your turn to make a wish
I said.
We watched as the star
skipped across the atmosphere
and she said
I just wish that all the other wishes
we've ever made, come true.

All these years later
she's married
and pregnant
and living in Oakland.
I hope that means
all the other wishes finally came true.

FUMBLY NIGHTS AND FOGGY MORNINGS
SF Sounds; 2017

When you've been in San Francisco or Oakland for a while, it's almost impossible to date someone who hasn't fucked somebody you know. Like it or not, our fingerprints are all over each other's lives. Our histories are tangled up in each other's sheets. Our shadows are etched on each other's bedroom walls, left over from whatever detonated – the heat of which may have lasted for years or just a single night.

You can't spell San Francisco without a few exes. You've probably read that line from me before, but that doesn't change the fact that it's incredibly accurate. When you've spent years tumbling through beds, searching for something that you can't quite define, sometimes you accidentally find it. One morning, you wake up and the person next to you is still sleeping, breathing in a Morse code that can only be deciphered by the telegraph machine inside your ribcage.

Artwork by Robert Liu-Trujillo

And fucking becomes making love, and hanging out becomes dating, and this person becomes your person. We become one, and you become part of each other.

Then, one day (in the vast majority of cases), it all cracks apart, and you have to sand down the jagged edge where the two of you were connected. You have to solve possibly the most complex math equation in history: Us − You = Me. All the while knowing that the person whose scent was the only thing you consumed each morning before coffee is out there doing anything but being with you. Plus, they still have your favorite hoodie.

Everyone you meet has at least a little bit of somebody else's broken heart permanently caked underneath their fingernails. The longer you live in The Bay, the more likely it is that you'll know whose heart that was. If you care enough about that person, you let their ex pass on by, and if you don't, then you let your heart — or your loins — lead the way.

Sex isn't always about love, though, and dating in the 21st century, especially in the Bay Area, means blurry boundaries and muddled histories. Being in a place where only a couple of degrees separates everyone means having to make interesting decisions. Turning down a good friend's recent ex is a no-brainer, but what about the person your friend was just casually sleeping with? Is there a grace period before it's ok? And how important is it to ask? What about the ex of someone you don't even like that much, but who you know you'll see around? Banging your frenemy's ex is certainly satisfying, but isn't having a frenemy complicated enough to begin with?

We live in a time and place where boundaries around sexuality and relationships zig and zag depending on the souls involved. A monogamist in one relationship can become a polyamorist in the next. Casual lovers can become life partners, and exes can become someone you continue to sleep with every once in a while for years. Fumbly nights become foggy mornings, and the previous evening's flirtations become today's "what are you looking for?". And if you're dating multiple people, who do you spend Valentine's Day with? The only thing that stays constant is that fucking your roommate is a stupid idea.

The science behind sighs is imprecise. The space between the head and the heart is often miles apart. And every time I find someone I want to fall in love with, they're already in love with somebody else. Sometimes, they are just in love with themselves. Sometimes, just in love with the idea of love.

So, we move on and keep swiping and texting and going on first dates, all the while wondering what the hell we're actually looking for.

This is where we stand in 2017. Or in this case, this is how we lie down.

THE VAST MAJORITY OF PEOPLE AREN'T SUPPOSED TO BE LOVERS FOREVER

Slouching Towards Neverland Zine, Limited Edition; 2022

Walking through Shanghai
as the rain flirted bashfully with the ground
my hand on your lower back
as we peeked into stores
trying on weird clothes

We exist somewhere between the
tree-lined streets of the French Concession
and the cobblestone corridors of Xintiandi

Which makes sense because
we are neither growing
nor exactly bumpy and hard

Sometimes when we were far
you seemed closer to me than you are now
That's ok, the vast majority of people aren't supposed to be lovers forever.

I ONCE FELL IN LOVE AT THE LONE PALM
7x7; 2012

Somewhere there's a photo of me and my ex-girlfriend in which she's sitting on my lap and we're very obviously in love. We'd just started dating, probably hadn't even slept together, and you can tell just by the way we're wrapped around one another that the brain chemicals which make you fall in love are absolutely fucking exploding in our heads. The photo was taken at the Lone Palm after the very first reading I ever did. I spent a lot of time at the Palm back then since it was a block from my house, and even though I rarely see the bar or my ex-girlfriend these days, I still love them both. Immensely.

I first got turned onto the Lone Palm when I moved to the Mission in 2004. My friend Jason had been living in the neighborhood for several years, and once we got settled, he immediately took my roommates and me to the bar.

Upon walking in and seeing the dark interior lit mainly through candles, streams of neon light, and a TV screen playing black-and-white movies, I knew I'd found my new haunt. Little bowls of goldfish crackers dotted the white cloths that covered the tables where people were sitting. They sat either in groups, talking and laughing about some private thing I'd never know about, or as couples gazing into each other's eyes, sending out signals of love and lust over the rounded lips of their martini glasses. And then there were the regulars, the ones who make camp at the short end of the bar: the shit talkers and the fire starters who always see the bar as their own. There were the two Scotts, Max, Ashrav, and the Danish (maybe Swedish) girl whose name I can never remember, and more. Within a short time, my roommate JT would be among them as well. They'd all become a part of my life for those years I spent in drinking, drowning, laughing, yelling, wobbling, jabbering, and whatever else you do when you've spent a few lifetimes at a bar a block from your apartment.

They say the Lone Palm is a good bar to take a date. I wouldn't know. Taking a date to a bar where you're a regular and your friends are too is a recipe for disaster.

I could just see one of the Scotts or JT telling my date that I had some unmentionable disease while I was in the bathroom, just to fuck with me. What can I say? My friends are assholes, and I wouldn't think twice about doing the same to them.

Stuart Schuffman

In my early and mid-twenties, the Lone Palm was where we went to celebrate things, to drink in sorrow, and to make shit happen. So, when I had my first public reading at Dog Eared Books, the most natural place to make merriment afterwards was the Palm. And it was there and then that Tobias took a photo of two people in the midst of falling deeply in love. Trapped in its art deco wonder at the corner of 22nd and Guerrero, The Lone Palm never seems to change, but I do. We all do. Love comes and goes, apartments are moved into and out of, and individual friendships bob up and down in importance throughout different parts of your life, but the Lone Palm is exactly the same as it was when I first walked through the doors all those lifetimes ago.

OUR LOVE WAS LIKE A PALINDROME
BrokeAssStuart.com; 2016

The pencil shavings left over from your
makeup are still here
as is some hairspray
and the champagne glass you stole for me.

Your essence is strewn around my room
like smoke stains from a fire
but you're not here
nor will you probably ever be again.

The cars and the craziness still motor by my window
but the loudest sound I hear
is that of your absence
the bombastic quietude of you being gone.

Picking up the pieces of you left around my room
they will live in the drawer
where all my other failed loves go.

Ours was like a palindrome
it ended just how it started
with loneliness.

PARADISE BY THE NETFLIX LIGHT
Love Notes & Other Disasters Zine; 2014

Amy Winehouse breaking my heart
moaning dead tunes that crackle
from the speakers of your cell phone
while we fuck on your bed
in your living space
in your ex-boyfriend and his wife's
living room
The only separation being
three curtains which, with the wall, make a box.
The only other separation being my heart from my cock.

Which is inside you now.

The TV screen illuminates the room
dim and mute
as I pull your hair
and your nails dig into my back
my left hand closes around your neck
and you gasp
harder.

Paradise by the Netflix light.

At the Hemlock earlier you told me
let's go home and fuck
but you can't spend the night
I looked at your hands
older than they should be, given your
perfect all-American face
and I thought of the tattoos that cover your
perfect all-American body
that say things I don't remember
but mean
"I am lost."

I am too, we just wear it differently.

Stuart Schuffman

This bed is not quite a futon
but more a love seat that folds out
and it's not quite a love seat
because this isn't love
you're incredibly beautiful
and remarkably broken
and I could never love you
but I do love these moments,
sweaty in this living room
weaving ourselves together
like being part of a living loom.

And once we're done
I kiss your arms
and I kiss your neck
and I kiss your shoulders
and I kiss your back
Little nips of intimacy
that make this feel less like a handshake.

And then I go home
as per your request.

SMELLING THE THINGS SHE DREAMED OF
BrokeAssStuart.com; 2014

One of the best things in the world is
kissing the person you love
just as they are waking up.

The orange eastern light
sneaks in through the clefts
between your grey curtains
and the off white walls
and for this moment alone
there are no sirens
or shopping carts
or madmen screaming
on Folsom Street below.

You kiss the soft corner between
her eye and her temple
smelling the things she dreamed of
tasting the way she feels
just before she stretches.

For these brief seconds
there is no talk
of things you have to do
or plans you have to make
or ways you've let each other down.

There's just the quiet strum
of pulmonary rhythms
synced by sleeping near each other
and love.
So much love.

She is yours alone
until the day fully breaks
and takes her from you.

WILD PARROTS
Previously Unpublished

The wild parrots
squawk outside your window
as you sleep

I am in your dining room
working on my computer
counting down the days
till you leave

It's a weird thing
to love someone
and dislike them so much

Or maybe it's that I dislike
the person I am

Stuart Schuffman

when I'm with you

Regardless, you moving
out of San Francisco
can't come soon enough

I NEVER GOT TO
Previously Unpublished

I never got to
buy you dinner
or take you for drinks
or give you an orgasm
as a friendly way of saying
thanks.

So I hope a little poem
is enough to say
the late night asexual
intertwining of our bodies
that left us somewhere
between being lovers and
being friends was somehow
perfect.

The smell of you fresh
from the shower next to me
as your phone made
our faces glow in the
East Hollywood darkness
of your room made me feel
good.

And maybe next time
we see each other I'll
be able to buy you dinner
or take you for drinks
or at least give you something
else.

THE DAY AFTER YOUR WEDDING
Previously Unpublished

It's the day after your wedding
and I just spent part of my morning
looking for the photos you sent me
when we were first in love

Nearly ten years have gone by
since then
and I'm more lost now
than I've ever been

You were my big one
thus far
the love of my life
second only
to San Francisco
who's now married to someone else as well

My heart is broken at the moment
not because you've found
someone else
but because
I haven't

I find myself now
fresh out of a relationship
that always hurt
and made me compare it
to the one you and I had
one that was good
and healthy

And here I am
all these years later
surrounded by people who
sing my praises
but aren't really my friends

Stuart Schuffman

I'm lonely
so so lonely
and you've found love

I had to find those photos this morning
digging through my old computer
that you urged me to get
and whose lifetime
lasted about as long as our relationship

Five years is a long time for a computer
and a long time to love someone
especially one
that you end up
pushing away

So I found these photos
of you so young
and beautiful
and I don't know why

I needed to find them
other than the fact that
they are the only private bit
of you
that I'll ever have again

I hope you're happy
like so fucking happy
because that's all I've ever wanted
for the people that I love

Hopefully he gives you
all the things
I never would.

THINGS PEOPLE HAVE SAID TO ME IN BED
Previously Unpublished

"Really Stuart? You already came?"

"I'm gonna cum!"

"I'm cumming!"

"I just came!"

"Did you already cum?"

"Wrong hole."

"WRONG HOLE!"

"Be gentle"

"Harder!"

"It's ok, it happens to everyone at some point."

"OhMyGoddddd."

"STUART!"

"I love you so fucking much."

"I could've gone home with any guy there, and I picked the guy who's too drunk to get it up."

"Oh shit, I just came so hard."

"Mmmm....hi."

"You licked out my hood piercing??"

"How can you be such a mean and cruel person?"

"How are you so sweet?"

"You can't spend the night"

"You're gonna spend the night, right?"

"No."

"YES!"

"I told myself I wasn't gonna fuck you."

"Choke me."

"Spank me."

"Pull my hair."

"Tell me how dirty I am."

"I've only slept with three other people"

"I'm sleeping with two other people right now."

"I'm a total slut."

"Can we order some pizza?"

"I just wanna be like this forever."

"Let's just run away with each other."

"You're the worst thing that's ever happened to me."

"Fuck me Stuart!"

"Fuck you Stuart."

"Don't feel special. I cum easily"

HOW TO SURVIVE A SAN FRANCISCO BREAK-UP
The Bold Italic; 2012

I'm currently sleeping on my cousin's couch in the Castro. Well, that's not entirely accurate. I'm sleeping on a couch that was mine, and in my apartment until recently, when my girlfriend and I broke up. When I moved out, I took my couch with me and gave it to my cousins. It's their couch now, and I'm sleeping on it. I kinda feel like a turtle, carrying my home on my back wherever I go.

Strange, right? Well, most things in San Francisco are a little strange, and ending a relationship in this town is no different. From not being able to move out for a few months due to the expense of this city to knowing that the only way you won't run into your ex is if she moves out of town, breakups in SF might be a special breed. What follows is a little guide to surviving a San Francisco breakup. That is, of course, after you figure out who gets which tutu from the costume box.

Get Out of Town.

When you've spent a long time with someone, your lives have a way of melding together; you become an island of two. You have your own language, your own customs, your own way of interfacing with

Art by Heather Tompkins, courtesy of The Bold Italic by GrowSF

the world that only the two of you fully understand. After a breakup, everything from the Tesora blend at Philz Coffee to the groceries you buy at Rainbow reminds you of the little sovereign nation you used to inhabit. So, the best thing you can do is get the fuck out of town for a little while. Go somewhere that holds no nostalgic memories for you and your ex, like Berkeley. Really, when was the last time you actually went to Berkeley? Yeah, it's still over there across the bay.

Get Laid.

With a breakup comes writing sad poetry at Caffe Trieste, drinking too much in Mission District dive bars, and riding Muni to work with a general feeling of malaise. But you know what else comes with breakups? New booty! That means you can hook up with that dude who found you on Facebook and got amazingly more handsome since you last saw him in junior high. You can finally holler at that girl you have a crush on who works at Tartine. You can go home with the redhead who always ends up at the same parties as you. Being single means you can fuck all those people you've fantasized about while you were tied up in monogamy. It also means you can finally live out your fantasy of getting tied up. Wicked Grounds did just reopen, you know...

If you've been screwing the same person for a long time, it might be kinda weird to get naked with somebody else. But it's also unbelievably exciting to explore the curves and nerves and tastes and purrs of a brand-new body. And sure, they may not do that one thing that your ex used to do. But the first time you hook up with someone is incredibly hot. And more than anything, it gives you an ego boost. It helps you realize that you're still sexy and attractive and that people want you.

Be Prepared to Run into Your Ex.

This is San Francisco, a city that's only seven miles by seven miles. You are, without a doubt, gonna run into your ex. It is unavoidable. If you're lucky, it'll be during the daytime while you're both sober and on your way somewhere else. If you're unlucky, you'll be out drunk one night and end up an emotional mess after running into her and her friends at The Residence. If you're really unlucky, you'll run into him while you're drunk and fragile and he's out with someone else. Most likely, all three of these things are gonna happen. So just be mentally prepared.

Be prepared for the way they can take your breath away just by entering the room. Be prepared for him to act like he's totally over it. Be prepared for her to seem happy with somebody else. Be prepared for them not to want to have a drunken conversation with you at Otis about all the things you could've done better. Be prepared for them to seem like they've gotten their shit together while you're still an emotional casualty. They likely feel the exact same way as you – they just don't wanna let you know. It's called self-protection. It hurts. Be prepared. Shit, you probably can't. At least try, if not for yourself, then for me. No one wants to see you crying in public, unless it's because the Niners just lost the playoff game.

Stop Going to the Same Spots.

This goes along with the last point, but try changing up your routine a bit. If you go to all the same places, you're more likely to get all nostalgic. Plus, you're more likely to run into your ex. So, switch from Four Barrel to Blue Bottle. Try the Union Square location of Cafe La Taza instead of the Castro one. Sit on Gay Beach at Dolores Park instead of Hipster Terrace. Hang out in North Beach instead of the Marina.

Start Saying Yes to More Things.

One of the great things about being single is that you no longer

Love Notes & Other Disasters

have to consider someone else with every decision that you make. Start saying yes to things you wouldn't have said yes to before. Take up that friend on the promised surfing lesson. Go for the midnight bike ride up the Wiggle, through the park, and out to the beach. Try dating girls. Have a threesome (that's what I'm hoping for). Have an "uncool threesome" (you know, the MMF one). Go to the Power Exchange. Do too much blow in Delirium's bathroom and go home with someone way too young for you. Bang a cougar you meet at Balboa Cafe. Do some shit you might regret, but will make a good story eventually. It's amazing how this all ends up going back to sex, isn't it?

Don't Fuck Your Ex's Friends.

There are a million reasons not to go there. Just don't. Plus, do you really think no one is gonna find out? This is San Francisco, for fuck's sake. Gossip moves through this town quicker than herpes.

Try Not to Keep Fucking Your Ex.

I know this one can be hard. You're wasted one night, stumbling out of Beauty Bar, City Tavern, Badlands, or some other meat market, and your opportunities totally underwhelm you. You think to yourself, "I should really call ___." It sounds like a good idea at the time. The familiarity, the comfort, the fact that you know your itch will get scratched. All I'm saying is that it's not a good idea. You're just picking scabs from a wound.

Art by Heather Tompkins, courtesy of The Bold Italic by GrowSF

Get Back in Touch with Old Friends.

There's a great line from "Break Up the Family" by Morrissey that goes, "Let me see all my old friends/let me put my arm around them/because I really do love them." And once you go through a breakup, that shit totally resonates. You wanna surround yourself with people who love you. Plus, let's face it, you've been totally neglecting your friendships. And hey, they might have hottie friends to hook you up with. I especially enjoy hanging out with my married friends and sharing all my ridiculous dating stories to make them jealous. And they really are ridiculous. How is there not a reality show about the strangeness of dating in San Francisco?

Don't Listen to Too Much Morrissey.

Or any other sad music for that matter. Yeah, I know I just quoted him and all, but sitting around listening to sad-ass music is just gonna make you a sad ass.

Throw Out the Stuff That Reminds You of Them.

Get rid of some of that clutter that piles up during a relationship. Things like your matching Bay to Breakers costumes, the Britney Spears songs that somehow got on your iPod, the stubs from that Giants game you went to last year, that weird piece of furniture you found on the street that your ex insisted you bring home, the shitty piece of art that you've loathed ever since she bought it off some kid on Haight Street. But keep the photos – you'll want those someday. Just make sure you hide them from yourself for a while.

Lately, I've been thinking that love can only be measured by the scars it leaves. But if that's the case, then maybe a breakup can be measured only by the way you heal. Hopefully, some of the tips above will help you mend. If not, there's always booze.

All Of This Is The Natural Byproduct Of Not Dying Young

(DEATH)

I have an unfortunate skill of being able to write really good eulogies for people. One of the unavoidable byproducts of living is seeing friends, loved ones, and heroes die. I feel very lucky that this is the shortest chapter in this book.

The title of the chapter comes from a line in the story "When San Francisco Fails Those Who Love It" which is actually in the Slouching Towards Neverland chapter, but it just seemed like the perfect title for this one.

R.I.P MAYOR ED LEE, MY SOMETIMES NEMESIS
BrokeAssStuart.com; 2017

When the alarm went off this morning, I looked at my phone and saw I had eight texts, all from a variety of unconnected people. Considering my birthday is in four days, my first thought in that foggy, not quite awake state was "Is it my birthday?" I looked at the date and it wasn't, so my next thought was, "Oh shit, what did my big mouth get me into now?" It wouldn't be the first time I'd woken up to a shit-storm of my own creation.

I opened the first message and saw the news "San Francisco Mayor Ed Lee Dead at 65". Bolting up in bed, I said to my girlfriend, "Holy shit! Ed Lee died!" and as I clicked the link, my phone followed suit. "Fuck, my phone just died too. Can you call me a cab? I need to get to my computer."

My distaste for Mayor Ed Lee is no secret. Before, during, and after the 2015 mayoral campaign in which we were adversaries, I hammered him relentlessly for political corruption and for selling out San Francisco to the highest bidder. His dislike of me was also well known. While acknowledging me publicly would only give credence to my position, sources at City Hall informed me that I was referred to as "an abomination" within the Mayor's Office. If it's true that you can only judge a man by his enemies, I must be doing something right.

Before I continue, I need to lay a few things out: this is not going to be the hit piece some of you are expecting. I may not agree with much of what Ed Lee did as San Francisco's Mayor, but I do believe he loved this city and wanted the best for it. Unfortunately, his vision of what was "best" for San Francisco often excluded anyone who made under $150,000 a year. This also isn't an attack on him as a human being. From what I've been told by nearly everyone who knew him, Ed Lee was a kind and caring man who loved to joke and was genuinely fun to

All Of This Is The Natural Byproduct Of Not Dying Young

be around. My heart goes out to his family and friends who are mourning him on this sad day and are heartbroken by his unexpected passing. It's also important to acknowledge that Ed Lee was San Francisco's first Chinese-American and first Asian-American mayor, which is an incredible achievement, especially given SF's ugly anti-Chinese history. Thank you, Mayor Lee, for breaking that barrier.

So no, this will not be a hit piece. What this will be, however, is an anchor to the reality of what has befallen San Francisco under Ed Lee's stewardship. As all the articles rolling in right now only give the mayor praise — for fear of speaking ill of the dead — it's vital that we not let his untimely passing wash away the irreversible damage his policies have done to the fabric of San Francisco. It's essential that those of us who lost our home, both literally and metaphorically, get to have our voices heard in how his legacy is defined.

To be perfectly blunt, Mayor Ed Lee oversaw the destruction of much of what made San Francisco special. Despite the hills and the Victorians and the fog and the bay, the thing that truly set San Francisco apart from everywhere else in the world was the people. For decades, San Francisco was the place you went if you didn't fit in anywhere else. If you were queer, an immigrant, an artist, a polyamorist, an anarchist, a freak, a dreamer, or just someone who wanted to live as their true self, San Francisco is where you went. It was also home to a thriving pro-union working class who were just as proud to say they lived in San Francisco as the weirdos who kept washing up on the shore. But all that disappears when a city becomes so unaffordable that the median rent is $4300. And while Mayor Lee wasn't the one actually raising the rent, the policies that he set forth provided the perfectly fertile ground for greedy landlords and rapacious real estate developers to do anything they damn well pleased.

While the idea behind the "Twitter Tax Breaks" wasn't terrible, what they wrought was. Sure, they allowed San Francisco to have one of the lowest unemployment rates of any major city after the Great Recession, but the problem was that those jobs didn't go to San Franciscans who had lost their jobs in 2009. People were imported from all over the world to fill the newly created jobs and the homes vacated by the jobless. And it was there, that very moment, that set the tenor for what San Francisco was to become. Ed Lee and his big-money tech industry backers had a vision of San Francisco as the tech center of the world, and since 2011, they've done a damn good job of making it so. All it cost was the soul of the most interesting, vibrant, and unique city in America. A handful of people became tremendously wealthy, while everyone else was left with an apartment that cost them half their salary in rent.

Ed Lee started out on the side of the people. He fought against landlords and struggled for poor and working-class people. He even organized a rent strike in Chinatown to protest fucked-up living conditions. He then decided to join the system he had fought against, aiming to change it from the inside. It seems it changed him.

Despite being a housing rights activist in his younger days, San Francisco saw skyrocketing evictions during Ed Lee's time as mayor. However, when given the opportunity to slow this down by pushing stricter laws for Airbnb – laws that would make it more difficult for people to evict tenants and convert their properties into poorly regulated Airbnb hotels – he stepped aside. He essentially allowed Airbnb to write the law governing it. It was no secret that Mayor Lee's most prominent financial backer was Ron Conway, a major investor in Airbnb.

The same Twitter Tax Break that kept these tech companies in SF allowed its beneficiaries to avoid paying $34 million in taxes in 2014 alone. Imagine what that money could've done if we put it towards affordable housing or our homelessness epidemic.

Speaking of the homelessness epidemic, Mayor Lee's treatment of the homeless during Super Bowl 50 was despicable. The City of San Francisco spent $5 million on a party for a football game happening 45 miles away. Because of that, the mayor had the police push all the homeless folks out of downtown so that they wouldn't be on camera for the rest of the world to see. Instead of fixing our problem, he swept it under the rug...or at least under the freeway where the homeless encampment stretched a mile long.

Under Lee, San Francisco became a Dickensian story of wealth disparity. I called it a Tale of Three Cities in my SF Examiner column. We have a worse wealth disparity than Rwanda. While homelessness has always been a problem in San Francisco, over just a few years, we became a place with such an immense consolidation of wealth that our homelessness epidemic wasn't just a problem; it was an embarrassment. With initiatives like the Navigation Centers, it often felt like Mayor Lee's heart was in the right place, but he didn't have the political will to do anything about it.

Ed Lee wanted to be thought of as "The Tech Mayor," and I honestly think he deserves that title, but not in the way he imagined. His devotion to the all-mighty dollar of the tech industry did very little for the people of San Francisco. It's given us horrible traffic, egregious rents, an exacerbated homelessness crisis, and a city full of self-entitled assholes who don't actually give a shit about San Francisco because they don't plan on being here long enough to do so.

The thing about San Francisco is that while we fight vehemently about the things we disagree on, we also tend to agree on a great deal of liberal principles. Ed Lee would've been considered a pretty liberal mayor in many other cities, but San Francisco is at the vanguard of progressivism, and for most of us, he just wasn't liberal enough. That said, for a guy who rarely took a stand, it was heartening to see him stand up for immigrants and sanctuary cities.

The Political Right has used the tragic death of Kate Steinle as a bludgeon to attack immigrants and the cities where they live. I remember seeing Ed Lee on national TV, standing up for our immigrant neighbors in the face of hateful conservative rhetoric. I turned to whoever was standing next to me and said, "I don't like much of what that guy stands for, but I love that motherfucker right now." And at that moment, I really did.

This morning, somebody directed me to the comments section on the Breitbart article about Mayor Lee's passing. All of the 1000+ comments were hideous and nasty, full of venom and hate for immigrants, sanctuary cities, and many of the values we San Franciscans hold dear. And it was then that I felt closest to Ed Lee, closer than I had ever felt before. While he and I disagreed about pretty much everything about San Francisco, we at least agreed on one thing: all those racist, homophobic, white supremacist Trump supporters could kiss our beautiful San Francisco asses.

    Rest in Peace, Mayor Ed Lee.

Stuart Schuffman

FOR ALL OUR FRIENDS WHO DIED WAY TOO YOUNG
BrokeAssStuart.com; 2016

Fletch was the first person my age I knew who died. I was 19 and in college, and Sato had called and left a message on our answering machine, weeping, "Fletch is dead. He died in a car crash" over the telephone lines that stretched from San Diego to Santa Cruz. Fletch was Filipino, or maybe Mexican, with a mediocre mustache and brown skin. He had a blue bong. We called it Smurfette because of the Smurfette sticker on it, and we'd say things like "Where's Smurfette. I want to kiss her."

Weed was the thing that held many of us together, that and boyhood kinship, and there were up to 20 of us some nights sitting in parking lots in strip malls in San Diego's endless suburbia. Fletch had just shown up one day with a guy named Drummer John, and we were all 15 or 16. Drummer John was married to a girl named Gabby from somewhere like the Ukraine, Poland, or the Czech Republic. They were married, but they kind of hated each other. I guess it was the only way she could've stayed in the country.

"Fletch is dead. He died in a car crash." We played the message a couple of times. Fletch was dead. He couldn't have been more than 20 years old. The dumb motherfucker was racing his car, doing things you do when you're not more than 20 years old, and crashed it. He burned to death in the Rice Rocket he was so proud of — he was the first person I heard use that term, which makes me think he was Filipino after all.

That was a wonderful year. I was 19 years old and living in my first ever apartment. It was a one-bedroom. Jeremy and I shared a room, and we had a living room where we hosted parties every Tuesday night. If one of us was getting laid, they had to do so on the earth-tone paisley futon in the living room. I had that thing for years afterwards, and it got fucked on so many times. Thinking back, I don't know if it ever got washed. The goddamn thing probably had more DNA on it than a season of CSI.

That was a magical year. I know magic was involved because it was one of those times in my life where I knew what was happening to me was important, even at the time it was occurring, and I felt like a grown-up and acted like a teenager. It wasn't like now, where you just go through life and look at the date and say, "How the hell did it become November already?"

All Of This Is The Natural Byproduct Of Not Dying Young

No, the things that happened were important, and I knew so even though to this day, I can't explain how they were, considering that most of them were so banal. That little apartment in Cypress Point in Santa Cruz was a novella in itself, but maybe those are other stories for other times.

That was a terrible year. It was the year my grandpa died, and Danny shot that kid in the face, and George Canada died. And when George died, that was the one I really felt because I'd known George since junior high and we were friends, and I really liked the guy, even if he was kinda a fuck up. And he was probably kinda fucked up when that bus hit him while he was riding his motorcycle.

George told stories like "This morning I woke up in a bush," and he looked like a friendly stoned lion with his long blond hair that went far past his shoulders and the blonde scruff that covered parts of his face, almost qualifying as a beard. And in high school, there'd be keg parties in the dark corners of public parks or on high school baseball diamonds, and George would bellow "Community Bowl!!!" which meant that everyone with weed would convene and each of us would toss a little bit into a pipe and all of us would smoke it. Back then, we competed to see who had the coolest pipe and the coolest reusable keg cup. George's cup was the best. It looked like a tit, and you could drink beer out of the nipple, and you'd be there talking to someone, and George would walk up and shove the nipple in your mouth and make you drink beer from it—that sweet, sweet, dead young boy.

I don't know if I ever cried when George died. I didn't go to his funeral. It was Spring Break, but I didn't want to go back to San Diego. Danny shooting that kid and George dying were too much for me, so I went and hung out in San Francisco instead. I remember the last time I'd seen him was New Year's Eve, a few months before. But like I said, I don't remember if I cried for him when he died, but years later, when I was sharing a different one-bedroom apartment, this time with a girlfriend in San Francisco, I had a dream I was partying with George, and I woke up weeping. George was 20 years old when he died, and I was so sad because it wasn't until that dream that I really fully realized how young that was. I thought about all the stuff he never got to do, like legally drink in a bar, or bitch about things on Facebook, or even see the 21st Century. He's dead. Forever 20 years old, forever looking like a beatific lion bellowing "community bowl" to a group of people who now, 15 years later, can't even remember the last time they went to a keg party, let alone one filled with underage explorers trying so damn hard to figure out what the hell growing up means.

ANGIE
SF Sounds; 2017

When you're in your 30s, you don't meet people like you did in your teens or your 20s. You'll still call someone a "good friend" even if you haven't seen them in a few years, but you aren't the same person you were back then. That person is trapped like a fossil in amber, and can generally only be accessed by the people who knew you before. You simply can't be as close with all the people you used to be close with. You change, they change, life changes... and life changes you.

Angie and I weren't best friends, but she was always part of my life during my early and mid-twenties. We ping-ponged between Mission dive bars, sure of what we were gonna do with our lives even if we weren't exactly doing those things yet.

Art by Robert Liu-Trujillo

I'd gone to junior high and high school with Marina, who became a sort of social gatekeeper, introducing me to a new group of friends. Of them all, Angie was the most unforgettable.

Angie was all tattoos, crazy hair, and heart. Her voice was brassy and loud, and it seemed she didn't have a volume button. I don't even think the girl knew how to whisper. She always had a funny story to tell, which she often interrupted with her own loud laughter. She and Marina lived next door to Madrone, and it seemed the only drink they ever had was Sierra Nevada Pale Ale. I hate that shit, but I always ended up drinking it simply because it was there.

Angie's life and my life became deeply intertwined. We went to the same parties, hung out at the same bars, and popped by each other's homes if we were in the neighborhood. We became closest, though, when I was working on my San Francisco and New York books. Angie loved maps. She was a cartographer, so when I wrote my cheap living guidebooks, she made the maps. Back then, she talked a lot about a guy named Brewster.

All Of This Is The Natural Byproduct Of Not Dying Young

Marina eventually joined the Peace Corps and moved to Azerbaijan. Angie and Brewster became an item and later married. She became one of those people whom I only saw at going-away parties or ran into on the street. We'd hug and briefly catch up, and she'd show me her newest weird tattoo.

These kinds of things are typical in SF. As you get older, your group of friends becomes smaller. The people who don't move away become part of your city environment. You take their presence in your life, even if only peripherally, as a given. You take their existence for granted.

Recently, I got a cryptic text from Marina: "Angie passed away on Sunday night." I don't have all the details yet, but how she died isn't nearly as important as how she lived.

About a month ago, I saw Angie riding by on her bike. I was gonna call out her name, but I was in a rush and figured I'd just run into her again soon. Now, knowing I'll never hear her deep, loving laugh again, I wish I'd taken the extra five minutes just to say, "hello." The hardest part about getting older is discovering that not all the people you love will get to do so with you.

So, this is for you, AngiePants. The crafty girl who crocheted a holder for her TV remote control while she and Marina binge-watched "X-Files." The hilarious girl who laughed the hardest at her own jokes and never knew how loud she was talking. The sweet girl who gave great hugs and lit up every room she walked into. The one who was so deeply a part of my San Francisco that it will never be the same without her. I love you, Angie. If there is an afterlife, I hope it's full of maps and Sierra Nevada.

FUCKING BUBBLES
BrokeAssStuart.com; 2017

Fucking Bubbles. I don't know how many times I've said that phrase since I first met him in Dolores Park in 2014. In fact, anyone who ever met Bubbles uttered that phrase at least once, whether in absolute awe, complete exasperation, or both simultaneously.

Bubbles was Bubbles. There are a lot of other things we can tack onto that, like artist, DJ, rebel, queerdo, performer, and nightlife staple. He was even an activist in his own way. Simply existing and being himself in this world with unbridled confidence was an act of defiance and activism. But really, the only thing that adequately described Bubbles was Bubbles. He was truly one of a kind.

This is why his murder early on Saturday morning in the Tenderloin has struck San Francisco so hard. For so many of us, Bubbles was proof that San Francisco still had magic in it. That this city was still for everyone. That it was tolerant, and loving, and strange, and heartfelt. That if you didn't belong anywhere else, you still belonged in San Francisco. That The City allowed you to become who you were meant to be, and that it would take you back even if you fucked up.

And let's be honest, Bubbles did fuck up. A lot. It was part of what made him Bubbles. The list of bars he was 86'd from is almost folkloric, and his Facebook updates played out like a magnificent soap opera where he was often the only character. From live-streaming himself doing drugs to boasting that he was able to make rent because a "techie" paid him for a blowjob, you'd find yourself muttering the same refrain, "Fucking Bubbles".

But it's not like Bubbles gave a shit what you thought anyway. And that's what made him special. Bubbles lived his truth in a way that very few of us will ever have the courage to do. He wasn't just fabulous Bubbles when cloistered in the (imagined) safety of San Francisco; he was Bubbles with the mustache and the wig and the bikini top, even when traveling through places like Turkey. Bubbles was his own spirit animal. He did what Bubbles wanted, and only what Bubbles wanted, all the time. He could be a real motherfucker like that, but he was OUR motherfucker. And we loved him for it, even if sometimes begrudgingly.

I am absolutely gutted right now thinking of poor, sweet Bubbles bleeding to death on the sidewalk in the Tenderloin. That someone was so upset by the audacity of Bubbles' existence that they shot him to death in the streets of our city. Our city, where people like Bubbles are supposed to be safe. Our city is supposed to be a place where people like us – all of us who don't fit in anywhere else – are safe. Bubbles, identified as a man but with his mustache and his sparkly skirts and padded breasts, purposefully presented himself to the world as neither male nor female, but both, because that's how he expressed his true self. It hurts to know that the man who shot Bubbles. It hurts to know that the man who shot Bubbles argued

All Of This Is The Natural Byproduct Of Not Dying Young

with him outside the strip club and then chased him across the street and murdered him. It hurts to know that he probably just saw a queer freak in front of him instead of the richly complicated and complex individual that Bubbles was. It hurts to know that Bubbles was most likely murdered because he was unabashedly queer and was unwilling to compromise that under any circumstances. It hurts to know that Bubbles was killed in the same neighborhood that will soon be designated the Transgender Cultural District.

It hurts. It all hurts.

Fucking Bubbles. What's left of San Francisco's soul had another chunk taken out of it on Saturday morning when you died. I know you were planning on moving to Berlin at the end of the month and starting a new life there, but even all those miles away, you'd still be ours because there would be no Bubbles without San Francisco, and San Francisco will never be the same without you.

THE TIME I FOUND MY NEIGHBOR DEAD
BrokeAssStuart.com; 2013

It was 9:35 am, and I was starting down the stairs to catch a bus that would get me to work by ten. As I bounded down to the tiny landing that separated the first set of stairs from the first apartments, I saw him splayed out with his legs on the last couple of steps and his head blocking the door. I recognized him as the old man who lived two stories above me and smoked joints. Even though I'd never seen a dead body before, I also recognized him as dead the first second I saw him lying there.

"SIR! SIR! ARE YOU ALRIGHT?" His face had a bluish quality about it. He must have tripped and hit his head. There was a slight scratch on the door from where his glasses scraped against it.

"FUCK! Sir..."

I ran back upstairs, managed to tell my roommate, Peter, what I had found at the bottom of the stairs, and called 911 in the same breath.

"Shit, who is he?"

"I think he fucking lives two above us, with the little fucking plants."

"Fuck, I'll go knock and see if anyone knows him."

I brought the cordless phone down with me to the old man and talked to the operator while Peter flew upstairs to knock on people's doors. In a trembling voice filled with umms and and's, I explained to the operator what I had found.

"Is he unconscious?" The operator was just a shade less calm than the man lying next to me.

"I told you he's not breathing, he's fucking blue."

"Has rigor mortis set in?"

"What?" I knew what it was, I just couldn't think straight.

"Has he gone stiff?"

"Uh, yes, I guess I don't know."

"Is he stiff?"

"Uh..."

"Bend his arm, see if he's stiff." His arm wasn't stiff. I bent it. It was heavy like a real person's.

"No, it's not stiff." Upstairs, there was noise. Peter had found someone who knew the old man. I could hear him coming down the stairs.

"Dennis?" He said the name like someone preparing himself for tragedy. When he hit the landing and saw the old man, his voice revealed no preparation for the tragedy. "OH MY GOD! DENNIS! OH MY GOD!"

"Have you given him C.P.R.?" The operator's voice brought me back.

"I don't know how"

All Of This Is The Natural Byproduct Of Not Dying Young

"DENNIS! OH MY GOD! YOU'RE GONNA BE OK BUDDY! STAY WITH US! OH MY GOD! DENNIS!"

"Do you want me to instruct you?" I could hear the sirens now. Things started to swirl a little.

"Hello?"

"Yeah?"

"Do you want me to instruct you on C.P.R.? It's your choice."

"Uh..." I turned to the neighbor. "Do you know C.P.R.?" He didn't answer me; he just moved in and began C.P.R. I heard the sirens getting really close and the paramedics pulling up, so I got off the phone and said, "We're gonna have to move him so the paramedics can come in."

"We're not supposed to move his head," Peter answered.

"But how the fuck are the paramedics gonna get in?" The neighbor said nothing and moved Dennis out of the way the best he could. Blood streaked across the white tile floor as the neighbor slid Dennis's body across it. I sat back watching as the neighbor did C.P.R. and the paramedics tried to wedge their bodies inside the small space created by Dennis's body and the door. The last thing I saw before I went back to my apartment was the paramedics ripping open Dennis's shirt and one of his buttons flying up the stairs and landing next to my foot.

I sat in the funky-smelling orange chair that came with the apartment, gazing out the window at the proceedings unfolding outside the building. I knew that I was gonna have to go down and talk to the cops, since I was the one who found Dennis, but I just didn't want to have to see the body again. I stuck my head out the window.

"Hey, do you wanna talk to me? I'm the guy who found him."

A white motorcycle cop with a handlebar mustache answered incredulously, "Yes, of course, we have to talk to you. Come down now." Why do motorcycle cops always have handlebar mustaches?

I went down the back stairs and hopped a fence on the side of the building. I did not want to see Dennis again. The cops were just sitting around joking and filling out paperwork when I came around the building. What is it about the American police force that makes the "good cop, bad cop" routine applicable to all situations? Handlebars was treating me like a felon while an Asian dude was trying to console me for being intercepted by a dead guy on the way to work. After answering their questions and giving them my info, I split. The whole thing was too heavy for me, and I needed to leave.

I walked around for a while, freaked out, calmed down, called my parents, freaked out, calmed down, got some food, walked around, and finally, after a couple of hours, decided it would be okay to go back. After stepping through the door of my building, I was amazed at the efficiency of the paramedics or the morticians or whoever it is that cleans up dead bodies. No one would have thought that there was a corpse there less than two hours earlier. The only thing left from that morning's madness was the one button that had landed next to my foot.

A POEM FOR NOAH TAO
BrokeAssStuart.com; 2020

I'm wearing my Lucky 13 shirt
with the legendary logo
of that ornery cat

But this time the cat's face
is half covered with a bandanna
that says 2020 on it
like it's warning you to stay away

Noah made sure I got this shirt
because he knew how much I loved that bar
and he knew it was going away
but more importantly because he was my friend

That's who he was

If you were his homie, he was
on your team
which meant you were in
his heart
which meant you were
someone he loved

which meant he would
think of you in those unexpected moments and reach out to say
"I got you" in a million different ways

Noah was the first person to tell me
"Loud Pipes Save Lives"
and in a way that sums him perfectly
too nice to be a biker
too biker to be that nice

A habitual button pusher
line stepper
shit talker
ball buster
mirth making
rat bastard sonofabitch who
lit up every fucking room he was in
even if he was burning it down

I loved that man and
this world is worse
without him in it

Unfortunately, loud pipes aren't enough
to save everyone's life
but I have a feeling they will be the music
that brings our boy Noah home

AS THE ATROCITIES PILE UP, THE CLOUDS FEEL DARKER
San Francisco Examiner, 2017

There's a duskiness hanging over the Bay Area that shouldn't be here. This is usually our warm season, our "Indian Summer," when the sun is supposed to shine and the people are supposed to shimmer. But there it is, a haze clutching our skyscrapers, a visual reminder of the darkness that has been 2017.

Waking up these past few mornings, the first thing that I sensed was the smell of burning. The fires despoiling the North Bay have brought the horrors of the past year to our doorstep. From Houston to

Puerto Rico, from Las Vegas to Mexico City, we've watched disasters and atrocities slash across our screens as we felt safely removed. Some of us had loved ones in these places and watched on helplessly, but the majority of us only paid attention for a few days before moving on to the next thing.

I'm not pointing any fingers; it's hard to stay focused when some new wicked savagery seems to assault our world each week.

As if that weren't enough, many of the values and ideals that we feel define us have been under bombardment since January. This administration has attacked our weakening environment, our hard-working immigrants, our insufficient health care system, and declared war on people of color, who are just asking to be treated fairly. It's also promised tax cuts for the wealthy, relaxed regulations for rapacious corporations, pardoned racists like Sheriff Joe Arpaio, and defended the actions of white supremacists around the country.

We thought 2016 was bad, but it was just the appetizer — hell, maybe just the *amuse-bouche*. I'm not sure any of us could've known how bad 2017 would be.

That gloomy haze hanging above us all week may be smoggy air pollution wafting down from the terrible fires claiming lives and livelihoods in the North Bay. Still, in its own way, it's also the physical manifestation of the desolate weight we've been carrying every day since Nov. 8, 2016. Every morning since then, we've awoken to news that has filled us with anger or anxiety or both.

As each of these atrocities piles up, the clouds feel darker.

Fortunately, all of this has made our community stronger. When the current administration attempted to ban Muslims, we shut down the airports. When they threatened to rescind DACA, we surrounded the Federal Building.

When white supremacists, emboldened by the Molester-in-Chief, tried to rally in our cities, we showed up in legion and let them know they're not welcome. There's no doubt that we have plenty of local problems that we need to reckon with, but when the shit hits the fan, it's incredible to see how the Bay Area stands up.

It's been heartwarming to watch people all across the Bay throw and attend fundraisers to help the victims of recent disasters. But seeing the way folks have reacted to the fires tearing through the

North Bay has completely filled me with love and admiration for our community. My social media feeds are full of people offering up beds, couches, and bedrooms to people who've lost their homes. Storefronts are acting as depots for people to drop off clothes, toiletries, and other necessities. Some individuals are circulating information on available resources and safe places, while others are passing around GoFundMe campaigns to help people get back on their feet. Seeing the community come together to look after our own during a disaster has been nothing short of humbling.

Yes, it has been an awful year, and there doesn't appear to be an end in sight. But watching how this community unites in times of need only strengthens my conviction that, ultimately, if we keep working hard and keep taking care of each other, we're going to be alright.

ME AND BOURDAIN

BrokeAssStuart.com; 2018

I only met Anthony Bourdain twice. We weren't friends, we didn't hang out, and he probably didn't even remember me at all. That said, he had a tremendous impact on my life. At a point where my career was just really starting to blossom, he inspired me to do things my way and proved that you could be successful while playing by your own rules. He was a beautiful writer, an empathetic storyteller, a high priest of travel, and the ultimate rebel. He used food and travel as a vehicle to prove that there is more love in people than there is hate and that you can learn so much about a person by sitting down and breaking bread with them. Today, we lost one of the rarest kinds of humans, someone whose thoughtful words and deeds opened us up to our own compassion and curiosity. Anthony Bourdain was the word "yes" in a world full of "no".

I first learned about Tony Bourdain in 2007 when I was living in Brooklyn and researching *Broke-Ass Stuart's Guide to Living Cheaply in New York*. I somehow had a free morning between exploring the city and waiting tables, and I flicked to the Travel Channel. That was the moment Bourdain entered my life.

Nearly every other TV travel host I'd ever seen was annoying and fake and made me want to puke a little bit, but suddenly here was this guy who just didn't give a fuck. There were no stand-up shots of him in front of the Eiffel Tower, smiling too hard and saying something hokey like "Have you ever seen anything like this?" There were no moments of dining in touristy restaurants that no real traveler would want to set foot in. There was no appeasing the network's agenda of family-friendly and wholesome content. Anthony Bourdain felt like an outsider, like he'd seen things you weren't ready for. He seemed like the kind of guy who didn't seek out the underbelly of a place but still managed to end up there regardless of his actions. Anthony Bourdain felt authentic, and he felt dangerous.

What really made him special, though, was that there was reverence in his irreverence. His bad boy exterior only barely hid the fact that he was very deeply a humanist. As my friend Candace wrote in her Facebook update today, "Bourdain reflects that the beauty of traveling the world is coming across people who have no reason to be kind to you, and yet are." That to me is the essence of Tony's work.

As you can imagine, after watching my first episode of *No Reservations* that morning in my Brooklyn apartment, I was hooked. I began watching it as often as possible, and it inspired me to do a travel show of my own, which I finally achieved in 2011.

It also made me obsessed with Bourdain's New York. I wanted to find the places he talked about and maybe even run into him. His favorite dive bar was a place called Siberia, but unfortunately, by the time I found out about it, the bar had closed forever.

A few months after I first watched *No Reservations*, I found out that Anthony Bourdain was doing a book reading and signing in Manhattan. I am the furthest thing from a starfucker, there's a tiny handful of famous people I'd care to meet, but Bourdain was one of them. So, I trudged my way down to lower Manhattan and waited in line for an hour. I was the only schmuck who didn't bring or buy a Bourdain book to get signed. Instead, I did the most Stuart thing ever and signed a copy of *Broke-Ass Stuart's Guide to Living Cheaply in San Francisco*, which had just come out, and gave it to him. I actually wrote about the experience as one of the very first posts on BrokeAssStuart.com.

As the years went by, I continued to watch Bourdain's shows and read his books. I was a total fan boy. He embodied exactly what I wanted to do with my life. In 2011, the year I co-created and hosted my travel TV show *Young, Broke & Beautiful*, I was living back in San

All Of This Is The Natural Byproduct Of Not Dying Young

Francisco. One day, the local blogs were abuzz with the news that Bourdain and his crew were in town shooting The Layover. I figured this would be a great chance to meet Tony again and give him a copy of my NYC book. Plus, I wanted to tell him how watching his show had inspired me to do my own.

After chasing down a few rumors, Valerie Luu told me that they were filming part of *The Layover* at her Rice, Paper, Scissors pop-up, and it happened to be down the street from my house. So, I ran over there, book in hand, and hung out for a while with a bunch of other folks who were excited to meet their hero. Tony eventually strode in with Oscar Villalon (managing editor at ZYZZYVA magazine), since Oscar was part of the shoot. After waiting for the mob to recede, I walked up to Bourdain and gave him my book, saying, "Not sure if you recall, I was the schmuck who showed up to your book signing with a copy of my own book a few years ago and gave it to you. Since you're a New Yorker, I figured you should have this one too."

While I'm pretty sure he had no idea what book I was talking about, he thanked me for the NYC book, saying that, since he's never there anymore, he might actually need it as a guidebook. Then we chatted for a bit about making TV shows. He'd actually heard of *Young, Broke & Beautiful*, and I got to tell him, "Watching your show inspired me to want to do one of my own. I said to myself, 'If they gave this guy a show, they'll give one to anyone.' We both laughed, and then I left him alone, hoping that maybe in the future we'd meet again and have a drink.

Unfortunately, that drink never happened. Despite the friends we have in common, I never saw Anthony Bourdain again in person. I was crushed this morning to wake up and find out that it won't ever happen because Anthony Bourdain, the patron saint of square pegs, tired of being expected to fit into round holes, took his own life.

For all of us outsiders looking in, Bourdain seemed to have the perfect life. He got paid very well to travel the world, meet wonderful and interesting people, eat their food, and make clever and poignant observations. It's literally all I want to do with my life. But what do we know? It's obvious today that Tony Bourdain was wrestling with demons that his adoring fans didn't know about. We only saw the public side of him, the side that inspired us to explore, travel, and take risks. And while that public side felt very candid, we didn't know what things he wrestled with and what monsters he struggled to keep under the bed.

So today I want to thank Anthony Bourdain for lighting a fire inside so many people. I want to thank him for bringing so many different lives and ways of being into our homes through his shows and his books. In a time where the very fabric of our world feels like it is fraying, we need more people like Bourdain, people who show us that we're all far more alike than we are different and that sometimes all you need to understand someone better is to sit down and share a meal.

Thank you, Tony. Thank you for everything.

EULOGIES FOR THE LIVING
San Francisco Examiner; 2017

There's a scene in the movie *Empire Records* where all the record store employees hold a funeral for Deb, even though she's still alive. Earlier in the movie, Deb had tried to kill herself. So, her friends and co-workers held the mock funeral so she could hear all the reasons she was loved.

I was thinking about this on Monday afternoon as a few hundred people gathered at Slim's to say our last goodbyes to our friend Angie Hathaway. Our lovely, generous, hilarious, spirited Angie had passed away suddenly the week before, and we were all there to hold each other up and share the thousands of reasons we loved her. For so many, Angie was a staple of San Francisco, so the crowd ranged from strait-laced folks to those who had tattooed knuckles on their neck.

Angie and I had been tight in our mid-20s, and since one of her many talents was cartography, she made the maps to my San Francisco and NYC guidebooks. We hung out a lot back then, but it

All Of This Is The Natural Byproduct Of Not Dying Young

had been a decade since those salad days, and as happens so often in life, we'd drifted apart. We'd become those San Franciscans who, when our paths crossed, gave each other really good hugs and chatted for five minutes before continuing on our ways. So, I'd never gotten to tell her how absolutely fantastic she was, how her loud laugh and exuberant energy lit up rooms and lifted people, how her many craft talents inspired people to try new things and to create.

These sentiments and many more were passed around Slim's that day like a collection plate, while babies toddled and screamed, and cute dogs chased each other through our legs. It made me realize we should hold memorials for our friends while they're still alive, so we can shower them with the love we somehow hold back until they die.

I shared this idea on Facebook, and many people chimed in, saying this is what a birthday party is. And while I get that, I'm thinking it has to be something more. Don't get me wrong: Birthday parties are great, but they are rarely the profound outpouring of love, admiration, and appreciation that we see at memorials. Life's hard as it is, so why not make a point of gathering people together to tell someone just how important they are? It could be similar to a roast, but instead of saying hilariously twisted and messed-up things about someone, we could get up and share what makes this person such a blessing to have in our lives.

A few years ago, one of my roommates did this for her birthday. (She actually scared the shit out of me because I got invited to it by email and, at first glance, I thought she had died). I wasn't able to attend, but when I asked her about it, she said, "It might've been the most narcissistic thing I've ever done, but I was in a weird place at the time and hearing from so many people why they loved me really helped me through it."

We live our lives in our own heads. We only really get the sense of how the people we cherish feel about us by what they allow themselves to show. But we shouldn't wait 'til someone is gone to share what makes them special enough to keep them in our hearts. So maybe that's what we should start doing.

Pick someone you love and throw them a living memorial. Gather their friends together and take turns absolutely fucking gushing about them. Tell them why you look up to them, what inspires you about them, how they make you feel, and, most importantly, what your life would be like without them. Because, otherwise, you might never get to tell them at all.

ACKNOWLEDGMENTS

First and foremost, I need to thank everyone who has ever supported me and BrokeAssStuart.com financially. Whether this was on Patreon or Paypal, buying a beer passport or a shirt, attending an event I threw, or purchasing a zine or a book. I literally could not have gotten here without you. I couldn't have gotten anywhere.

I'd also like to thank anyone who has ever supported in other ways like reading articles and sharing them, posting about the stuff I'm up to, or spreading the gospel of Broke-Ass in any other way.

Next, I'd like to thank Robert Buckley and Terran Empire Publishing for publishing this weird and insane retrospective of my work. It's an incredible thing to look at a volume that spans the entirety of my career, and I'm so thankful Robert has given me the opportunity to put it all in one place and share it with you.

My deepest thanks goes to my incredible wife, Kayla Brittingham. She's the best thing that's ever happened to me. The world would be a far better place if everyone had a love like ours. Thank you to my parents, Jay and Janice Schuffman and my brother Ross for always believing in me. Thanks to the rest of my big, crazy, Jewish family for always having my back.

Thank you to my business partner Alex Mak for being ½ of BAS. It would've collapsed a long time ago if it weren't for him. Thanks to Amiee Kushner for being the "CFO" and voice of reason at BAS. Thank you to the literally hundreds of writers, editors, photographers, and artists who have contributed to BAS over the past two decades. Your hard work helps shine a light in an often dark world. I still wish I could pay you better. Thanks to the whole Brand Marinade team for helping us with all our zany merch. Thank you to Michael Silver and Ric Cohen for their many years of friendship and legal advice. Huge shout out to Melissa Keith who was the first travel writer I ever met and who made me realize it was something I wanted to do.

Thanks to all the publishers and editors who have taken a chance on someone dumb enough to call themselves Broke-Ass Stuart. This includes the folks at Lonely Planet, David Gomberg and Justin Heimberg at Seven Footer Press who published my previous three books, Michael Howerton, Greg Anderson, and Deborah Peterson from the San Francisco Examiner, Mary Polizzotti at 7x7, Marke Bieschke and Steven Jones at the SF Bay Guardian, Dan Gentile and Grant Marek at SFGate, Jennifer Maerz at The Bold Italic, Eric Arnold at SF Sounds, Jennye Garibaldi at Everfest, and anyone else who let me scribble all the silly little words that make up this book. Thanks to Grow SF for allowing me to use the work I created for the Bold Italic in this book.

Shout out to Sam Erickson, 44 Pictures, and IFC for helping make an incredible TV show all those years ago. *Young, Broke, & Beautiful* was so special, and if it had just been a couple years later, during the streaming age, it would've been huge. Thank you to Anthony Bourdain for inspiring me to do travel TV.

A big thank you to all my friends who've supported the semi-quixotic dream that is BAS. So much love to Tia, Krista, and Ashley who inspired some of the work in this collection, while also helping me grow to be the person that I am. And thanks to all the other women whose late-night escapades with me made their way into my writing. Big ups to all the people toiling away in media and journalism who do such incredible work for so little money. And thanks to them again for showing so much love over the years to all my weird endeavors.

Thank you to the people of the Bay Area for embracing me so deeply and allowing me to be such an embedded part of this beautiful culture.

And of course, thank you, dear reader, for buying this book. You have no idea how much it means to me. Seriously, thank you.

Thank you to anyone I forgot to say thank you too.

I Love You All!! Thak You!,

(I Just thought I'd throw one more in For good Luck),

Help BrokeAssStuart.com Survive!

Photo by Peter Snarr

Did you know it costs us nearly $20,000 a month to run Broke-Ass Stuart?

You already know independent journalism makes very little money. We don't get paid more if we expose corruption, we don't get a bonus for giving free exposure to small businesses, we don't get lucrative contracts for interviewing local artists or defending the Bay Area's progressive ideals.

We're only able to keep doing this because of readers like you.

If you find anything in this book or on the website helpful or important, I hope you'll become a member of the Broke-Ass Stuart Patreon.

Join over 500 people who support our independent journalism each month.

Plus, you'll get rad perks for doing so!

http://patreon.com/BrokeAssStuart

www.ingramcontent.com/pod-product-compliance
Lightning Source LLC
Chambersburg PA
CBHW050337010526
44119CB00049B/582